Women in Soviet Fiction, 1917–1964

Women in Soviet Fiction
1917–1964

Xenia Gasiorowska

THE UNIVERSITY OF WISCONSIN PRESS

Madison, Milwaukee, and London

1968

Published by the University of Wisconsin Press
Box 1379, Madison, Wisconsin 53701

The University of Wisconsin Press, Ltd.
27–29 Whitfield Street, London, W.1

Printed in the United States of America by
Kingsport Press Inc., Kingsport, Tennessee

Library of Congress Catalog Card Number 68–16060

TO *Zygmunt*

Preface

This book is an excursion into virtually unexplored terrain: no major study, either in Russia or in the West, has been dedicated to the typology of Soviet fictional women. The venture therefore has been fraught with dangers. I do not claim—indeed, do not intend—to provide a true picture of life in the Soviet Union: the role of literature and the publishing conditions there would have frustrated any such endeavor. Yet, a sociologist is likely to reprove me for failing to do just that. I do not try to determine the place held by a Soviet heroine among her Western counterparts: she does not belong to their family. Yet, a scholar of literature may insist that such a place should have been sought by means of accepted methods of literary criticism. My object is to demonstrate that the hundreds of women characters inhabiting the stylized world of Soviet fiction can be reduced to a certain number of typical patterns portrayed within their respective environments.

This proved to be an arduous if fascinating task and one that took many years to accomplish. Some aspects of this study were developed in my articles which appeared between 1953 and 1962 in the *AATSEEL Journal*, the *Antioch Review*, the *Modern Language Forum*, *The Problems of Communism*, the *Russian Review*, the *Slavic and East European Journal*, and *Studies in Russian and Polish Literature, in Honor of Waclaw Lednicki*, ed. Z. Folejewski et al. (The Hague, 1962).

The preparation of the manuscript itself presented problems familiar to those scholars in the Slavic field who hope that their work can serve both the specialist and the general reader. For the convenience of the general reader, I include a bibliography of Soviet works of fiction mentioned in this book which are available in English translation and a glossary of frequently used Russian terms. Russian documentation is confined to the notes, but the Index provides both English translations of titles as used in the text and transliterations of the original Russian titles. I use the transliteration systems of J. Thomas Shaw's *The Transliteration of Modern Russian for English-Language Publications* (Madison, 1967). System I, facilitating correct pronounciation by the reader unfamiliar with the Russian language, is used in the text, Glossary, and Index; and the international scholar System III, for bibliographical materials in notes and for words as words. Each title is accompanied in the text and the Index by the date of its first publication, as serialized in a journal or in book form. Dates in notes, however, may occasionally differ from these, because some quotations were taken from later editions—always provided these quotations had not undergone changes during textual revisions, a not uncommon occurrence in the Soviet Union. All translations of the quotations in the text are my own.

The writing of this study was made possible by research leaves and salary support grants from the University of Wisconsin, for which it gives me great pleasure to express my gratitude to the University Research Committee.

In conclusion, a word of tribute to all those who helped me along the road. Above all, I wish to express my profound gratitude to Professor J. Thomas Shaw for his judicious reading of the manuscript, stimulating encouragement, invaluable advice, and excellent suggestions. For his unflagging interest in my work, patient sympathy with its vicissitudes, and constructive criticism I am indebted to my husband, Zygmunt J. Gasiorowski. And sincere thanks go to Professor Edmund I. Zawacki, who unsparingly gave of his time to help me unravel many a stylistic snag.

I greatly appreciate the courteous, efficient aid of the staff of the Memorial Library of the University of Wisconsin—particularly that of Miss Marguerite A. Christensen, Mrs. Jacqueline Kelly, Miss Elizabeth J. Donohue, and Mr. Alexander J. Rolich—as well as that of the staffs of the Library of Congress, the New York Public Library, the

British Museum Library, and the Bibliothèque Nationale. I also wish to thank Mr. J. Kenneth Pawoski for his dedicated assistance in preparation of the manuscript, and Mrs. Mildred Busse for prompt and skillful typing.

Madison, Wisconsin   XENIA GASIOROWSKA
January, 1968

Contents

Women in Soviet Fiction, 1917–1964

Introduction

The study of conventional literary types is important: it widens the field of literary criticism and sheds additional light on the techniques of the craft of fiction. Moreover, the mass literature of a given period provides real insight into the various aspects of the period's mores, values, and conditions. Great literary figures do not negate conventional characters; on the contrary, they confirm their credibility. The unique Becky Sharp, setting out to find a husband or perish, marches at the head of a legion of anonymous girls—living and fictional—whose lot was typical of the life in Victorian society.

The typology of Soviet fictional characters can be of special interest because of the peculiar and obligatory relationship which exists between literature and society in the Soviet Union. This study does not purport to make sociopolitical disclosures, and any exhaustive treatment of historical developments is obviously outside its boundaries. Yet, the drama of a mass literature is played against the backdrop of real life, and what is left unsaid, or is kept dimly lighted, can be just as revealing as the carefully staged and brilliantly spotlighted scenes.

There have been numerous studies of male characters in Soviet literature, both in the Soviet Union and in the West, but fictional women have been, in comparison, neglected. Yet, while heroines in Soviet fiction hold a position secondary to that of the heroes—just as human emotions in it rate lower than social duty—their role is significant and deserves attention. The existence of recognizable patterns of

Soviet heroes and antiheroes is well known. This study, by examining in detail the characterization of Soviet fictional women from 1917 to 1964, will show that they too can be reduced to a limited number of basic types, like actors in the *commedia dell'arte*, who respond in an established fashion to the situations of a few standard plots.

The existence of all these stock characters is conditioned by certain peculiarities of Soviet literature. One is that the traditional Russian quest for a positive hero has largely deteriorated into an imposition on the reader of a model character allegedly already existing in real life. Next, there are the limitations to artistic creativity caused by the Soviet writer's formal and indisputed duty to educate readers ideologically. Nor can one dismiss the practical inducements for authors to bring forth works acceptable within a system where periodicals and presses, stage and screen, bookstores and libraries are owned and run by the State. Most important is the role of Socialist Realism, the official literary doctrine introduced in 1934, a date which came to be considered a watershed in the history of Soviet literature.

No exhaustive survey of Soviet literature can or need be included in this study, but for the purposes of type evaluation, literature will be divided into three periods: the years between the Revolution and the establishment of Socialist Realism (1917–34), the era of its absolute domination (1934–53), and the period following the death of Stalin in 1953.

The first period, still free of State controls over the arts, is characterized by an abundance of writers' groups and associations, as well as by feuds over and experiments with literary forms. The two basic schools, however, were the independent writers, called at that time Fellow Travelers (*poputčiki*), and the *engagé* writers, usually, though not necessarily, of proletarian or peasant descent. The main distinction between them lies in their attitudes towards the purposes of their creative work. The *engagé* writers, then as later, were intent on presenting reality (slanting it, if need be) in a way which would influence the reader's thinking. Their characters were meant to set up standards of exemplary behavior, and in the process these characters tended to become standardized themselves. The independent writers, on the other hand, were always interested primarily in painting life and the human condition as they saw it. Their characters were designed to prove no point, except perhaps the complexity of both life and people, and neither deliberately established nor followed models.

Artistically the work of the Fellow Travelers was much superior to that of the proletarian writers, few of whom had talent and most of whom were further handicapped by a lack of education. Both groups were fascinated by the themes of the Revolution and of an individual's reaction to social change, which, nevertheless, they treated from completely different ideological angles. The proletarian writers can be termed precursors of Socialist Realism, and in the next two decades many of them became its pillars, while the Fellow Travelers—dead, or exiled, or silenced—played no role in the world of Soviet fiction within the framework of Socialist Realism until they reappeared after 1953 in modified guise.

The second period of Soviet literature falls between the First Congress of Soviet Writers (1934), at which the principles of Socialist Realism were first announced by the spokesman of the Party, Andrey Zhdanov, and the Second Congress (1954), at which their interpretation was not only discussed but, for the first time, challenged. During these two decades the works of Soviet writers, restricted by the scarcity of acceptable themes and the required uniformity of their treatment, became increasingly alike. All authors belonged to the Union of Soviet Writers, a professional organization which was founded in 1932 following the dissolution by Party decree of all the numerous literary groups of the 1920's. And with a few exceptions scarcely any writer could be readily identified by his individual style.

Henceforth only one mode of writing—Socialist Realism—was possible; one—Marxist—school of thought was recognized; and one group of writers—"Soviet workers of the pen"—existed. As a result, Russian literature instead of forms and trends developed patterns. There were topic patterns, such as the ennobling influence of work; plot patterns, like the perennial tale of a young Communist improving the lagging performance of a factory; and character patterns, the wise Party Secretary, for instance, and the gruff, honest chairman of the *kolkhoz*.

The peak period of Socialist Realism can be subdivided into the 1930's, when the authors were learning, at Stalin's behest, how to be "engineers of human souls" and to conform to the literary rules; World War II, when the rules were relaxed; and the postwar decade, which promoted "Soviet patriotism" and came to be criticized eventually for "lack of conflicts" and "varnishing of reality" in fiction. This last period, while it led literature into a dead-end street, is nevertheless most important for the purposes of this study. It was then that the main patterns of "typical" Soviet women became firmly established and mass produced amidst extensive discussions by literary critics and the reading public.

Once the demands of Socialist Realism were met—the adherence to Marxist-Leninist ideology (*idejnost'*), the spiritual commitment to the Party's aims and policies (*partijnost'*), the rendition of Russian nationalism as Soviet class-consciousness (*narodnost'*)—little opportunity was left for flights of the imagination. Nor were they encouraged; the domain of the irrational and the subconscious are excluded from Marxist esthetics. Within Socialist Realism an atmosphere of optimism founded on the doctrinal certainty of social progress is obligatory; fiction, while using constructive criticism, must portray reality in its "revolutionary development," that is, as a process of uninterrupted improvement; and the Soviet people are seen as a Party-led team of builders of a future Communist State. Such characters, allegedly average men and women shown in everyday work and life, lend themselves well to being classified as "typical." Mass produced, they also tend to be rigid, two-dimensional, and predictable in word and action.

The third period—the post-Stalinist decade—is characterized by some relaxation of the rigid literary controls of the preceding era. The progress of this "thaw"—so-named for the first timid harbinger of change, I. Erenburg's novel *The Thaw* (1954)—was first checked by Khrushchev's pronouncements on Soviet arts in 1957. Further authoritative warnings against ideological coexistence of Soviet and non-Marxist esthetics were repeated on several occasions, such as the Third Congress of Soviet Writers in 1959, the Twenty-Second Congress of the Party in 1961, and Khrushchev's address to a group of writers in 1963.

These fluctuations are understandable. Under Soviet conditions the very existence of the latest trend depends on its acceptability for the purposes of current Party policies. Nor did the thaw affect the two basic premises of Soviet literary life: the State ownership of publication media and the status of Socialist Realism as the official creative method. Needless to say, books written by Soviet writers and critical of the Revolution or of the Soviet regime could be published only abroad, and even then they often appeared under an assumed name.

The post-Stalinist changes consisted firstly in that themes hitherto unmentionable were made available for criticism, provided it stayed within proper limits and did not extend to subjects not yet declassified. These themes ranged from terrorism of the secret police to labor camps, from inefficient bureaucracy to juvenile delinquency. All were blamed on Stalinism, particularly "the cult of personality."

Secondly, the body of Soviet writers was no longer homogeneous. One group, the stalwarts of the previous decade, firmly continued within the confines of Socialist Realism, like defenders holding a besieged fortress, and waged battle on dissidents. They routinely adjusted to the new trend, and judiciously cautious, did not introduce any drastic changes into their works. Another group, though unquestionably loyal to the Party, most frequently became the target of official rebukes because of their candid and impatient portrayal of various aspects of Soviet life. These heirs of the proletarian writers of the 1920's and of the prerevolutionary realists denounced current reality in the name of a better society of the future. Soviet-educated (most of them were in their thirties at the time of Stalin's death), they stayed without apparent effort within the boundaries of Socialist Realism, which, however, they constantly tried to widen. Their most significant contributions to that goal were their bestowing on villains the standard virtues of Soviet positive characters and their attempts to get away from characters who are all black or white.

Finally, a third group, comparable to the Fellow Travelers of the postrevolutionary period, dwell on the very fringe of Socialist Realism and occasionally venture beyond it. These writers, prevalently young, seldom engage in social criticism and have no didactic message for the reader. They are wont to record their travel impressions, to describe hunting scenes and nature, and to probe human emotions without passing judgment on them. They still cannot afford to experiment with form and style, nor to choose among different literary methods, but some of their works are on a high artistic level. In general, since the beginning of the thaw, the style of recent Soviet fiction has been showing steady improvement.

Marxism conceives of human beings as products of their social environment. Since the world of Soviet fiction in the sense of its psychological climate has only one environment, all its inhabitants share in some degree its spiritual characteristics. Faith in the Party's infallibility, for instance, has been the hallmark of positive characters and the redeeming feature when found in negative ones; occasional villains who lack such faith are considered spiritual cripples, outcasts from a wholesome Soviet community. Consequently, it is primarily by their physical environment that Soviet fictional characters are differentiated, as much by its material conditions as by the mores it creates and its whole way of life. A milieu in Soviet fiction is not a backdrop against which a drama is enacted; rather it may be said that plots are built to portray people within a certain milieu: a collective farm, a factory, a research institute, or even a whole country ravaged by war. And the characters, acknowledged as the offspring of the milieu with which they are integrated, acquire traits considered typical for both.

These considerations caused this book to be divided into four parts, each tracing the development of a group of female types intrinsic to Soviet fiction from its beginnings after the Revolution of 1917 to the eclipse of Khrushchev in 1964: the peasants, the proletarians, the Soviet Amazons (female participants in the Civil War and World War II), and the intelligentsia. Where continuity in types was found to exist, reference is also made to prerevolutionary characters. Works by Russian *émigré* writers, works published by Soviet writers abroad, and literatures of the peoples of the Soviet Union other than Russian have not been included. As it is customary for Soviet works to be revised in subsequent editions in conformance with political changes, the difficulties of establishing canonic texts are familiar to all students of the literature. In this book it seemed best to accept the first versions and to point out changes whenever necessary.

The first part traces the transformation of the peasant housewife—a mere domestic drudge before the Revolution—into the model kolkhoz heroine of streamlined Soviet fiction. Because the first female pioneers of emancipation had to fight the centuries-old restrictions of their conservative milieu, village life of the 1920's is discussed in considerable detail. Special stress is put on the subsequent changes in the conditions and mores of the village, changes paralleled by those in the heroines' characterization.

The second part concentrates on the problems, primarily ethical, of young working girls and on their relationship with the Communist Youth League (*Komsomol*), whose role is more prominent in Soviet fiction in the 1920's than at any other time. It also studies typical proletarian women at the height of their popularity as heroines of the "industrial" novels in the decade following World War II, and shows their retreat into insignificance with the advent of the thaw.

Because the Amazons belong to all the strata of Soviet society, the portion of this book dedicated to their characterization follows the sequence of the general development of Soviet fiction. Thus, it reflects the romantic as well as the political rendition of the Civil War by the relatively untrammeled fiction of the 1920's and the rigid patterns of patriotic heroism demanded by Socialist Realism. The Amazons of the post-Stalinist era are few and have not developed into a separate type.

The last part, dedicated to the upper middle class, distinguishes two groups. The first consists of prevalently negative characters; through the 1930's they are the useless women of the former bourgeoisie, and in the two postwar decades, the wives and daughters of the upper crust of Soviet society, dubbed by Western critics as the "priviligentsia." The second and by far the larger group comprises the flower of the authentically Soviet intelligentsia: the young women who have no ties with the prerevolutionary past, have been educated professionally and ideologically in Soviet homes and schools, and are dedicated workers in their professions. This type developed in the postwar decade and became particularly prominent in the post-Stalinist period. It is among these career women that cases of psychological conflicts generally occur in Soviet literature, and therefore their attitudes to work, duty, and emotional problems have been found to warrant the most attention.

This study, concerned solely with the typology of Soviet fictional heroines, does not undertake to compare them with their Western counterparts, nor to evaluate consistently the artistic level of the works used. Works of higher artistic value frequently do not contain significant female characters, as in the case of A. N. Tolstoy's trilogy *The Road to Calvary* (1919–41); or they feature heroines who, like Aksinya in Sholokhov's *The Quiet Don* (1928–40), a conventional *grande amoureuse*, do not influence the development of the New Soviet Woman. At the same time, a mediocre novel or short story with no other claim to distinction than its being representative of a kind may contain a character essential to introduce a certain type. It should be noted that certain minor characters may serve the purpose as effectively as protagonists and will therefore be given equal consideration. Lastly—but importantly—since mediocre works, streamlined by the requirements of Socialist Realism, have been by far the more numerous in Soviet literature, much of the material used will necessarily consist of them.

Readers cannot expect to find a faithful picture of contemporary Russian life in Soviet fiction, even though fiction professes to hold a mirror to reality. Fictional Sovietland is a carefully stylized reflection of that reality; it is not a phantasy, because to be emulated it must be recognizable to the reader, but it is actuality shown in the process of *becoming* what it is eventually expected to be. In order to understand Soviet fictional characters—their behavior and motives—one has to discuss them within their own world, which, in turn, has to be accepted on its own terms.

The Soviet fictional world is orderly, has a stable psychological climate and permanent ideological laws scrupulously enforced and unquestioned. Its inhabitants are presented to the reader by an omniscient author who reports on their thoughts, feelings, and activities in a straight narrative innocent of devices except, sometimes, a flashback. Nobody has access to their subconscious lives, whether author, reader, or the characters themselves. Their behavior is presented only on a rational plane; their emotions can be—and usually are—controlled; conflicts between passion and duty are resolved in favor of duty. They expect no miracles except from science; Communism is their creed; work is their way of life; they can unhesitatingly tell right from wrong, reality from fancy, truth from deception. They are not universal types—for this they lack individuality—but each is a Soviet Everyman moving through the cycle of birth, love, work, and death within the framework of his finite existence.

The fact that this study is dedicated to female characters entails the discussion of certain specific aspects bearing on their characterization, such as morals, manners, and domestic life. Emotions, too, acquire a higher pitch and wider range but remain subordinate to matters of public importance. In Western or prerevolutionary Russian fiction the main factor in a heroine's life was, of course, love. Tender maiden, passionate mistress, custodian of the home as wife and mother, she dwelt in an emotional world to which all other matters were external as being the domain of men.

Not so in Soviet literature, where positive women characters (and they are mostly that, varying in degree and offset by a few less-than-perfect exceptions) equal men in dedication to the welfare of the Soviet Union. They are, if anything, more enthusiastic in the performance of their professional duties, just as eloquent in expressions of loyalty to the Party, almost as ready to put duty above love. Yet a heroine has not been allowed merely to exchange feminine virtues for masculine ones. In Western terms one may say that a Soviet heroine, having assumed a gentleman's code of behavior, has not been excused from being a lady. Kind, modest, unselfish, chaste, she thus has a double set of distinguished qualities, civic and feminine. Correspondingly, she also has a double set of duties, civic and domestic.

The Revolution did not keep all its promises to the New Woman, who was supposed to be granted not only equal rights but also the means to exercise them. Communal kitchens and State-provided care of children and the household envisaged in 1918 have not materialized for practical reasons. What is more, by the middle of the 1930's it was realized that such institutions, destroying family and home, would have been socially and morally harmful. As a result, however equal in social rights and education, the emancipated heroine has remained handicapped in her competition with the hero.

In his case, no demands are made upon his time and energy beyond that of providing for his family, if he has one, and so he is free to engage wholly in the pursuit of larger goals—social, ideological, and professional. Work for the inhabitants of Sovietland is not just the means of earning money, but an individual's contribution to the common welfare, a noble and demanding duty. Whatever their education, they strive to improve it while also participating in socially useful projects and organizations. Obviously a hero's life is not easy. Yet the heroine, while similarly engaged and not an iota less busy, is also expected to look attractive, to take interest in the hero's career, and if married, to run a household and to bear and raise children.

Her magic talent for somehow stretching the limits of time and effort is a significant factor in the characterization of the fictional New Woman. It enhances her didactic value and influences her position in Sovietland. It should again be recalled here that while positive characters are assumed to be typical of their living counterparts, their *raison d'être* is to educate the working masses by inviting emulation. At first glance, to emulate a paragon such as the New Woman would seem a hopeless endeavor, but actually her outstanding qualities and the rewards they bring can be acquired by any female reader willing to try hard enough. A daydreaming moviegoer in the West may identify with a manicurist on the screen who marries a millionaire, but she has no hope that this will happen to her. A Soviet girl, on the other hand, may not only hope to marry a brawny Stakhanovite hero such as she sees on the screen—socially and financially he is her equal—but she may also aspire to become a Stakhanovite in her own right, as the heroine usually does. Thus, making her dreams come true depends to a large extent on her own effort and performance and always is in the realm of the possible.

There are other factors in the typical heroine's characterization which make the reader feel she belongs to the masses. Though seldom a beauty, she is usually attractive, her routine assets being a fresh complexion, a long braid, and a pleasant smile. Her scant wardrobe consists of a few pieces of everyday clothes and a—just one—dress for festive occasions. The same could be said of her psychological outfit: her thoughts and emotions are sensible and predictable and include no extravagant items. An average Soviet woman should not find it difficult to look, act, and think like a fictional heroine.

Possibly it is this injunction to be an average person, as much as the double load of duties, that limits the scope of the New Woman's ambitions. Her equal rights are never questioned; on the contrary, they are pointed out with pride as an exclusive Soviet bounty. She is respected as a mother, valued as a helpmate and efficient worker, offered perfume and flowers on International Woman's Day in token of recognition. She is not, however, cast as a leader, a dreamer, seldom if ever as an executive, poet, scientist, or ranking Party official. These roles are routinely assigned to men.

This is not discrimination on the part of authors. It is just a reflection of the fact that men in fiction are not conceived of as primarily the males of the human species; whereas femininity has always been the indispensable ingredient of any heroine's makeup. A typical Soviet hero is a builder and a fighter—for the Communist Cause, as it happens—but otherwise he is not unlike other heroes in world fiction. He is, of course, also shown as lover, husband, and father; but these are only secondary details in his characterization, and they do not warrant an International Man's Day or affect studies dedicated to men in fiction. A typical Soviet heroine, however, is an interesting phenomenon, presenting a smooth, if artificial, blend of feminine instincts and of those civic and spiritual faculties which in non-Soviet fiction have been traditionally ascribed to men.

The quest for happinesss of Anna Karenina and Madame Bovary is enveloped by an aura of intense femininity; it is improbable that Ibsen's Nora, having slammed the door of her home behind her, embraced a cause such as the Master Builder's; and contemporary heroines of Western fiction increasingly are seen as primarily biological entities. Soviet women, on the contrary, tend to be soulful and moderate in their demands for personal happiness and emotionally involved in their professional work. If their small universe is rather unexciting and bare, still they keep it tidy and functional and seem to yearn for no broader vistas.

Perhaps in conclusion it is appropriate to specify more closely the nature of Sovietland. It is, of course, the world of Soviet fiction governed by the laws of Socialist Realism. As we have seen, its emergence does not coincide with the official proclamation of these laws in 1934. The typical—or positive—characters who are the legitimate inhabitants of Sovietland can be traced to Gorky and even to Chernyshevsky, and in postrevolutionary literature they became prominent from the very beginning. Their days of glory were the two decades between the First and Second Congresses of Soviet Writers. Nor did they wane or even change significantly in the post-Stalinist period. During the 1920's and again since the mid-1950's, however, these autochthons have reluctantly coexisted with aliens—the atypical characters living, so to speak, on the outskirts of Sovietland.

It should be stressed that aliens are not the same as negative characters, because the latter, even though allegedly nonrepresentative of Soviet reality and branded as leftovers of the Old, do belong in Sovietland; they even have useful functions there, such as conniving intrigues for the New Men and Women to defeat. As in photography, negative characters are positive characters reversed, and like Vice and Virtue of a morality play, both are used for didactic purposes.

The aliens, on the other hand, are not meant to be typical and do little towards the education of the masses. Smuggled into Sovietland by a few nonconformist authors, within plots with inconclusive and seldom happy endings, they also are often antiheroes, frustrated by the very conditions in which the natives thrive. Needless to say, they have so far constituted a small minority, but without actually destroying the laws, they tend to be a disruptive element in the orderly texture of Soviet fictional life. Most importantly, aliens do not serve as models for mass production of stereotypes, possibly because, having no didactic value, they are not in demand with publishers and, Soviet critics insist, do not appeal to wholesome Soviet readers. It is not inconceivable that at some time, as aliens increase in number, they will affect the established character patterns, or if the Party finds it advisable, they will be expected to become standardized themselves. It should be remembered, however, that they are as independent as their authors, and that rather than conform, they disappeared after the 1920's and were not heard from again until the thaw.

Nevertheless, a distinction should be made between the mass-produced stereotypes and the original typical characters on which they are patterned. Individual positive characters, particularly those created by talented writers, often do come alive even for Western readers. Some have charm, a certain depth of feeling, impressive will-power, or winsome naïveté. But even a worthwhile character if endlessly duplicated by mediocre writers is bound to lose its artistic value.

There is a Russian toy, a wooden doll called Matryoshka. Produced for centuries by village craftsmen, Matryoshka represents a typical Russian beauty: dark-browed, blue-eyed, red-cheeked, she is wrapping a brilliantly colored shawl around her plump body. The doll can be taken apart; inside is found another doll, different only in size and color of her shawl. This one, in turn, contains still another replica, and so on, until at least half a dozen of them stand around the original Matryoshka. They all look different from the toys of any other land— gaudy, solemn, demure, somehow a little secretive. This comparison is not meant as an insult to the Soviet fictional heroine. On the contrary. The crowd of stereotyped characters obscures the picture: the heroine, the original model, does deserve to be noticed by the literary critic, to be sought out, as it were, among the crowd. She will differ from the heroines of non-Soviet fiction in that her characterization is standardized and sketchy and in that she can be judged and known only through her behavior—but then, so are our neighbors in real life. Also, it must be remembered that, however stylized, her characterization cannot but be based on that of the real women of the Soviet Union. To this extent (if no further) heroines do have a claim not only to being "typical," that is, representative of the average, but "types," that is, original personalities who also embody the distinctive qualities of a peculiar group.

I

THE PEASANTS

I

The Russian Village in
Postrevolutionary Fiction

The village theme dominates postrevolutionary Russian fiction from its beginnings, continuing throughout the 1920's, and culminating with the period of collectivization, 1928–32. Apart from and because of the tremendous problems—economic, social, political—which the village posed to the Soviet regime, it offered to fiction writers a wealth of material of an unprecedented scope. The handling of this material, however, differed considerably, depending on the ideological and artistic orientation of the writers.

One group of writers, best represented by Boris Pilnyak, was the Fellow Travelers who were continuing the Symbolist tradition and saw the village as a dark, mysterious, semi-Asiatic Russia, swept by the blizzard of the Revolution. Entrenched in this stronghold of the past, primordial peasantry resisted the onslaught of progress which was being led by leather-clad robots, the commissars from town. This fictional village served as a backdrop for the short stories dedicated to the Civil War which abounded in the years 1921–23, but it did not survive beyond this period.

A second group, composed of Fellow Travelers gravitating to the realistic school and of the peasant writers, saw and portrayed the actual, everyday village: bewildered by revolutionary changes, bled and ruined by seven years of war, apprehensive about the redistribution of land. They knew that village well, having been born or taught school there, or both; but they made different uses of the material it provided. The realist Fellow Travelers' interest was primarily that of artists: rich in dramatic characters and situations, the milieu offered them impressive "slices of life." In their works they sided with the Soviet regime in its struggle against reactionary peasantry but subordinated the political aspects of that struggle to the human passions it generated. In Leonov's *The Badgers* (1924), for example, the commissar wins, but it is the defeated peasant rebel who comes alive for the reader as a suffering human being; and the female partisan, Nastenka, who hails directly from her Dostoevsky namesake, is quite unconcerned about politics. And in Seyfullina's *Mulch* (1922) the hero's utter dedication to the Soviet cause, resulting in his own and his family's death, is overshadowed by his tragic, lustful infatuation with a foolish little schoolteacher. Stylistically, this group favors a direct, flowing narrative, lucid if often ornamental, and the narrative genre *skaz*, a story told allegedly by a witness.

As to the peasant writers, though some of them—Panfyorov, for instance—create their own "rustic" style, generally their language is simple; and making no attempt at psychological insight in their character drawing, they concentrate on telling their story and on emphasizing its political moral for the reader's benefit. Not only are they themselves on the side of progress (which they equate with the Soviet regime), but so are all their positive characters, who are shown as courageous, broadminded, and fighting the dark forces of reaction. The enemies are *byt*—the complex of customs, beliefs, and manners which determine a way of life—and the *kulaks*—the rich, greedy peasants who oppose the change.

If this approach makes peasant writers precursors of Socialist Realism, most of them still belong to prerevolutionary Russian literature in that they respect their heroes as individuals. They do hold their characters up as models for the reader to emulate, but not as mere puppets in a show. While their plots dutifully emphasize class stratification (*klassovoe rassloenie*) and the clash of the social forces of good and evil, the drama is still enacted within the lives of the protagonists. Such, for instance, is the method of Neverov, a self-educated peasant, champion of the landless poor and of the downtrodden woman.

Unfortunately for the artistic value of these works, the emotions involved in promoting progress cannot be shared by the readers so readily as the less exalted but more familiar passions. As the history of Soviet literature under Socialist Realism was amply to prove, ideological grafts do not thrive in fiction's orchards. Even very talented Soviet writers have failed to make, say, rural electrification fascinating, and the majority of the writers under discussion, such as Zamoysky or Korobov, were not even very talented. Their lack of cultural background and of education was a further handicap. Sholokhov, of course, stands apart by virtue of his art, but even so, a comparison between the respective heroes of *The Quiet Don* and *Virgin Soil Upturned* (1932, 1960) supports the point at issue. Melekhov, groping for a political faith, is poignant, while Davydov, secure in the rightness of his Bolshevik loyalties, is at most edifying, even to a Soviet reader.

This is not to say that village novels with a social message had no foundation in reality; in fact, many of their characters had living prototypes, and the contemporary press and statistics bear out the truth of their plots and setting. But because they were meant to prove a point, they neither told the whole truth nor refrained from embellishing it. As a result, some writers, Kochin, for example, were criticized for exaggerating the stubborn medievalism of the Russian village, while others, like Panfyorov, were reproved for minimizing the regime's difficulties in reforming the village, for making it look as saccharine as the bucolic scenery of Karamzin.[1] Most critics, including Gorky, felt that in any case the village and its inhabitants were being given too much attention, and that the bourgeois slogan of the "power of the soil" over the peasant had no place in Soviet literature. They insisted that both the establishment of the new and the abolition of the old should, rather, be shown in the workers' milieu in the city. But the theme of the turbulent village *byt* continued to fascinate writers until, like all Russian art, its flow was directed into the narrow cemented canals of Socialist Realism, where it took whatever course was currently prescribed for kolkhoz life in fiction.

It has been accepted as a truism by literary historians that in the 1920's, village fiction portrayed the process of change. In theory, the process was twofold: the transformation of backward peasantry under the new order's economic and psychological impact, and the breaking down of the old *byt* and the prejudices it bred. In practice, however, fiction concentrated on the second aspect, by far the more dramatic of the two. Naturally, the transformation was in the center of the plot, promoted by protagonists, obstructed by negative secondary characters; but the breaking up of the old byt, rich in the wreckers' dilemmas and their opponents' tragedies, held an irresistible appeal for writers.

The mixture of old times' debris and the young order's innovations practically begged for a framework of fiction. There were ingenious substitutions for basic Christian ceremonies, such as the "Red weddings," discussed later, and the decline of the patriarchal family. There was the peasants' reaction to the ban on religious practices and to the new institutions such as the Children's Corps of the Pioneers of Communism (*Pionery*), the Communist Youth League (*Komsomol*), the Party Women's Section (*Zhenotdel*), and the village councils. And finally, there was the sweeping reevaluation of moral values and the changed status of women. The peasant's efforts to cope with this unprecedented upheaval provided fiction with the element of suspense.

Contrary to the protestations of Soviet literary historians, contemporary fiction did render the Party's guidance and the political influence of the city; it just did not conceal their limited scope. The Party, at this crucial period of its own internecine struggle for power and of the urgencies of its New Economic Policy (NEP), could not spare much attention to the permanent problem it had in the Russian village. The city (meaning, of course, the proletariat, not the cowed intelligentsia, the hostile bourgeoisie, or the NEP-bred speculators) had numerous difficulties of its own. Fiction writers, then, had the village—vast, awesome, and isolated—all to themselves.

Revolution had been made in the city, and it was pledged to establish the dictatorship of the proletariat, not of the peasants. Compared to the peasantry, which constituted over 80 percent of the population, the proletariat was numerically insignificant. But, though semiliterate and, it was allowed, as yet imperfectly class-conscious, it had the means of participating in revolutionary change. Even before World War I, a worker could go to the theater, read papers, borrow books from a library, and send his children to school. Culture—cheaper, shabbier, of lesser quality than that of the intelligentsia—was nevertheless within his reach; he could, and often did, get involved in politics. But none of these things existed for the peasant, ensconced in his village, illiterate, and politically a blank. After 1917, the village was glad to see its men return home from the front, ready to cultivate the land which had been expropriated from former landlords. Up to this point the Revolution was acceptable, indeed welcome, but the peasants wanted no change beyond the realization of Lenin's promise to them of "peace and land." They would had been content to let the town go its own way and leave them to go theirs.

The bloody experience of the Civil War and the ensuing victory of the Soviet regime proved that this was not to be the case. The village, as it had always done, resigned itself to the inevitable. However different the new laws were from the old, they too came from the town, where, as before, omnipotent authorities issued orders and sent their emissaries to enforce them.

Dealing with underlings was routine for the village; over the centuries it had known those of the khan, the tsar, the squire, who, themselves, could not be reached to hear complaints. "God is too high above, the Tsar is too far away," said the proverb. The village thus bore, on the whole patiently, with the activities of the political neophites in their own community, few at first but steadily increasing in numbers; and an occasional petty tyrant or impostor took easy advantage of their ignorance and gullibility. But they did oppose by plot, sabotage, passive resistance, and even violence if necessary, the two aspects of the change which touched the very core of their existence: peasants' private ownership of the land and the byt.

Many a Communist from the city was killed while requisitioning food during the Civil War and the years of famine which came in its wake, as was many a Party official during the collectivization years. Their deaths, connived by grain-hoarding kulaks, continued to lend dramatic highlights to works of Soviet fiction until well into the 1930's. Love of property, invariably shown by writers as ruthless greed, served as the basic characteristic of members of the reactionary camp. And the struggle between them and those from the progressive camp, who had no property to love and allegedly yearned for none, was the standard subject of village novels.

The struggle over the byt went deeper and, in a way, was fiercer because it affected the rich and the poor alike, and though it went on in the town as well as in the village, it meant more for the latter.

The religious issue loomed large. The Soviet regime took, officially and emphatically, a hostile attitude towards religion, denouncing it as the "opiate of the people," promoter of ignorance and prejudice, and an institution perpetrated by reactionary clergy. The anti-religious campaigns, usually conducted by the Komsomol, were noisy and intentionally brutal, in spite of Lenin's expressed opinion that blasphemy could only create revulsion and make enemies of the faithful instead of enlightening them.[2]

It is difficult to ascertain (and no attempt will be made here to do so) how much religion actually meant to the illiterate peasants, acquainted with its ritual rather than with its spirit. Prerevolutionary fiction, and presumably contemporary reality, abounded with peasant folk attending church services, mothers praying for their sons fighting in the war, and housewives welcoming wandering pilgrims into their homes; they all crossed themselves and invoked the Mother of God and the saints on any occasion, but not even Tolstoy really showed a peasant face to face with his God. Even Soviet writers—though obviously in a spirit opposite to that which might have been expected of their predecessors—have given more attention to the subject. Still one cannot but assume that to a peasant and particularly to his wretched wife faith in God's mercy, in the Holy Mother's intercession, in a miracle even, must have provided some, perhaps the only, comfort. Moreover, religion promised a reward in future life for the sufferings borne on earth, and gave the solace and the emotional release of prayer. How could peasants welcome the news that God was a fraud perpetrated by the priest and that both had now been expelled from the village? Lenin, "smiling and frowning" in the gilded frames from which icons were removed, "Karla Marxov hanging side by side with the Holy Mother of God"[3]—what miracles would they have to perform in answer to a prayer, what comfort offer, in order to atone for the blasphemy?

Family arguments over icons' removal, church weddings, and baptisms play a prominent role in early Soviet fiction. Usually, these quarrels are treated humorously, but occasionally a tragic note is sounded, as in "Superstition" (1928) by N. Kolokolov, in which an old woman catches her death of cold praying in a storm on the crossroads for her Communist son's return to faith. The prayer is not answered, and the son, torn between filial love and Party duty, refuses to summon a priest with the Sacraments to her deathbed. Generally, though fiction's cynical kulaks merely feign religious feelings and landless progressives have none, the bulk of peasantry is plainly shown as clinging to theirs in spite, or perhaps because, of the efforts of anti-religious propagandists.

Loyalty to the Church was caused not only by spiritual, but also by practical considerations. Even should the peasants believe their priest to be a fraud, still his services were vital. He was needed to perform the basic rituals of civilized life: to baptize, to marry, and to bury the dead. Otherwise, as the village saw it, the children had no names, the young brides were no better than hussies, and the souls of the departed could have no rest. After a while, clumsy, halfhearted efforts were made to compromise between the religious ceremonies deeply rooted in the village *byt* and the civil formalities with which the Soviet State was replacing them.

Funerals seem not to have caused too many difficulties; at least, trouble over them does not figure prominently in fiction. Pioneers of progress were laid to rest by their comrades in red coffins, with appropriate graveside speeches and some guitar or accordion music substituted for religious services.[4] Otherwise, if available, a priest would still officiate, as he did even in "Superstition," mentioned earlier.

But christenings and weddings, which, besides being religious ceremonies, were also the principal social events of village life, became real bones of contention. Wives, politically "unenlightened" (*nesoznatel'nye*) and usually prompted by their even more conservative mothers, stoutly opposed giving outlandish names, such as Terror for boys and Revolyutsya for girls, to their children. They also refused to substitute "Octobering" (*Oktjabriny*)* for baptism, even at the cost of severe domestic crises and damage to their progressive husbands' careers. "Kittens and puppies may run about unchristened," a wife exclaims, "but I am a respectable woman and will not allow you to have my baby disgraced in such a fashion, you pagan monster!"[5] "Enlightened" mothers, on the contrary, flaunted their freedom from old-fashioned prejudices, which, to them, included baptism. "My baby needn't fear the evil eye," asserts one of these; "he hasn't been baptized."[6]

Marriages, of course, were the key issue. It was not a question of doing away with wedding festivities: except for the omission of a few customs now considered obsolete (such as the bride's ceremonial wailing at her "having been sold to go away to an alien land"), weddings remained unchanged and were celebrated with as much drinking and brawling as ever before. "The Party platform contains no objections to wedding customs," a Communist father explains, "so, if we are to make merry, let us do it right, in the Russian fashion."[7]

The brides, however, again with their mothers' support, insisted on

---

* A short-lived effort replacing baptism with a ceremony of naming the baby, so-called in honor of the October 1917 Revolution.

being married "properly," i.e., by a priest. The protests of the groom, usually active in local politics, availed him but little: even Mishka Koshevoy, the famed representative of the Soviet victory in the Civil War in Sholokhov's *Quiet Don,* had to submit to being married secretly at midnight in the very church he had recently succeeded in closing for services. He did insult the officiating priest, who could not resist the temptation of reminding the young Bolshevik of how he had led the attack on the priest's house, but this did not save him from feeling humiliated.

A very good example of the situation is provided by the mass wedding performed by a defrocked priest in A. N. Tolstoy's *Road to Calvary.* It is October, the month of the feast of the Holy Virgin's Intercession, when, the harvesting over, the Russian village since time immemorial has celebrated its weddings. "We've thrown out the White priest," the mothers yell to the Soviet commissar. "Now give us a Red one! It's time to start weddings; our girls are getting restive!"[8] The resourceful commissar obliges. Sixteen brides, decked in finery for which pork and flour had been bartered with the hungry town intelligentsia the previous spring, are solemnly married by "the Soviet preacher who has had an argument with God," and the feast lasts three days.

The Komsomol's endeavors to promote civil marriages are usually presented in a humorous vein:

> On the door of the local Soviet an announcement was displayed: "Long live the free family life according to the international new byt! The day after tomorrow in the school building an unusual worker-peasant Red wedding will take place, without bridal crowns, priests, or opiate, in the presence of any citizens interested in the aforementioned event . . . with greetings, your worker-peasant best man, [Signature]."[9]

Another civil marriage is performed by the village mayor, who addresses the young couple in the following terms:

> "Do you promise to follow the path of Communism as bravely as you are now opposing the church and the old people's customs? Are you going to make your children serve as Young Pioneers, educate them, introduce scientific farming methods, and fight for the world revolution? [Then,] in the name of our leader, Comrade Vladimir Ilyich Lenin, I declare the Red marriage completed. Hurrah!"[10]

The reception follows. In the front yard, under a triumphal arch, glasses of vodka are served at a table decorated with Lenin's portrait.

But the next morning two dead dogs are discovered swinging from the top of the arch, bearing an inscription: "A dog marriage deserves dog honors." Village reactionaries show their disapproval even more drastically at still another Red wedding, in which the young couple kneels to receive the customary parental blessing with a portrait of Lenin used as replacement for an icon: during the reception, the groom is murdered in a drunken brawl especially staged for the purpose.[11]

Whatever good was introduced by Soviet innovations or preserved by village tradition was, unfortunately, overshadowed by the elements of evil inherent in both. The picture presented of village life in the 1920's is frightening:

> Everybody drinks—it's hideous. Schools are closed: sagging porches, collapsing chimneys, broken windows; men teachers work on kulaks' farms, repair old overshoes; girls become kept mistresses of wealthy peasant louts. Hospitals and dispensaries stand idle; the village is racked by typhus, scarlet fever, diphtheria, syphilis. Neglected kids are chasing dogs, smoking, swearing like troopers—all money and grain is used to make the home-brewed poisonous vodka [*samogon*].[12]

The excerpt is from a sketch (*očerk*), a borderline genre reporting on facts in fictional form which has been traditionally popular in Russian letters. Portraying contemporary reality was easier for a country correspondent (*sel'kor*) than it was for a fiction writer because the former could claim, at least in the 1920's, that he was merely writing as an eyewitness, reporting facts. The writer, on the other hand, countering accusations of pessimism and exaggeration of facts, was reminded that portrayal is not photography; that the first rule of realism is selectivity; and that for a proletarian artist selectivity should have an ideological slant. The job of the country correspondent, therefore, though dangerous (many were beaten, a few murdered by peasants for "prying") was simpler, and his stories can be credited with veracity.

It is these stories that corroborate fiction's gloomy image of the postrevolutionary Russian village as forsaken by God and man. They tell of huts buried in the snow, haunted, as in the times of Kievan princes, by prowling wolves; of wise women (*znaxorki*) and sorcerers; of sickness and filth; of obscene languages, fistfights, beatings, rapes. And they tell of blind, brutish, ruinous drinking: how whole families—women, old folks, children, as well as men—were getting drunk on samogon vodka.

But what, one may ask, of the clergy? of teachers? of those better educated, cleverer, among the peasantry itself? Finally, what of local representatives of the Soviet regime? The frightened, impoverished clergymen were struggling to keep their families from starving; many teachers were former White officers content to be forgotten in their obscure corners; village NEPmen, the kulaks and the speculators (*mešočniki*), some of them survivors of local Party purges, were busy getting rich;[13] and while one community of six hundred homesteads allegedly lacked leadership because it had only two Party members, another was terrorized and robbed by its council chairman, an ex-Tsarist policeman turned Communist, a case not at all exceptional.[14]

The situation was not altogether new. As reflected in literature before World War I, the morals of the Russian peasant were low, Tolstoy's beliefs to the contrary notwithstanding. Works of Bunin, Chekhov, and Uspensky in particular show many a rural scene of licentiousness, brutality, and drunkenness, staged against the grim backdrop of ignorance, poverty, and filth. The main difference was that, of old, vice had been recognized as such even by the wicked, and the precepts of virtue, however little practiced, were clearly spelled out and accepted. In the wake of the revolutionary strife, though, not only did the village morals deteriorate further, but the very validity of their standards was challenged. Sexual morality was the prime target. Labeled as prejudice, it could be discarded at will by the followers of the new Soviet way of life. And until the principles of Communist morality were defined and established, these followers could boast of their being free from obsolete superstitions and turn a deaf ear to accusations of profligacy and godlessness coming from the enemy camp.

In the middle of the bitter kulak-versus-pauper struggle, it was easy for zealous innovators to mistake old-fashioned license for progressiveness, and for the cynical to take advantage of this confusion in terms. Both sides—the supporters of the regime and its adversaries—blamed each other for the demoralization spreading like wildfire, and recognized the issue as both ethical and political, since not only were the standards of personal behavior at stake, but the whole institution of the family, as well.

In the early postrevolutionary period, Communism, having denounced the family as the seat of oppression and the bastion of reaction, supported its ideological stand with concrete measures. A decree on marriage and divorce and one on inheritance were issued by the Party within a few months after the Bolshevik coup. Next, on September 16, 1918, the first Code of Laws of the Russian Soviet Republic relating to Civil Status and Domestic Relations was adopted by the All-Russian Central Committee. Henceforth, divorce, almost impossible before the Revolution, became available at the request and presence of one party, while the other could be notified *post-factum*, even by an ad in the papers. The only restriction in the marriage law was a ban on union between first-degree relatives. Abortions were legal and free. Illegitimacy was abolished; all parental rights were terminated at the age of sixteen for daughters and eighteen for sons; children no longer inherited, for the parents' property went to the State.[15]

The results, as the contemporary press and literature testify,[16] were so alarming that the Party saw fit to take some action and invited the opinions and the participation of Russian society. In 1926, a new, much stricter law was passed regulating divorces, marriages, alimony and child support payments, and outlawing abortions, and while it did not immediately alleviate the crisis, the unusual concern shown by the public testifies to the gravity of the situation. The press and law, literature and public opinion exercised their influence as of old, primarily in the city; the village had its own ways of dealing with such problems and its own reasons for using them.

As in the case of religion, the family issue had two aspects for the village: spiritual and practical. Communism set about destroying the image of the dignified, pious peasant home, where several generations, living under the same roof, were ruled by a wise patriarch, where all sons were industrious, all daughters virtuous, and all parents knew what was best for their children. After the Revolution, while the illusory quality of this idyllic home had been long apparent, the older generation was not only shocked by young people's disrespectful and loose behavior, but also frightened by the financial threat it presented. An unmarried daughter's baby had always meant not only dishonor for her family, but also the expense of raising it; under the new law, a bachelor son could also be sued for child support, for which the whole family was responsible since property was owned in common. Moreover, young couples now refused to live with their in-laws, demanding their share of land and cattle, and it was plain that old-fashioned family unity was rapidly melting away. Free love and common-law marriages, though considered in the city to be the epitome of progress, were unacceptable to the peasant because they gave no guarantee of stability or of a secure future household. Desertion and divorce not only meant broken hearts, but also endangered family property, and the latter consideration was by far the more important. "Marriages have to be lawful," peasants insisted. "A peasant family is like a cart: once you're harnessed, you've got to pull it for all you are worth, and no kicking either! It's not like in factory life here; we've got the land to consider."[17]

The village Komsomol, in spite of its small membership, had an important part in undermining the old-fashioned family. Sanctioned by the Party, the ancient conflict between "fathers and sons" was becoming a road leading to a youth's life career, and his defiance of parental authority acquired the glamor of a battle for progress. In the all-out war waged by the Soviet government against what Marx had called "the idiocy of village life," the Komsomol's activities ranged as high in importance as did anti-religious propaganda and the liquidation of illiteracy committees. But the most deadly weapon was the emancipation of women. Men were providers and protectors: they dealt with the dangers of the outside world—taxes, requisitions, civil war; they worked the land and laid down the law at home. Women—the unpaid workers, the nonvoting members of the village community—were nevertheless in charge of the basic rituals of its life. Matchmakers, mourners, midwives, gossipmongers, and custodians of social propriety, they had for centuries been carrying on their bent shoulders the whole structure of the family *byt*. When they suddenly straightened up and demanded freedom, the structure developed fissures. It is not surprising, therefore, that fiction writers, searching for characters representative of postrevolutionary change, first chose peasant women.

2

Peasant Women in Postrevolutionary Fiction

❧

BEFORE THE REVOLUTION

Peasant women have never been as prominent in Russian literature as the strongly agrarian nature of the country and the intelligentsia's preoccupation with the peasant problem might lead one to expect. Russian fiction had concentrated on the portrayal of the landed gentry and of the bourgeois milieu. The peasants, especially women, were seldom protagonists, and even then they were not so much persons as means of illustrating a point. The point could range from Karamzin's discovery in *Poor Liza* (1792) that "even peasant women are capable of love" to Tolstoy's assertion of the power of sin in *The Devil* (1889). But it could be made by any ingenue in the role of Liza and any *femme fatale* in that of Stepanida, while Natasha Rostova, for instance, or Dostoevsky's Nastasya Filippovna are personalities impossible to duplicate. Even the tragic heroines of Grigorovich's, Leskov's, and Pisemsky's famed works serve primarily as illustrations of the dark sides of the peasant byt.[1]

As secondary characters, though, peasant women were popular with Russian writers; young girls, particularly, are generously endowed with charm and beauty. Griboedov and Pushkin cast them, pert and pretty, in the classic role of the heroine's confidante. They roam the genteel world of Turgenev, shy and gentle young creatures, humbly accepting their tragic lot, be it "deep love such as is known only to a simple Russian girl" (Malanya in *A Nest of Gentlefolk*, 1859) or a loveless marriage at the mistress's whim (Tanya in *Mumu*, 1854). Chekhov is full of sympathy for tender young Lipa (*In the Ravine*, 1900), who sings like a lark as she scrubs the floors; Tolstoy, for the simple Marina and even for the poor, half-witted Akulina (both in *The Power of Darkness*, 1887). They are uncomplaining victims of a senselessly harsh society and an indictment against it.

Like theatrical extras, peasant girls are so numerous and unobtrusive that they belong to the setting rather than to the plot. Barefoot, apple-cheeked "serf wenches" dance and sing in the harvest festivals of eighteenth-century musical comedies and bustle contentedly enough around the country estates in Aksakov's, Gogol's, and Goncharov's novels. But by the end of the nineteenth century the picture darkens. The village belles with a reputation for vocal and choreographic talents (*pevun'i, pljasun'i*) are replaced by Shchedrin's brutish, miserable "slaveys" (*xolopki*) and by the ragged, ignorant girls of Uspensky, Bunin, and Chekhov—the "extra mouths to feed" in the huts of landless peasants.

The role of old peasant women is even more insignificant. Even humane Korolenko, at the miniature Last Judgment of "Makar's Dream" (1885), demands justice for the hapless hero but forgets his anonymous old wife. Infirm grandmothers, ancient as the icons they resemble, moaning, praying, scolding their daughters-in-law, are prerequisites in every peasant hut. So, in well established households, are the kind, faithful nurses who dote on their young charges and counterbalance the evil influences of French governesses on the Russian gentry's education. They exist so that the main characters—Pushkin's Tatyana, Turgenev's Liza—can turn to them for comfort. In *War and Peace* it is a habit with the Rostov girls to cry out their sorrows on the soiled, pink feather bed on Nanny's trunk in a draughty passage, the trunk which contains all her earthly goods.

This curious lack of personality, of a unique, individual lot in life peculiar to the female peasant in Russian literature is particularly noticeable in the case of married women. And it is the more surprising because no Russian fictional character is more pitied—and pitiful—than is the proverbial "much-enduring peasant wife" (*mnogostradal'naja baba*). Nekrasov in *Grandfather Frost* (1863) sums her up in these famous lines:

These are the hardest lots devised by Fate:
One is to wed a slave; and yet another
Is to obey a slave—a lowly state;
The third—to be a slave's unhappy mother.
And all these loads united in the end
To crush the women of the Russian land.

There is no need to recall here the concern over the fate of the peasant shown by Russian writers, acutely conscious of their moral and civic obligations toward "the younger brother." Serf or pauper freeman, helpless victim or ruthless kulak, repository of national virtues or ignorant drunkard, the peasant had been prominent in Russian literature from its very beginnings. His plight was movingly portrayed; numerous suggestions were made for means of improvement. Abolition of serfdom was long considered a panacea; then, after it did not prove to be one, it was land and judiciary reform, educational programs, the constitution, and the Revolution. Practically every intellectual and political school of thought offered its solution to the peasant problem, and so, through their own emotional media, did the arts. Yet, even if successfully accomplished, none of these reforms was (nor was ever claimed to be) able to solve the problems of the peasant woman, because she had the additional handicap of being ensnared in *byt*.

A *baba*'s path was, as the proverb puts it, "from the stove to the door" of her squalid, overcrowded hut, extended, of course, to the boundaries of the village. In this tiny inferno, from the age of five she nursed her still younger siblings, helped her mother with housework, tended geese and sheep. At fifteen she was, irrespective of her wishes, married off and moved to another hut, perhaps another village, thus exchanging her parents' grumbling and occasional cuffs for a husband's beatings, a mother-in-law's abuse, and only too often, a father-in-law's lasciviousness.[2] From then on, babies were born every year, a few of whom survived; backbreaking work in primitive conditions—house and farm chores, hoeing, harvesting—never abated; then, all too early, came old age, then death.

A judicial or land reform could hardly affect the baba: in spite of a lifetime of hard work, she earned no money, owned no property, had no influence on family affairs, except such as any shrewish wife can achieve within a wrangling household. Even the abolition of serfdom could do little to improve her lot: within the patriarchal peasant family she remained her parents' slave, then her husband's. The poorest, the most stupid man, despised and insulted by everyone else in his native

village, still could find another human being who would bow to his
will, work for him, and show him the respect denied by everybody
else: all he had to do was to marry. Drunkenness, poverty, and physical
deformity were no obstacles; he was still her master: church, law, and
custom all agreed to that. At a village wedding, the father of the bride
would bless the kneeling couple with an icon and then strike his
daughter with a whip and hand it to the groom. Henceforth, it was to
the husband that the duty of "teaching" the girl was transferred. Then
the wedding party would leave for church where, as part of the
marriage service, the priest warned that a wife should fear her husband.
If, in the course of her married life, she were to muster enough courage
(or were desperate enough) to run away from her husband, the law
allowed him to bring her back through the police. But, of course, she
never tried: village life did not breed rebels, except perhaps occasionally one who would risk her salvation in heaven and whatever sem-
blance of status she had on earth for the brief respite of an illicit love
affair. Otherwise, to a respectable married woman love seldom meant
anything besides an ever acquiescent performance of her marital duties
towards her usually sullen and brutal husband.

Under these conditions, then, what kind of fictional heroines could
babas become within Russian literature? Nekrasov wrote moving
poems about their tragic lot as peasant mothers and widows; Grigorovich, Leskov, and Turgenev vividly painted their loveless marriages;
Pisemsky, a desolate romance; Chekhov and Bunin, their everyday lives
of miserable drudgery. But the women themselves could not be remembered other than as representatives of a species, for they actually had
no separate, individual existence. Their plight was so obvious, their
feelings so predictable, that authors did not attempt to elaborate on
them. Neither did they themselves speak out. They were martyrs:
starved, beaten, abused, in need of help which was not forthcoming.
So, like visitors at the bedside of an incurable patient, the writers—and
the readers—sighed in sympathy, and chastened, tiptoed away.

THE PEASANT WOMAN'S
EMANCIPATION

In postrevolutionary literature, the peasant woman suddenly came out
of the shadowy wings and advanced to the brightly lit center of the

stage. She belonged there. In the first place, Russian literature had long been interested in reflecting the social aspects of contemporary reality; next, the impact of the ever docile baba's rebellion on family life held a dramatic appeal for fiction writers; lastly, class struggle and the emancipation of women were basic parts of the Marxist program. As heroine, the destitute, downtrodden baba boldly assuming her newly acquired rights met all the specifications, and so was immediately granted the freedom of the Soviet realm of fiction.

The works of Fellow Travelers of the formalist school were an exception. As a literary group, they were indifferent to social problems in general and to those of the village in particular; since they were not given to mystic nationalism, they had little use for the peasant woman as a symbol of Russia, such as had fascinated Blok, and alien to Marxism, had none for a baba freshly promoted to the status of a Soviet citizen. Therefore, the woman's role in the phantasmagoric village of their creation was limited to that of the female of the species *par excellence*. It was through the realist school of Soviet writers that the new peasant woman became a key literary figure.

Protesting women had been known in pre-Soviet Russian literature, but they had not included peasants. Here, then, was a new fictional character without precedent or model in the past: the semiliterate baba who dared to challenge every principle traditionally held sacred in her environment, a pioneer of progress. Her characterization presented some difficulties, because on the one hand, she was required to possess an unusual personality, while on the other, she was alleged to be representative of the rank and file of the needy (and therefore progressive) peasantry. Literary critics resolved the contradiction by acclaiming these first pioneers of emancipation as a "type," a rare and happy summation of features characteristic of her whole kind. Yet she could not claim to be the image of the Russian peasant women, because in reality she stood for a small minority among them.

The Soviet regime, having in the past repeatedly declared itself the champion of women as the exploited victims of bourgeois society and having from the beginning granted them equal rights, could have expected women to be staunch supporters of their liberators. Actually, the "much-enduring peasant wife" proved exceedingly difficult to liberate.

The reasons were practical and psychological. A peasant woman could not suddenly leave her hut and walk outside that proverbial door.

Who would take care of the children, do the farm chores, wash, and cook until the communal nurseries, kitchens, laundries, and the rest of Kollontay's socialist dream came true? Also, how well were these women equipped to accept Lenin's invitation to "participate in governing the State"? " 'There are millions of them,' " one of Tolstoy's wise old peasants had said in *The Power of Darkness*, " 'and all like beasts in the forest. As she grows up, so she dies. . . . A man, he may at least learn something in the pub, or in the army, or in prison, maybe. But a woman!' "[3] Small wonder then, that when overnight these wretched creatures became free and were called to action, their response was not enthusiastic, and the few volunteers were overwhelmingly outnumbered by laggards.

The blame for that was laid at the old regime's door. Women, it was contended, had been stultified by neglect and brutal treatment, and so, many of them simply could not immediately appreciate the happy change in their situation. These should be aroused from torpor, educated, and encouraged to accept their new rights and duties. Surely, these recent slaves could conceive of no greater joy, and had nothing to lose but the yokes of tyranny? It was nevertheless apparent that the sound of chains breaking did not make equally pleasant music to all women, and to more timid souls was frightening because, conservative by nature, they felt insecure in the face of change.

Since the solid front of opposition encountered by the small avant-garde of progressives included both the determined supporters of the old forms of village byt and its spineless victims, the peasant women in early Soviet fiction fall into three groups: pioneers, reactionaries, and weaklings.

PIONEERS OF PROGRESS

The pioneers' isolated position and their small numbers did not, of course, detract from their importance; on the contrary, it was the courageous few who starred as fiction's protagonists, while the large conservative camp was represented only by secondary characters. The drama of the peasant woman's awakening was shown against a backdrop of unrest, known as "the bitter, obstinate class struggle within the postrevolutionary village." The plot, which also provided the pattern for character development, was standard: the story of female slavery, the heroine's revolt against the reactionary environment, and finally, her transformation into a conscious follower and full-fledged co-builder of Soviet society.

This miracle of the ignorant baba discovering and doggedly follow-ing the path of progress was explained by her "social instinct." The definition itself was coined in later years, but the principle was ac-cepted from the start.[4] Since class consciousness was considered an attribute of the proletariat, the proletariat alone qualified at the time as the toiling masses; the peasants did not arrive until the 1930's, after the kulaks had been liquidated and the poor and "middling rich" peasants had joined the kolkhozes. In the meantime, however, the poor were credited with "revolutionary consciousness"—a natural, built-in hatred towards the rich and a desire to support the Soviet regime—and it was as part of this larger phenomenon that the emancipated baba, the female pioneer of progress, emerged in postrevolutionary fiction.

The genus is fully represented by Neverov's "Marya the Bolshevik" (1921), one of the first prose works to be published after the Revolu-tion. It is a short-short story, almost an anecdote, allegedly told by a witness, and its heroine can rightfully claim the title of the very first "New Woman" in Soviet literature.

Spiritually, she is undaunted; physically, she resembles a large kewpie doll and is mated, in an intentionally ridiculous contrast, to a small, ill-tempered husband. Before the Revolution, Marya made a great show of being an obedient wife, duly afraid of her puny lord, but during the Civil War she suddenly awakens. She stoutly refuses to perform her former duties, including that of bearing children; elected "for a joke" to head the village council, she rules it with an iron hand, becomes active in organizing a local Zhenotdel, reads books and newspapers, renounces religion. Finally, she divorces her harassed husband, dons a man's blouse and a pointed cap with a red star, and when the Cossacks temporarily seize the village, leaves with the retreating Bolsheviks. "She was seen in another village, but perhaps it was someone else, there are so many of the likes of her nowadays," the narrator ruefully comments.

There must have been, if the readers' reactions are any indication. Marya was praised, congratulated, and invited to visit kindred souls in other villages. In the event that her address at the moment was un-known to Neverov, he was requested to advertise since, fortunately, her full name had been mentioned in the story.[5]

However true to life, Marya as a fictional character is not a personality but a terse summation of the new peasant woman's essential characteristics. All postrevolutionary village heroines follow the same blueprint: like Marya, they are bubbling with vitality, eager to destroy the obsolete forms of village life (particularly social and religious prejudices), intrepid in their actions, and impervious to the censure they provoke in the conservative camp. They claim no ideologically approved program for their rebellion—Dasha Chumalova of *Cement* (1925), the proletarian heroine, will be the first to do that—but they know full well what they are rebelling against, and do it with gusto.

Within the narrow boundaries of the short story, Marya stands like a poster: sketched with a few bold lines, colorful, and two-dimensional. The protagonists of the first Soviet peasant novels—we will choose A. Korobov's *Katya Dolga* (1925) and L. Seyfullina's *Virineya* (1924) as representatives—are painted like portraits, in a more leisurely manner and with a brush more attentive to details. They are, to be sure, far from sophisticated; the authors are either too naïvely careful to preserve the heroine's resemblance to a living model, or too anxious to focus all the light on her. Virineya's story faithfully reproduces that of Arina, janitress of the school where Seyfullina was teacher,[6] though the fictional beauty's fiery temperament stems from Dostoevsky and her awareness of social wrongs, from current political trends in literature. And Katya's full-length portrait takes up all the space, eliminating the landscape, reducing her village to a dimly outlined background, with all other characters in the novel barely sketched in.

Katya Dolga has no niche in the gallery of Soviet fictional heroines and from the artistic standpoint deserves none.[7] Yet she is a landmark on the road to the Russian woman's emancipation, perhaps even comparable to Dasha Chumalova of *Cement*, precisely because she is the precursor of the artistically mediocre, standard type of a kolkhoz woman. Like Marya the Bolshevik, she is buxom and beetle-browed; like her, too, she is spiritually and physically a head taller than her husband, who, returning from the war a cripple, became involved with kulaks and black marketeers. Forced into a loveless marriage at eighteen, Katya at the time of the Revolution is twenty-five and mother of two children. She has known nothing but drudgery and poverty, but this allegedly helps her to find her way instinctively to the Revolution, which she at first opposed, having mistaken it for the commissars' requisitioning bread from peasants.

Soon she is participating in village government, organizing women, supporting the activities of a budding Komsomol. In the latter interest she is prompted by more than just social zeal: the head of the Komsomol, Ivanok, a boy of eighteen, is Katya's lover, and she has by him a child whom she refuses to have baptized. When Ivanok is murdered by the kulaks (a hero's end, destined to become classic in Soviet literature), Katya dramatically presents her baby to the mourners assembled at his funeral and urges all women to help her continue the struggle for the New, of which Ivanok was a pioneer.

Admittedly, she is no romantic heroine, certainly not a decadent one. There is nothing of the dreamer in her, nothing mysterious nor hysterical. Her love for Ivanok is frankly sexual, though their liaison is properly ennobled by a common interest in the Komsomol. She is very practical: even her conflict with the Church, obligatory in a "progressive" character, began with her protesting what she considered a too generous land allotment to the village priest; and she is well aware not only of the ideological, but also of the economic advantages of the village commune system. But she is not unfeeling; she readily supports her invalid husband and refuses to let him go to the poorhouse, when he himself considers this a fair solution.

She has more than just a touch of masculinity in her physique and disposition—as well she should, in order to claim a man's job and place in the village community. Whatever she achieves within it is done through hard work, plain talk at village meetings, and faith in progress. She performs no miracles singlehandedly; the author sees to it that Katya has the support of the young and the poor, dialectically balanced by the hatred of the rich and the censure of the reactionaries. But she fights her own battles, and these are numerous, particularly in the terrain of customs and morals, where everything about Katya incenses the gossipmongers: her illicit romance, her illegitimate and unbaptized baby, her meddling in village politics, even her literacy—she "attended school for two winters"—and her love for cleanliness.

The latter, in Katya's case, could be considered symbolic of her mission as a pioneer of progress. Her efforts to cleanse the village way of life resemble those she had made on entering her in-laws' hut as their son's bride.

> How was she to live here? You could plant vegetables on the floor; on the walls soot was an inch thick; festoons of cobwebs covered the ceiling. An awful stench was coming from under the stove. After a week or

so, she began by scooping out the stuff from under that stove, and there was plenty of it: rotten potatoes, putrid cabbage leaves, dirty rags, and even a dead cat. . . . The family was angry with her: "We don't need your fussing, Catherine; we've been living fine this way without it."[8]

Such is Katya: strong, loud-voiced, matter-of-fact; as a wife, erstwhile humble, then emancipated and yearning for a free union with a man who shares her political ideals and work; as a mother, dedicated, in spite of numerous outside activities; eagerly seeking education but limiting it to fields of immediate import—the rudiments of Marxism and farming; an efficient social worker, an organizer with a gift for leadership, trusting and seeking the Party's guidance always but, realizing her limitations, not unduly hasty in joining it. Such is Katya and such, under different names and with minor changes of details paralleling those in government policies, will henceforth be the other peasant heroines in Soviet fiction. Katya will start from ideological ignorance, her own and that of her milieu; from hardships economic, social, and those imposed by the byt; and will conquer them all. She will achieve personal happiness by subordinating it to work for the common welfare, and this, with appropriate variations in other villages and later in other kolkhozes, will also be the story of her successors.

Virineya, the heroine of Seyfullina's novel, escapes from the hardships of an orphaned childhood to work as a servant in the city at fifteen. She soon returns to the village with a lover, and they openly live in sin until she tires of him and leaves. She leads a dissipated life working on a road construction until she meets Pavel, a Communist just home from the war. She becomes his devoted though still unwedded wife, the mother of his child, and his helper in partisan activities. In the latter capacity Virineya is killed by the Cossacks.

Though the acknowledged star of the early village literature, Virineya did not contribute towards the establishment of the type of the kolkhoz woman, because she limits her fight against the old byt to the narrow confines of sexual freedom. She could have, nevertheless, qualified as a rebel and an innovator—peasant women preferring common law unions to a church marriage did not appear in prerevolutionary fiction—but her joyless, desperate drinking bouts and promiscuity could have hardly set her up as an example for Soviet womanhood. In addition, her bitter enjoyment of the power which her sultry beauty held over men's senses had enough decadent flavor to exclude Virineya from the premises of sound proletarian art.

In a sense, Virineya's story could still be termed an awakening, a former slave's sudden realization of her rights and duties in bringing about a new social order, if only it resembled less the traditional bourgeois story of a fallen woman rehabilitated through love. Soviet critics have done their best to have Virineya accepted as a New Woman. They have pointed out her flouting of the village traditions of propriety, her independent spirit, her anti-religious sallies, even the fact that "if she did sin it was with poor people like herself," while scornfully rejecting rich, would-be seducers.[9] Still, the question of her ideological spontaneity, of whether she came to love Pavel because he represented Communism or vice versa, has remained controversial,[10] and thus no later kolkhoz heroine came from the same mold as Virineya.

Virineya's case points to the necessity of distinguishing in Soviet literature between the authentic pioneer of progress and just a mutinous soul; the former fights for independence, the latter for personal happiness, as they are, respectively, moved by political awareness and by intense femininity. Virineya, who has a complex psychological makeup for a Soviet fictional character, is utterly feminine in that she is motivated solely by her emotions. Marya the Bolshevik has no time for romance; in Katya Dolga's busy schedule, Ivanok and her baby take no precedence over the affairs of the village council; and both women calmly disregard public gossip. But Virineya is proud and sensitive; she suffers; and her self-inflicted degradation becomes a hysterical challenge to society. Sensuous, but not really dissolute (she just pretends out of spite that she has many lovers), she is not a *grande amoureuse* either: Pavel is her only love, and he can hardly be called a passion. Her real vocation is motherhood; what she wants, in her own words, are children, born moreover properly, "of a husband and into his family."[11] Had she survived the partisan phase of the revolutionary struggle, she would have probably dedicated herself to raising babies rather than to the Zhenotdel. In fact, she even dies as a mother rather than as a partisan, because, having escaped arrest, she stealthily returns home, "drawn by her milk to the babe"—and perishes.

Sholokhov's Aksinya, the incandescent heroine of *The Quiet Don*, qualifies even less as a pioneer of women's emancipation, though she too has been hailed as such by literary critics. Her rebellion against old-fashioned morality is regarded as "one of the symptoms of the advancing great social storm," as "the fresh wind ushering in the coming of freedom," and even Grigory Melekhov becomes "not only the man she loves but a means of escape from the hopeless circle in which she is imprisoned by the reactionary Cossack byt."[12] Actually, except for her proud defiance of her brutal husband and of village opinion, Aksinya never steps onto the revolutionary path. Had she been led along it by Grigory, as Virineya was by Pavel, she would have followed him gladly. But since he himself forever vacillates between the Red and the White causes, Aksinya fights against the "dark realm" of Cossackdom only insofar as it keeps her and her lover apart.

Enthralled by the intensity and completeness of her passion the "Cossack Anna Karenina," as she is often called, shows no interest in women's emancipation, or for that matter, in any of the fateful political events exploding around her. For this reason, in spite of the period in which most of *The Quiet Don* is set, and except for the dates of the novel's publication, Aksinya does not really belong among the heroines of the Soviet literature. She certainly did nothing to help establish the pattern of the New Woman.

Thus, while Virineya continues the tradition of the Russian romantic heroine—high-strung, passionate, and tender—Marya and Katya are blazing the trail for the future heroines who, like themselves, will be blessed with energy, enviable health, and lack of imagination. All three, however, have a certain disarming candor, the result, perhaps, of their authors' enjoyment in portraying these courageous young women, whom they acclaimed as harbingers of a new and happy breed. The heroines of the works appearing a few years later, such as Anka in K. Gorbunov's *The Ice Is Breaking* (1927) and Steshka in F. Panfyorov's *The Village Bruski* (1928–37), will have lost the redeeming quality of naïveté. They are generously endowed with appropriate progressive traits (one can almost visualize the authors checking their list against the by then established blueprint); but their love affairs are vulgar, their speech graceless and didactic, and even their enthusiasm has a wooden quality. As fictional characters, they can no longer be compared to portraits or even to posters; they are stencils, and within another few years, they will be used for mass production of "typical female pioneers" under Socialist Realism.

In one of the earliest Soviet works of fiction, *Andron the No-Good* (1923)—an epitome of "class struggle within the village"—Neverov, the author of "Marya the Bolshevik," shows another pioneer baba in a poster-like apotheosis. Anna, having disposed of her home duties by passing them on to her husband, signs papers in the local Party's office, side-by-side with its chairman: "One banner is over his desk, another over hers; both are red, gold-fringed, and bear an inscription. His says, 'Proletarians of the world [unite]!' and hers, 'Comrade women [unite]!' "[13]

Anna's triumph is not an exception. As reflected in contemporary fiction, women's invasion of public affairs met with less opposition than did their emancipation at home. Possibly, a man did not feel as strongly about somebody's wife speaking at a village meeting as about his own wife's refusal to cook his dinner. In addition, men were inclined, at first, to treat women's rights as a joke, until they found out too late that it was not, as in the case of Marya the Bolshevik's election to the village council. Finally, these women's rights were backed by the government, and obstructing them could lead to trouble with the authorities. Thus the opposition, spearheaded by the kulaks, usually acted indirectly, including the heroine in its plottings against the regime. Her real troubles began at home.

There, the main antagonist was the husband, invariably a domestic tyrant and puny in contrast to his brawny spouse, so that the plot was narrowed to the Soviet version of "the battle of the sexes." The struggle lacks romance. Unlike her predecessors in prerevolutionary Russian literature, a pioneer baba turns against her husband as against an oppressor, not as an unloved man and not because she loves another. She may eventually find, usually among members of the local Komsomol, a worthier mate, one who would not resent her being a "de-married" woman (*razženja*); but basically she demands economic and political, not romantic, independence. She will no longer submit to beatings and abuse, insists she will come and go as she pleases, but goes to a Zhenotdel meeting, rather than to a rendezvous with a lover. Perhaps, busy neophyte of Marxism, she shuns the time-consuming intricacies of a love affair; perhaps she does not even believe in love, having been for so long a mere drudge, valued less than cattle and treated with less consideration. " 'Are we human?' " asks one of Neverov's heroines bitterly. " 'Horses, that's what we are, and so we are valued—as horses. As long as we are young and healthy, they make us pull the cart, and they also sleep with us, but once we are squeezed dry, they kick us out.' "[14] Another woman echoes: " 'People talk of love.

What is it like, love? I've lived with my husband for fifteen years and never found out, not once. All I got out of it was a big belly, year after year.' "[15] Virineya agrees. Romance is just a pretty lie invented by people in the cities:

> "All sorts of talk about love [in books]. Our village fellows have no use for that. They don't even waste sweet talk on girls, let alone on their wives. They will sometimes call a cow a pet name, or a horse, but a wife?—Never. He married her to do the work and to bear kids, not for petting. And even at work men will have some consideration for cattle, but not for a woman."[16]

Were they allowed by fiction writers to present their side of the argument, husbands might have said that perhaps they were incapable of tenderness and ignorant of love because they, too, had been stultified by hard work and poverty; and that to a peasant family, women's emancipation was not the least of postrevolutionary hardships. But old-fashioned husbands—and progressive heroines were always married to these—just obstinately insisted on what they considered their natural rights: " 'A sparrow pecks his female,' " protests a character in *Andron the No-Good*, " 'a rooster pecks his; why can't I beat up my woman?' "[17]

The third opponent of the progressive heroine, sometimes more formidable than kulaks or husbands, was the reactionary female, the real representative and faithful custodian of the old byt. To this sneering, lamenting gossip, Marya was a worse offender than Virineya. Virineya's behavior was scandalous but not unusual, simply a case of another wanton woman; but Marya's behavior was shocking, because it upset the established, normal order of things. Her participation in political activities could not, strictly speaking, be called sinful, but it was felt to be deeply immodest, unwomanly, and unprecedented.

This, essentially, was the main issue—the positions stormed by the progressives and defended by conservatives in postrevolutionary warfare over the byt. The progressives demanded female equality with men in matters economic, political, and personal. The conservatives, on the other hand, insisted that since a woman had never had equality before, she should not have it now. Throughout the 1920's a bitter fight went on between progressive heroines and reactionary villainesses in Soviet fiction, while the rank-and-file women hung back bewildered and undecided.

THE CONSERVATIVE CAMP

Villainesses

In Soviet literature villains are important: for a plot constructed on the dialectic principle of clashing opposites, negative characters are as necessary as positive ones. The Soviet writer's task is to present a situation in which the victory of the New is not only possible, but also artistically justifiable. The representatives of the Old must therefore be repulsive enough to set off the attractive qualities of their progressive antagonists and sufficiently strong to make the struggle impressive. After all, even St. George cannot prove his valor unless he meets a ferocious enough dragon; tame dragons caused a serious crisis in Soviet fiction after World War II.

The difficult point then is not so much the harm done by the villains in Sovietland, as the reasons for their existing at all. Why, indeed, should there still be reactionaries in Soviet society? In the early 1920's the answer was easy: these were the remnants of the Old, bred by the prerevolutionary environment. But as time went on, this explanation became no longer applicable to the younger generation, and the blame was laid on the latent influence of the former *byt* on the new Soviet way of life. Thus, younger women found themselves on the wrong side of the ideological tracks because of selfish indifference to society and progress, a spiritual heritage of the old *byt*. Having been exposed in their formative years to new ideas and opportunities, they should have been able to overcome such failings as vanity or sloth. Since they are seldom guilty of worse offenses, they are deficient in modern virtues rather than afflicted by obsolete vices, and constitute a milder strain of reactionaries, unquestionably negative, but not quite as wicked as those of the old generation. Rehabilitation for these young women is possible and at various stages of Soviet literature has been used as a welcome device for enlivening the plot, giving fuller play to a hero's talents, or providing a happy ending. The transfer of a character from the conservative to the progressive camp, however, was rare, and was more likely to take the form of a victim's awakening than of a villain's conversion.

The sinister cohort of reactionary females in Soviet fiction of the

1920's is headed by village hags. They are a frightening lot that could easily compete with the weird sisters who worked Macbeth's ruin. Wizened, crippled, mumbling prayers and witch formulas, they live alone at the far end of the village, in filthy shacks full of dry herbs and dark icons. It is to them that foolish, desperate young women come stealthily for help, bringing a string of beads or a dozen eggs to pay for a love potion or for an abortion. A brew of frog's bones and "magic" herbs, a potion laced with lye, knitting needles, dispensed with suitable incantations which invoke both evil spirits and saints impartially—these are their stock-in-trade. These malevolent hags, responsible for the death of several fictional heroines of the 1920's including Natalya Melekhova of *The Quiet Don*, vanished from literature at the end of that period.[18]

Numerically, the hags are few, sprinkled through the vast expanse of village fiction like toadstools through a forest, but reactionary, middle-aged babas are a large group. A stolid, massive body, they are like a hydra, whose many heads—round, angry, red faces under gaudy kerchiefs—challenge the heroic young followers of the new order. It is they who spread venomous slander about members of the Zhenotdel, obstruct husbands' efforts to join village communes, force daughters to marry profligate kulaks rather than industrious if indigent lovers. Unlike the timid victim type which will be discussed later, these women are neither dazed by the new legal and moral code that the Revolution has ushered in, nor ashamed of their own inability to adjust to it. On the contrary, they consciously reject it all with hostility and take pride in doing so. Writers spare no efforts in making them repulsive, morally and even physically.

A good example is Anisya, in F. Gladkov's *The New Land* (1930). The daughter of a kulak, she is vulgar, slovenly, and grasping. She nags her husband, Andrey, who fails to "reeducate" her, and ruins his career as chairman of a village commune. Engaged in petty local plots jointly with the village priest, she neglects her children while refusing to place them in the "godless" commune nursery. Finally, she attacks a young teacher whom she suspects of having an affair with her husband and is expelled from the community.

Anisya is an overt class enemy, viciously fighting the Soviet regime, until her whole kind is defeated and becomes extinct in the course of the village dekulakization. But Ula, in Panfyorov's *Village Bruski*, has no desire to fight the regime; instead, she selfishly tries to enjoy life within it. Far from disappearing from literature—and presumably from real life—her kind thrives, and in the 1930's, asserts itself as a regrettable Soviet phenomenon: a young woman who refuses to enlist in the ranks of heroines and so becomes a villainess by default. If Ula cannot claim to be the prototype of these Soviet neo-bourgeoises, she is certainly one of the earliest models. Since she is not of kulak origin, she cannot claim environment as her justification.

Her main vice is indolence: she has no interest in her husband's work, no desire for useful activity for herself. She is plump, sensuous, illiterate, and fond of pretty clothes. Daughter of a destitute peasant widow, she first marries a kulak's son, a sickly youth (the degenerate rich in Soviet literature are uniformly plagued with poor health), but leaves him to become the second wife of a local Party executive, the much-married Zhdarkin,[19] and wallows in sloth. When Zhdarkin demands that she put their baby in a nursery and take a job, she finds a less conscientious Party executive, and apparently lives happily ever after. Her literary descendants, the lazy females of the decade following World War II, were seldom allowed to go thus unpunished and usually lost their husbands to a worthier rival.

Victims

The militant women, reactionary as well as progressive, had the advantage of knowing their goals and their enemies. Good or evil, they were strong, purposeful, and exceptional: they acted. The majority of peasant women, though, were too shy to oppose either the old or the new, and so became victims of both. To them, postrevolutionary change was overpowering and incomprehensible; instinctively, they recoiled, faced, as it were, with a choice of two ways of being unhappy, the traditional or the modern.

The group includes wives who, betrayed, resignedly continue along the beaten track of household duties; younger wives who resort to old, desperate remedies; and old women, dazed and passive. It is the first type—a middle-aged mother who cannot afford the luxury of nursing a heartache, and squares her shoulders to take on new responsibilities—who will survive in Soviet fiction. Eventually, she will even become a New Woman. The other two gradually wither away, together with the old byt which had bred them.

The role played by female conservatism—partly inborn, partly bred by environment, and varying in degree and form—could not be disregarded by fiction. Were it indeed true, as Marxist theory has insisted, that all women had been cowed into domestic subservience by tyrannic males, this situation could have been remedied by the passage of appropriate laws alone. But the average wife proved quite willing to stay at home and take care of the household and the children. Of course, she wanted the home to be reasonably comfortable, but as long as her husband was a good provider (at least by the modest village standards), she would not insist on economic independence. Nor did she feel an irresistible urge to exchange domestic problems for political and social activities—"these things," said an old adage, "were not meant to be solved by a baba's mind"—and she was content to leave them to men. If this made her position in the household secondary, it also gave her a feeling of security, and there were other proverbs which actually boasted of the fact. "If I keep behind my husband's back, it protects me like a stone wall," says one; "he may be a poor husband, but he is a shield; once I get myself behind him, I have nothing to fear," says another.

Moreover, this secondary position gave women a certain moral status: by village standards a humble wife was a good wife, a respectable woman. Even if her virtue of patient humility was not rewarded, it was recognized by others and treasured by herself. As she grew older, she became a link in the chain of tradition which had been passed to her by her mother, and which her own daughter would inherit. Breaking this continuity was a step not easily taken by the majority of women, who had still to learn to value independence enough to fight for it.

Besides security and status, religious considerations also contributed to conservative attitudes in marital relationships. By the established village code a husband was not a tyrant in need of deposal but the God-appointed head of the family, to be obeyed and honored "even if *his* head was softer than a boiled turnip."[20] Wife beating ("teaching" was the term used in the old Russian byt) was his almost holy privilege, and most women continued to accept it as such. Fiction until as late as the mid-1940's abounds in large, sturdy women unprotestingly submitting to maltreatment by small men.

> "The holy books [a village Solon explains a sample case in 1929] say that a wife should fear her husband. Because of this, strength flowed into Pete every time [he 'taught' his Anchurka]; otherwise, to be sure, he would not have had a chance; she could have squashed him like a cockroach, with one finger."[21]

Much, of course, depended on husbands, whose treatment by Russian fiction under Socialist Realism underwent changes more drastic than those in women characters. Although domestic tyrants were little affected in the process, having always been barely outlined and equipped with villains' standard paraphernalia, Communists, beginning with the 1930's, acquired choice virtues, of which not the least was clean personal life. In the postrevolutionary decade, however, unfaithfulness was widespread among the progressives. And even the easy divorce which the regime had devised primarily as a tool to free the enslaved woman was used by devious male characters for reasons varying from ideological, to financial, to romantic. The reason which the characters themselves and the authors preferred was incompatibility: a union of a progressive and a conservative was doomed to end in divorce. This did not hurt female pioneers, who discarded their mates with ease, indeed, occasionally with glee, and started a new life; but old-fashioned wives simply continued their careers as long-enduring babas in changed conditions.

Husbands who had adopted new slogans outside the home but did not practice them within it seldom bothered to reform their outmoded married lives; instead, they usually found new wives. In a way, a conservative wife was happier in a marriage with a kulak, since both had at least common interests and desires, even if only those—despicable in the eyes of Soviet authors—of preserving their property and the old way of life. Moreover, a domestic tyrant would not desert his family, neglect the farm, or spend all his time in political activities which, so far as the woman could see, brought nothing except trouble.

It did not matter to such a wife (though to a kolkhoz woman it became of paramount importance) whether her husband was prompted by ideological zeal or by opportunism. She did not even know that such things existed. Used to being treated as an inferior, she did not resent her exclusion from the man's new interests and failed to recognize in them the source of her misfortunes. Instead, she looked for a female rival, and usually found her too: a city girl—a young lady or a factory worker—who, unlike the homewreckers of the past, claimed a wife's status.

Unfaithful husbands had not been a rarity in the Russian village, but these were only cases of male waywardness, passing whims which had no lasting ill effects on family security. The seducers—Russian folklore had always assumed the part to be female (*razlučnica*)—were wicked women exercising their power of sex appeal. This quality respectable women neither possessed nor, allegedly, coveted, and men always returned to their senses, and so, to their wives. What was happening to baba's marriage now was frighteningly different. How could she fight a usurper who treated her lord as an equal and took him irrevocably away by becoming his mate and companion, everything which a wedded wife alone had a right to be, even if she seldom was? Her old feminine weapons had suddenly become inadequate and she knew of no others. Arousing the husband's jealousy with an affair of her own would not do at all: an adulteress could expect no understanding, least of all from village women, who would turn overnight from sympathizing friends into hostile critics. Moreover, she usually still loved the man, for it should be noted that while the authors persisted in marrying their female pioneers to weaklings, old-fashioned wives were given handsome, virile men, whom, unfortunately, they lost all the easier to other women.

Goaded beyond endurance, a younger woman might make a futile attempt to win her husband back from her "flat-bellied" rival by drastic measures. In Neverov's *A Tale about Women* (1923), Darya, mother of five, secures an abortion from a village hag and dies, upbraided by her husband for her yokel stupidity.

Perhaps the best example is furnished by Katerina, in P. Romanov's "Black Fritters" (1925). Buxom and determined, she sets out from her village to pull the hair of the woman with whom her husband, Andrey, is living in town. The formidable rival proves to be a thin, shy girl who shares with Andrey a strange new world of Party and factory interests. And Katerina, in spite of her solid weight and three children left at home, seems to them as unreal as a ghost from the past. They are kind: Andrey gives her some money; the girl, in return for the customary village gift of black rye fritters, a parcel for the children. Subdued and confused, Katerina leaves, pondering on the power, greater than mere sex appeal, wielded by her husband's new wife. "What tempted him?" she wonders. "She, Katerina, could carry a full barrel of swill to the pigs. This girl could not even lift a pail of milk." In the end, "waving her hand in final farewell, Katerina made the sign of the cross and started on her way home."[22]

The case of Natalya in *The Quiet Don*, perhaps the most neglected wife in Soviet literature, is different. Grigory, her wayward husband, is not a Communist, and Aksinya, her invincible rival, is a peasant like herself and barely literate. Thus, if Natalya's married life begins with a suicidal attempt and ends in death from an abortion, the reason is the traditional sway of sexual attraction held by Aksinya over Grigory. It is, in fact, so traditional a situation that in Soviet fiction under Socialist Realism, it no longer fits into an acceptable plot pattern.

By the end of the 1920's, the topic of humble wives wronged by progressive husbands lost its popularity with writers. The moral standards required of the New Soviet Man were becoming increasingly higher in Soviet fiction, while patient humility in a woman came to be considered a reactionary attribute. Instead, abandoned wives became active in the Zhenotdel and began to help other victims. Matrena, in A. Zavalishin's "The First Try" (1927), challenges in a divorce court the decision of the People's judge, who happens to be her former husband, and wins the case for her protégée. The story of Praskovya, the heroine of P. Zamoysky's *The Bast Shoes* (1929–36), is very illustrative of this awakening, but it belongs to the 1930's and will be discussed within that period.

The old women are pitiful, even the kulaks' wives. Such is Klusha in *The Village Bruski*, who for three years has been carrying the family nest egg, a small hoard of gold coins, around her neck. Her husband, who is hiding the gold from the Soviet authorities, answers her whining complaints about sores on her breasts with a curt: " 'Sprinkle them with ashes. Bear up till I can think of a better hiding place.' " Poor Klusha herself, though a grandmother, is no more capable of thinking than an eight-year-old, and in any case, she too takes for granted that property is more important than its owner.

Soviet stories exposing this attitude, common in the peasant byt, are numerous. Among the most characteristic are A. Zavalishin's "They Signed Up" (1927) and P. Romanov's "The Blue Dress" (1928). In the former, an old couple ask to "sign up" for a divorce: the husband is willing to go on feeding his meek spouse of forty years, who has become an invalid, but wants to take a new, healthy wife to work on his farm. His grief when the sick woman dies suddenly at the end of the procedure is sincere, but is aggravated by the unnecessary expenditure of the rouble fee. In the second story, the husband, who, while drunk, has accidentally stabbed his wife at their daughter's wedding, plans on remarrying immediately in order to save the expenses of a hired helper. They discuss the chance of her living on as a useless invalid, but she reassures him on this score: she is definitely dying. In a way, this matter-of-fact, impersonal cruelty is more poign-ant than the brutal beatings to which the long-enduring baba was subjected in nineteenth-century Russian fiction.

The 1920's also feature a whole gallery of sad old mothers. The most tragic among these is Ostrovnov's octogenarian mother in Sholokhov's *Virgin Soil Upturned*. She had blessed him to join the Whites, who were plotting an insurrection against "the godless monsters who had closed the churches," and he murders the oldster when her garrulity threatens to betray them all.[23] Others hopelessly try to protect their children against the spiritual ruin they are bringing onto themselves by their blasphemies and new, immoral ways. Such is the mother of Vaska, Virineya's consumptive lover; Andron the No-Good's gentle mother; the victim of "Superstition"; Ilinichna from Sholokhov's *Quiet Don*—the list is long.

As time goes on, these poor souls, clucking like frightened hens who have fostered ducklings, disappear from the world of Soviet fiction. From the thirties on, they are replaced by gentle grandmothers, now treated kindly by their children, those busy builders of socialism. They cook, wash, and rock the cradle, and at village feasts join the chorus praising the achievements of the Soviet regime. Brought to poll stations in the kolkhoz car, they cast their votes with gratitude and pride; they tell their granddaughters about the bad old days of their own youth and remind them that they can fully appreciate the magnificent work done by Lenin's Party only when they get acquainted with the ac-cursed conditions of their mothers' and grandmothers' past. " 'Well, and so did my life slip by!' " one old woman sighs at a family cele-bration of a girl flier's visit home. " 'Now, I might have liked to fly, too!' "[24]

Their husbands, who nowadays would not dream of tyrannizing them, also take part in the chorus of praise, and moreover, try to put their feeble shoulders to the wheel of common effort. Indeed, old men "marching into Communism" early became a requisite of the standard pattern in Soviet fiction. But their old wives, appreciative and quietly happy now, still keep within the familiar shadows of the peasant woman's natural habitat: between the stove and the door of the hut.

3

Peasant Women
Under Socialist Realism

🍃

THE 1930'S: A PERIOD
OF TRANSITION

The developments in Soviet literature following the inauguration of
land collectivization in 1928 importantly affected women characters in
village fiction. Because plots turned from portraying the emotional
experiences of an individual to the economic achievements of a group,
emancipated heroines no longer occupied the center of the stage. The
village theme lost its dominant position to the industrial theme, and so
the interest in the baba's tribulations also waned. Yet the increasing
tendentiousness of Soviet fiction prevented her return to the
prerevolutionary limbo. If she was no longer needed to help destroy
old customs, she could now promote new ones, something the Katya
Dolgas had not been qualified to do.

Now passions had subsided, reactionaries were defeated, and there
was no need to apply drastic measures. Women's participation in
village government had become routine, Zhenotdels could be abolished
because members had already learned to exercise their rights, and "the
equality of the workday wages"* had freed them from domestic ty-

* *Ravenstvo trudodnja*, Stalin's definition of the economic independence achieved
by women through equal salaries for a day's work in a kolkhoz.

rants. A kolkhoz woman, economically independent, could simply show to the door a husband who, returning from the wars, attempted to maltreat her as of old; or he would be forced to mend his ways because his wife threatened to divorce him, and his children, to report a spanking to their kindergarten management.[1]

As times changed, extremes disappeared. Nobody nowadays insisted on church marriages nor on blessing the newlyweds, whether with an icon or with Lenin's portrait. Children were no longer baptized or "Octobered," but simply given names, and the names themselves had also changed. Ideological names, such as Vladilena or Kim (for Vladimir Lenin and *Kommunističeskij Internacional Molodeži*, respectively) were superseded by elegant ones, like Ludmila and Yury, a snobbism noted by peasant writers at various periods.[2] And if the old-fashioned Domna and Vlas had vanished, so had Revolyutsya and Terror.

Still, the times of Marya the Bolshevik—adjusted, to be sure, to revised patterns—were not forgotten. Sequels to the bestsellers of the 1920's and peasant *romans-fleuves* still featured the careers of the pioneers, now matronly, and of the liberated former victims. A heroine might even take a new lease on life in an extra volume, added for the purpose. For instance, Marka, in the 1928 edition of N. Kochin's *The Girls*, tried to escape her miserable life by suicide. But in the 1935 edition she "awakened" to her new rights, and by participating in Komsomol activities and taking a lover, provided the novel with the newly mandatory happy ending.

In P. Zamoysky's novel *The Bast Shoes*, the march of time is even more evident, because, while the plot takes place in the years 1923–32, the book's four volumes appeared between 1929 and 1936. The novel begins with Praskovya's Communist husband leaving her with four children, for a city girl. With the help (deleted in later editions) of her young son, a *Komsomolets*, Praskovya overcomes her grief. She learns to read and promotes the expropriation of the kulaks and the organization of a kolkhoz, of which she eventually becomes chairman. Dedicated and happy in her work, she rejects a reunion suggested by her now repentant husband (who has not been mentioned since Volume II), urges women in a radio speech to live up to Stalin's expectations, and returning home, discards in a symbolic gesture an old pair of muddy bast shoes. The humble resignation of a Katerina (in "Black Fritters") is no longer acceptable to the new Soviet woman.

Marka's transformation is a tendentious postscript to an earlier picture of contemporary reality. Praskovya's is only partly that, since only the last volume of *The Bast Shoes* conforms to the new blueprint; and so the ones previously published had to be revised. But it is the fictional career of Panfyorov's Steshka, in *The Village Bruski*, which runs parallel to the actual events of the period, that reflects fully the changing status of women in life and literature.

In 1928 (Part I), Steshka is a naïve girl who marries a kulak's son; in 1930 (Part II), she realizes that by being just a wife and mother she lets life pass her by; in 1933 (Part III), she leaves her villainous husband and gains kolkhoz recognition as a tractor driver. In 1937 (Part IV), married to Zhdarkin and mother of his son, she suffers a relapse into slothful domesticity, much as did Ula, her predecessor. But this time it is Zhdarkin who is to blame, and Steshka again escapes marital stagnation by returning to tractor driving. Like Praskovya, she ends in an apotheosis, broadcasting a speech during a visit to the Kremlin and Stalin:

> "Our feminine hearts are overflowing with emotions," she said, "and of these love is paramount. Yet, a wife should also be a happy mother and create a serene home atmosphere, without, however, abandoning work for the common welfare. She should know how to combine all these things while also matching her husband's performance on the job."
> "Right!" said Stalin.
> "How she has grown [spiritually]!" thought Zhdarkin,[3]

who, with other kolkhoz friends and relatives had been reverently listening to Steshka's speech.

Steshka's growth, drawn as a sequence of contrasting sketches like didactic kindergarten posters of a child alternatively grubby and scrubbed, has the simplest psychological design. Her speech, nevertheless, sums up the pattern of the new kolkhoz woman's behavior, and she can be considered typical of the emerging species. Since she is some fifteen years younger than Praskovya (at the time of the Revolution she was about twelve), she represents the generation of heroines who are awakening not to their rights but rather to their duties. Personal happiness these women can expect to achieve only as a bonus, by living up to the goals of social usefulness, and their youthful mistakes are corrected by the same means. A psychological climate similar to that accompanying the rise of the dictatorships in Germany and in Italy was becoming apparent in Russia. It found its expression in the 1936 constitution's pronouncements on the sanctity of family, which made abortions illegal, child support obligatory, divorce difficult, common law marriages invalid, and children born of them not entitled to the father's name.[4] And it was reflected in the fictional heroines' gradually increasing dedication to the German "three K's"—*Kirche, Küche, Kinder*—Soviet style.

THE NEW SOVIET BYT

Of the three, the kitchen—in the larger context of a household in general—remained sketchy throughout the 1930's. At most, only housekeeping chores were mentioned: promptly and efficiently dispatched after a full day of outside work, they contributed to the heroine's status. Since World War II, however, particularly in the first postwar decade, the peasant home has been described in some detail. Still a one-room hut, it boasts of a metal bedstead and an electric iron and is overflowing with sunshine and good food. At meals, the kolkhoz woman, just returned from a village council meeting, smilingly serves her family roasted meats, freshly baked bread, and golden butter which mysterious brownies must have prepared in her absence. Occasionally, a conscientious author provides an unobtrusive grandmother who is presumably helpful, but generally, the erstwhile baba lives up to the versatility outlined for her in Steshka's program speech and creates this plenty singlehandedly. Nevertheless, this modernized peasant hut is still barely distinguishable in design, and as before, serves primarily as a backdrop for the fictional plot—as a stage set filled with necessary properties rather than a home.

Religion, in spite of all the efforts of the regime, has not been completely eliminated from Russian life or literature. Under Socialist Realism, churchgoing is seldom mentioned, but icons, the sign of the cross, and prayers survive. And these old outward signs of piety serve as characterization devices for negative figures.

Denounced and reviled, practically equated with savage tribes' creeds and practices, Christianity in kolkhoz fiction is a standard attribute of vicious old hags and feebleminded, middle-aged women.[5] Younger women sometimes accept it, but under duress. They are being victimized by their pious families—real nests of ignorance, greed, and cruelty—but in the end are usually rescued by the alert village Komsomol or by an enlightened lover. One such lover even won the Party's approval for eloping with the bride of a young Orthodox priest (Eva, in L. Obukhova's *The Splinter*, 1961), though illicit romances are as a rule considered unworthy of a Communist. There are also instances of unhappy endings to young girls' stories, and even of suicides (Ksenya in N. Evdokimov's *The Sinner*, 1960), otherwise practically unknown in Soviet fiction.

Yet piety, in its modified Soviet form, continues as part of the peasant heroine's characterization. She still trusts in the wisdom and goodness of a distant, omnipotent deity and is guided by its representatives. The kolkhoz woman takes all her personal problems, marital included, to the Party organizer (*partorg*), just as her mother took hers to a confessor. She can quote and she practices the basic teachings of Communism, but claims no extensive knowledge of Party dogmas. In moments of joy or sorrow, she turns to look at the picture hanging in the hut's "corner of honor" (*krasnyj ugol*). The icons and the portraits of the Tsar's family there have been replaced, at different periods, by portraits of Marx, Lenin, or Stalin, but the gesture and the emotion behind it are the same.

All in all, "Church," in the sense of an unqualified acceptance of a supreme authority and its code of behavior, is a significant factor in the life of a peasant woman in Soviet fiction throughout the postwar decade. After the thaw, this piety, along with other typical characteristics, becomes blurred as the figure of the kolkhoz heroine recedes into the background of the literary scene.

The third factor, motherhood, has always been important, but Russian village fiction seldom drew a full-length portrait of a devoted mother. It could have hardly been otherwise, because a baba was a lifetime drudge in the peasant household, while a kolkhoz woman has had too many duties outside it. Neither could dedicate herself to bringing up her children.

Therefore, under the conditions of Russian village life, a mother in prerevolutionary fiction was shown as tragic rather than affectionate. The reader had glimpses of her weeping over a dead child, attending a daughter's inauspicious wedding, or watching a son's departure for military service; but not playing with a child or having an intimate talk with a troubled teenager. No wonder: harassed, overworked, she had no time to fondle babies, who were crying in a cradle suspended from the sooty ceiling, or crawling or toddling underfoot on the hut's earthen floor. She could not even ensure them proper care while she was away working in the fields. Children were left locked alone in empty huts or in the charge of senile grandparents and of older siblings, often five-year-olds; even the word "nurse" (*njan'ka*) in the Russian peasant's idiom means an older sister. Nineteenth-century literature has many pathetic figures of children who were injured in infancy—hunchbacks, cripples, idiots—and of babies scalded to death or eaten by pigs.

After the Revolution, it would have been difficult to tell from fiction alone whether conditions were improved. The writers' attention focused on the peasant heroine's struggle for liberation from domestic slavery, and her home life was simply glossed over. The few children appearing in the fiction of the 1920's all looked alike and resembled stage properties rather than living human beings. It was, for example, as if the same baby doll, labeled "unbaptized and illegitimate," was used in every drama of feminine emancipation. As to what happened to them while mother was engaged elsewhere, it was assumed by the early 1930's that nurseries were available. These, it is true, looked unprepossessing. Visitors found "milk and soured cream in unwashed pots, a dishevelled nursemaid in a greasy blouse, cots resembling mangers . . . dirty windows, bare walls with cracks full of cockroaches, a peeling stove with bricks missing,"[6] and elsewhere, "all the windows in the room were closed; writhing in the cots and crawling on the filthy floor, babies, covered with flies, choked in a many-voiced chorus of yelling; but no adult was in sight."[7]

Such candid pictures, however, were rare. Unless a grandmother was on hand to babysit, a kolkhoz woman is shown as leaving her children in fine nurseries, which, along with the rest of Soviet life, were overlaid with the pink varnish of praise after World War II. In 1950, in S. Antonov's "Village Rhymes," visitors were requested to put on white overalls and slippers before being allowed to see the happy tots surrounded with toys or asleep in clean cots. E. Dorosh, whose *Village Diary* (1954–58) reveals many previously omitted features of kolkhoz life, also supports fiction's claim of the cleanliness and comfort in contemporary nurseries. He regrets, however, that these institutions are in operation only during harvest time.

Since Soviet fictional babies (blond, fat, and rosy, every one) are never sick, and brought home in the evening, either nap or gurgle contentedly, their mothers' satisfaction with the nursery arrangement is on the whole understandable. They obviously have no time—and show no desire—to sing a child to sleep with a lullaby or to watch it play.

As to older children, under Socialist Realism, they have been given small roles to act: model little citizens in their own right, they are also used to reveal some female chairman of the village council as a dutiful mother. At suppertime, she listens to their school news (collective projects, mostly) and dispenses the literary *plat du jour*—boiled potatoes in the late 1940's or cocoa in the following years. But there is no tenderness or rapport shown between a kolkhoz woman and her children, even after the thaw, and moreover, a bright, sensitive child such as in V. Panova's *Seryozha* (1955) is likely to be the schoolteacher's.

On the face of it, the kolkhoz woman does no more for her children than the baba did, but there is a difference, because it is assumed that hers is the wiser love. The Soviet mother, explains one critic, "encourages her children to acts of heroism and walks by their side in struggle and toil . . . and yet, how rich is [her] life in desires and interests which transcend that [motherly] love!"[8] Because of these outside interests heroism, in the words of another critic, "is a natural state to her who knows the joys of working for common welfare"[9] and so, unlike the ignorant baba, she educates by her very example. Demanding towards herself, she is also demanding towards her children, but they do not resent her sternness because "they realize that sternness is born of love."[10]

Motherhood in its purely biological form became fashionable in Soviet literature in the early 1930's, when several writers, notably Panfyorov and Gladkov, endeavored to replace the decadent presentation of sex problems with their own brand of wholesome earthiness. Motherhood was included in this effort. In Gladkov's *New Land*, a young girl, longingly watching a group of contented mothers nursing babies, exclaims: " 'Dear mothers, there is something touchingly cow-like about you!' "[11] And a woman leaves an excellent husband because she has no child by him to have one by a man she does not love. In Panfyorov's *Village Bruski*, during the fertile spring of the village's collectivization, two women (one, Anchurka, in her mid-forties) branded as barren (*nerodicy*) acquire new men and bear sons. And Ela, a sickly mother who had buried five children, has quadruplets. In this novel, in fact, every positive female character seeks and achieves pregnancy, within or without wedlock, and Zhdarkin sums up the author's attitude: " 'A woman, were it not for the instinct of motherhood in her, would be nothing but a stray bitch.' "[12]

As soon as the Party's stand on sex in literature was clarified—about 1936—such "wholesome earthiness" was discouraged. Henceforth, although prolific mothers were popular (eleven children were not considered too many by Vasilisa, in V. Kochetov's *Under the Sky of the Fatherland*, 1950) and the State rewarded motherhood with medals and granted money for each additional child, childbirth was handled in fiction discreetly, as were also erotic scenes. In new post-World War II editions, descriptions of couples bathing in the nude (the ultimate in risqué in Soviet fiction) were purged, and profligate women bootleggers (*samogonščicy*) were transformed into "young widows," occupation unspecified. The accent now was on civic duty rather than on primordial biological urges, and high standards were being set for the Soviet family.

The Soviet family, as writers and critics see it, "rests on the bedrock of Soviet society" and is cemented by "the enormous, organizing power of work." Its members are bound by genuine affection, mutual respect and friendship, common goals in life, and a profound understanding of family duty.[13] A woman's role in it is of paramount importance and is recognized as such. " 'Women are our comrades at work and captains of our families,' " a husband says at a kolkhoz party, and a toast "to treating women well" is drunk in token of approval.[14]

This scene offers a measure of the progress the peasant woman had made since Neverov, Seyfullina, and Kochin had pictured her wrongs. In the 1940's, the fictional heroine no longer fights for nor awakens to her rights; she exercizes them, while performing her duties. And, abandoning the insignificant role she had in the 1930's, she returns as protagonist in the 1944–54 decade, when the two main themes in fiction are wartime effort on the home front and that of reconstruction. "The enormous, organizing power of work" is the keynote of the period: it makes into a happy family not just individuals, but all of the Soviet people. And in kolkhozes people readily express their feelings in innocent reveling, curiously resembling that of their ancestors, the stylized peasants of eighteenth-century fiction. Discounting the ideological difference between work for a socialist state and the feudal *corvée*, their rustic songs sound very similar; even the rhythm is identical.

"Ours is a happy lot
We work at all the time,
We spend our whole day in the field
And we spend it making merry,"

a costumed peasant chorus sings in 1777. And in 1953, kolkhoz girls, similarly costumed for a Komsomol performance in colorful sarafans,* echo:

"We lead the singing, my friend and I,
We find it more fun [to work] together;
Our leisure we spend in cultural pleasures
And our life, among plenty.

[CHORUS:]

Oh, the vast,
the boundless,
the untrammeled,
country mine!"[15]

Pride in the Fatherland (a component of postwar Soviet patriotism) and in duty well done serve as incentives to still more efficient work. This, for a positive character in Soviet literature, means not simply good performance but a way of life; and because of that, the striking feature in the kolkhoz heroine's characterization is her utter dedication. Avdotya (in G. Nikolaeva's *The Harvest*, 1950) "would do nothing by half. She put [into farm improvement] the whole measure of her soul's forces, generously, withholding nothing, oblivious of herself—and those around her could not fail to realize that," comments the author approvingly.[16] So, Avdotya's authority grows fast, as does general recognition of her talents.

Recognition, however, is not granted the kolkhoz woman lightly; citizen, breadwinner, and homemaker, she is also expected to be modest and chaste. If married, she is faithful to her husband as a matter of course. If a widow, her sexual life is usually summed up by the author in a terse statement—"she led a decent life"—or not mentioned at all. These high moral standards, claimed as Soviet and new, are actually a revival of nineteenth-century attitudes in Russian literature, and the kolkhoz woman resembles her nineteenth-century counterpart more than her immediate predecessor, the pioneer baba of the 1920's. This is true also of her physical characterization, which includes the calm gaze, the dignified bearing, and the unhurried speech which Nekrasov and

* The Russian national dress for peasant women.

Turgenev admired. The Katya Dolgas were of necessity loud and brusque, as well as unafraid of old-fashioned sins such as adultery.

The peasant heroines' path has become smoother under Socialist Realism because husbands have also changed for the better. Not only are despots and philanderers a thing of the past, but men have come to appreciate in women that dedication to work for the community which is the hallmark of a positive Soviet character. With divorces and the marital triangle unknown in kolkhoz fiction and married love taken for granted, a couple's only possible conflict is within their work. They may disagree over the quality of their respective performances and over its recognition: a spouse publicly siding with the mate's critics is routine. But these misunderstandings—which furnish the fabric of the kolkhoz novels—are seldom the wife's fault, never, if she is the protagonist. It is the husband who resents holding a position inferior to the heroine's (a favorite setup in postwar fiction), while she, on the contrary, welcomes every opportunity of being proud of him. But her work is dear to her, and therefore a husband who belittles its importance is considered one of a kind with the old-fashioned wife-beater.

Fortunately, the relapses into despotism by a man of true Soviet convictions are strictly temporary, and marital happiness is always restored at the end of the novel. In 1934, a husband could still point at dirty, tear-stained children asleep on the floor, and shout: " '. . . and it's three weeks since you gave me a clean shirt, . . . the house is dirtier than the kolkhoz pigsty. . . . What use are your earnings to us?' "[17] But this husband was of kulak origin, and so the heroine could, and did, leave him for a worthier man. A decade later, the only conceivable villain would be a deserter from the army or a kolkhoz wrecker; and even he, expelled by his wife from their home, wandering like Cain in a hostile world, would respect her decision.[18] Generally, kolkhoz husbands match their wives' excellence, virtue for virtue, particularly in that of dedicated work.

THE TYPICAL KOLKHOZ WOMAN
OF THE POSTWAR DECADE

The Makings of a Heroine

By the late 1940's, the pattern of the typical kolkhoz woman had reached its full development, and peasant heroines have to be discussed not as individuals but only as representatives of a species. Moreover, while they do possess certain characteristics which distinguish them from members of other groups (for instance, proletarian women), within their own kind they are all alike. This is not a question of strong family resemblance, such as among several sisters, but of sameness, as of dolls bought wholesale by the dozen in a box.

They are alike in psychological makeup, in outward appearance, and of course, in way of life, which together with the identical plot patterns of the novels make this literary phenomenon of sameness possible. An analysis of this collective personality, referred to henceforth as the Heroine, mainly within three prize-winning representative novels will serve to support this contention. The novels are E. Maltsev's *With Heart and Soul* (1948), G. Medynsky's *Marya* (1946–49), and G. Nikolaeva's *The Harvest*.

War separates the newlyweds, Rodion and Grunya, in *With Heart and Soul*, and a few months later the bride is notified of Rodion's death. Work in the kolkhoz is her only solace; soon she is recognized as a talented agronomist. When Rodion returns wounded (he was rescued by partisans), he envies her success and misunderstands her offer of advice on his work. Hurt, she leaves him, but returns when he has realized his error and becomes an innovator. From then on they live happily, encouraged by the advice of a Party secretary who manages to hide his love for Grunya and by the coming of a baby.

In *Marya*, war takes the heroine's whole family away from her. Simon, her husband, and her young son are both called into the army and soon reported killed; her daughter leaves to work in a munitions factory. Marya is elected chairman of her kolkhoz and does an excellent job, wartime difficulties notwithstanding. When Simon, mistakenly reported dead, returns, he demands that Marya resign because people call him "Marya's husband" and because her work at home falls in part to him. He also misunderstands the character of Marya's friendship with a Machine Tractor Station (MTS) mechanic. A wise Party secretary averts the impending tragedy. Simon sets a record in wheat production, and husband and wife settle down to a life of mutual appreciation, common work, and love. Their daughter is happily married and has a fat baby.

In *The Harvest*, Vasily Bortnikov, mistakenly reported killed in action, returns home to find his wife, Avdotya, married to Stepan. The two men agree (though Avdotya is not consulted) that for the sake of the Bortnikov's small children, Stepan will leave. Vasily, a Communist, is at once absorbed by the task of reconstructing the war-ruined kolkhoz and discovers with amazement that his quiet homemaker Avdotya is holding a responsible position there. He resents this, as well as her enrolling in a course in animal husbandry in a distant town. Finally, hurt by his old-fashioned, masterful attitudes, she decides to leave him. When, however, Vasily falls victim to a plot organized by local reactionaries, Avdotya, helped by an understanding Party secretary, comes to his rescue. They make up and build a life of mutual respect, understanding, and useful work for the community. They also have another baby, fat and rosy.

It would seem, at a first glance, that the Heroine is just another Steshka of *The Village Bruski*, but this is not the case. Steshka, by a critic's succinct definition, is "not a person but just a sexual entity . . . a female of the species, incarnated and depersonalized,"[19] even though she is capable of mechanically following a social behavioral pattern; the Heroine, on the other hand, is more complex. She has a certain delicacy of feelings; offering personal sacrifices on the altar of duty costs her some anguish; she distinguishes right from wrong and makes decisions in favor of the former with the naïve seriousness of a good child. Thus, even though her thinking processes, narrated by the author, are of the simplest, and her moral principles, Christian and middle-class, are couched in Marxist vernacular, she does come alive even for the Western reader. The latter may even enjoy her acquaintance, if he enjoys that of Jane Austen's and Dickens' characters or reads the fiction section of American women's magazines.

It should be stressed, however, that such characters are to be found only among the original heroines created by writers who try, within the framework of Socialist Realism, to produce works of artistic value. But once their books are favorably reviewed or, especially, are awarded literary prizes, the heroines become established as "typical," and are in turn used by third-rate writers as molds for mass-producing the flat, identical characters mentioned before. It goes without saying that in the case of these a-dozen-in-a-box characters, no attempt is made at psychological analysis, and the reader can predict their behavior as confidently as the denouement of the plot. On the other hand, Avdotya, for instance, qualifies as an original typical Heroine, and the story of her two loves—a mixture of human emotions and editorial didacticism—deserves notice.

Vasily, abrupt and peremptory, is her girlhood's first love and the father of her children; Stepan, reliable and understanding, is a lover and a friend. And, like Shaw's Candida, Avdotya chooses the man who, contrary to appearances, is the weaker of the two and needs her most. In spite of its inevitable happy ending and the clutter of agricultural activities, the novel succeeds in conveying the image of a woman honestly trying to solve a difficult moral and emotional problem. Her numerous doubles in postwar Soviet literature simply follow the path of duty and collect the reward awaiting them at the path's end. Of course, since divorce in kolkhoz fiction is extremely rare, Avdotya's hesitations are just a manifestation of her subtler nature: the author would in no case allow her to do anything likely to shock the critics, who in the postwar decade were easily shocked. One of them, for example, indignantly asked whether Vasily should not have returned home before nighttime, so as to spare the readers "the coarsely naturalistic scene" of his finding a new husband in Avdotya's bed.[20]

While hard-working and dedicated, the Heroine is neither vain nor unduly ambitious. She always accepts kolkhoz chairmanship with humility, initiates daring experiments in wheat growing or milking with trepidation, and unfailingly seeks the Party's advice. Unlike male protagonists, she never has to be reprimanded for doing something on her own initiative. But one suspects that modesty in a kolkhoz woman is a virtue caused by necessity, that she realizes her limitations rather than underestimates her abilities.

Her basic handicap is lack of education. She has never been illiterate, of course. Even Marya the Bolshevik could syllabize articles in *Izvestia;* Katya Dolga had attended the village school for three years; Praskovya in *The Bast Shoes* took her first step towards emancipation by learning to read and so, against great difficulties, did Parunka in Kochin's *The Girls.* By contrast, negative characters, such as Ula in *The Village Bruski* considered the effort unnecessary. But the Heroine's formal education has been limited to several years of grade school attendance, and wisely, she does not court frustration by trying to go beyond that.

If she aspires to Party membership, she will study a few "soul-stirring" books—*The Short History of the Communist Party,* for instance—and acquire the basic Marxist vocabulary, much as a medieval nun acquired a smattering of Latin; reading newspapers regularly "in order to explain them to home folks" will then be necessary, particularly if she becomes a partorg. She may take a course in agriculture or in animal husbandry to improve the work in the kolkhoz and so to start along the road to distinction. She will then initiate some new farming method in planting or milking and will achieve a spectacular increase in production. Her photograph will appear on the kolkhoz "board of honor" (*doska početa*); her name will be mentioned in the county newspaper, perhaps even in *Izvestia*. She may make a trip to Moscow as member of some rural delegation; if the author insists on an apotheosis, she may receive the title of Heroine of Labor and may, finally, meet Stalin. If she is an administrative talent rather than an innovator, she will be elected chairman of the kolkhoz, make it a model of socialist welfare, and will be awarded the same honors. In both cases she would have reached the ceiling in her education, career, and happiness.

Should she, however, become "dizzy with success," she will lose her standing as a Heroine in spite of her achievements. To cite an example, the Stakhanovite beet-grower Stepanida (in V. Ovechkin's "Records and Harvest," 1946) was denounced by the author for assuming airs (she even had a secretary to help her handle reporters and photographers) instead of sharing the secret of her efficiency with other kolkhoz workers. Another Stakhanovite, Katyusha (in S. Voronin's *Useless Fame*, 1955), was promoted chairman of her kolkhoz on the strength of her outstanding performance as a dairymaid, but almost brought the kolkhoz to ruin by acting like a spoiled prima donna. She was consequently punished by the loss of her job and of her husband as well.

Such cases, it must be noted, are not meant to alter the Heroine's blueprint. On the contrary, they are exceptions which confirm the rule and the routine literary reflection of current Party policies. In Stepanida's case, it is the postwar substitution of the collective principle for Stakhanovism; in Katyusha's, the post-Stalinist indictment of bureaucracy. Most of the blame for the Heroine's mistakes is laid at the door of local (always *local*) Party bureaucrats. It is their responsibility to keep the peasant woman personally happy and socially useful, strictly within the scope of her limited qualifications.

The Heroine, then, appears as one of the two basic personalities: either the resourceful manager (a kolkhoz chairman or a partorg) or the soulful innovator. They are the Martha and Mary of Soviet peasant fiction, and each of them, allegedly, has chosen the better part.

The Resourceful Manager

As kolkhoz chairman, the Heroine is usually "an elderly woman of about forty."[21] S. Antonov's thirty-year-old Lusha, in "Auntie Lusha"

(1956), who was elected chairman at twenty after the war because there were no men left in her kolkhoz, is an exception. Grandma Katerina, in Medynsky's *Marya*, sixty-three and in the village government since the Revolution, is another. The Heroine is stout, has a weather-worn complexion and dark eyes, wears her dark hair parted and gathered in a bun, and has been dressed in a woolen navy suit and a large fringed shawl for the last twenty years, except in war time, when she usually appeared in a sheepskin coat and felt boots.

Herself a hard worker, she demands a maximum of effort from others. As a result, she has many enemies among the kolkhoz members and even among the bureaucrats, who do not bother to look for the reasons for this enmity. Such is the case of the protagonist in V. Ovechkin's "Praskovya Maksimovna" (1939) and its sequel "One of the Many" (1941). But she has the support of all the positive characters and, of course, that of the Party. The latter the Heroine trusts and follows without reservations, with the simple matter-of-factness which is her chief characteristic. Interviewed by the membership committee Marya explains:

> "I haven't got much schooling but I do side with the right whole-heartedly, and so I want the Party to make a whole woman of me."
> "And did you think it over thoroughly, comrade?"
> "I did."
> "Are you ready to tie your life with the Party?"
> "I am."
> "And your husband [who is in the Army], is he a member?"
> "No. That is, I don't know. But he'll understand."
> "And if he doesn't?"
> Marya hesitated, knotting the ends of her shawl, and whispered: "I'll come to you. You'll tell me what to do."[22]

Perseverance and efficiency are the Heroine's two other main features: in wartime she forgets heartache over the absence, and often the loss, of a husband or a son to provide shelter for refugees and to keep the kolkhoz producing food for the country; the war over, she helps with the task of the reconstruction.

She is kind-hearted: the sick, the old, and the destitute, widows and orphans in particular, can count on her for kolkhoz support. But she is not sentimental, and for her duty always comes first. During the war Marya, for example, sends her teen-age daughter, who ran away from impossible conditions at the construction site of a munitions factory, back, though the girl sobs out a story of cold and hunger in self-made dugouts, of moving heavy machinery, and of other hardships.

She is an excellent housewife, thrifty, provident, and orderly, and she runs the kolkhoz as she would her own farm. She may even show some slight conservatism in this respect; for example, Varvara (in V. Tendryakov, *The Outsider*, 1954) prefers horses to tractors. And the Heroine is invariably busy: talking to district Party officials, supervising work on the farm, occasionally straightening things at home, where her husband may be attending to chores—contentedly, as did Varvara's, or grudgingly, as did Praskovya's (in E. Maltsev's *Any Home You Enter*, 1960).

As a partorg, the Heroine closely resembles her chairman counterpart in dress and physique, though she tends to be even stouter. She is, however, less understanding and favors harsh disciplinary measures, especially when the culprit is inclined to make independent decisions—such, for example, is Darya in Kochetov's *Under the Sky of the Fatherland*. A zealous worker, the female partorg knows everything that happens in her kolkhoz and keeps the Party authorities informed. Needless to say, she has no initiative: "she firmly knows that people should be guided—where to is for the District Committee to decide."[23] It is possibly because of this stolidity that she is always cast as a secondary character and is never promoted to a higher position in Party hierarchy. While her lack of education could be a sufficient reason for her marginal status, men have been known to overcome this handicap in Soviet fiction.

The Innovator

As an innovator, the Heroine is younger than she is as a kolkhoz chairman; in fact, quite a few innovators are young girls, and women are at most in their thirties. She is slim, blue-eyed, with dark blond hair which is often unruly and usually worn in a crown of braids around her white brow. She likes pretty clothes: Avdotya's interest in them, as is proper for a mother of two, is evinced in her general tidiness and in her immaculate white shawls; but Grunya, the young bride, wears blue and pink dresses, and she owns silk stockings and patent leather pumps.

Shy and soft-voiced, the innovator makes no enemies and fights no battles, though she is quite capable of doing both if the success of her project is at stake; it was largely for the sake of their work that Avdotya and Grunya jeopardized their marital happiness. She regards improving farming methods as a holy quest rather than an agricultural experiment; indeed, the innovator's enthusiasm for and joy in serving society and Communism have a distinctly mystic, religious quality. She attends courses in farming in the spirit of a young acolyte. And scientists not only give her kindly encouragement, but also listen to her ideas, much as priests would listen to a country girl who has been having visions or hearing voices of saints. In contrast to Marya's sober, practical manner during initiation into Party membership, Grunya's and Avdotya's initiations are moments of ecstasy. Passages which illustrate this mystical attitude are not difficult to find.

Avdotya, admitted to Party membership, returns home to Vasily:

Her eyes, blinded by happiness to the sight of surrounding things, seemed to see something far beyond them, or perhaps deep down inside her soul. . . .

"Is everything all right?" [asked Vasily].

"Oh, fine!" She took a deep breath. "It all means so much, I can hardly make things out. . . . They asked me, 'Avdotya, tell us as a Communist, did you accomplish on your farm everything that is in your power?' And I suddenly saw all I should have done and didn't! . . . They accepted my word that now I would. . . . By fall we are to establish a model dairy farm. . . ."

Waves of fresh evening air, heavy with the smells of grass broke into the room through the open window. . . . Avdotya, deeply moved, sat still, her roughened little palms pressing her burning cheeks. Silently, Vasily embraced his wife, and she leaned her dark blond head against his shoulder. . . .

"So, now we are both Communists," Vasily said, "—both. . . ."[24]

Rodion sees Grunya off to be interviewed by the Party membership committee:

Grunya suddenly felt that she would like to be alone: wasn't this the day that would shed a new light on her whole life? . . . Walking along the narrow path, she often stopped to press her hand to the heart that would not be still. . . .

[She is summoned before the committee.]

"Why do you want to become a Party member?" she heard, without realizing who the speaker was. . . .

"I think [she answered] . . . that whoever wants to go forward and lead others with him should be with the Party. In it he will be stronger, and more courageous, and will have more to offer to the people."

"Right!" said the chairman. . . . "And what do you plan to do now?"

[Grunya, crooking a finger for each experiment, enumerates her plans for the farm's improvement until her hand closed into a tight fist. She is told she is accepted and may go home.]

. . . she did not remember later how she found herself on the porch, with the evening freshness caressing her burning cheeks. . . . Beyond the orchards the moon was rising, overhead a powerful loudspeaker was sending forth waves of a lofty, solemn music.

"Oh, how happy I am, Rodion, my love!" she whispered. She was standing, hushed and blissful, as if she had reached the top of a high mountain, and endless vistas were calling her from far.[25]

By the end of the postwar decade, on the eve of the thaw, kolkhoz women characters had lost all individual features and had reverted to the poster type. As such, Anna (in F. Panfyorov's *Mother Volga*, 1953) meets all the specifications for female excellence, national as well as socialist. She is big and blond and wears sarafans. Fortyish and a widow with a young son, she wins the heart of an Academy member who is dazzled by her rustic beauty, expert cooking, and agricultural achievements (though uneducated, she is a famed orchard grower), and marries him. The author adds the finishing touch by having Anna enroll in a correspondence course: a scientific cachet on the simple wisdom of the People. All in all, Anna can be considered the typical peasant woman, A.D. 1953.

THE THAW AND AFTER

The thaw, with its relaxation of the rigors of Socialist Realism and the official invitation to fiction to expose the shortcomings of Soviet reality, naturally also affected fiction's presentation of kolkhoz life. But, as in the early 1930's, the emphasis in literature shifted from the village to the city, and the kolkhoz Heroine, sharing the general village eclipse, starred in award-winning novels no more.

There was another reason for the waning of her popularity. She had failed to follow the mainstream of the new trend, and her image, instead of changing drastically within it, faded. After 1953, Soviet writers no longer presented a uniform front. Three groups—the conservatives, the progressives, and the independents—could be distinguished, and if they chose, they could deviate from established patterns. But only the independent writers chose to do so to any appreciable extent.

Independent writers, much as the Fellow Travelers in the 1920's, found the village attractive as a fictional background, but had little interest in kolkhozes as social milieux. They painted peasant homes, the rural landscape, the changing seasons, often with exquisite skill reminiscent of that of Turgenev or Chekhov. Of course, their village was not the elemental, symbolic Russia of postrevolutionary fiction, but neither was it the gingerbread kolkhoz of the postwar decade. The same was true of the women characters. Drawn with barely a few lines, they are nevertheless persons in their own right rather than representatives of the species "kolkhoz females." Wild, shy Manka, the village postwoman in the throes of a stormy first love (in Yu. Kazakov's "Manka," 1958); meek, guileless Matryona meeting the last ordeal of her long, miserable life (in A. Solzhenitsyn's "Matryona's Homestead," 1963); the plain, domineering, nameless Wife (in Yu. Nagibin's "The Groom," 1956)—they all, to use Nagibin's comment on the latter, "still do have something." In other words, they are feminine, unique, and elude classification by occupation, age, or marital status. But at the same time they are few, episodic, scattered through the short stories (a favorite genre) of their nonconformist authors, and generally seem to live on the peripheries of Sovietland: that is, they serve no didactic purpose.

Didactic purpose, on the other hand, continued to motivate the body of Soviet writers. The progressive wing took full advantage of the opportunity to develop their own brand of social criticism. It proved to be not always acceptable to the Party, but apparently both sides agreed that a writer's duty is to chastise society in order to improve it. The progressives' main targets were bureaucracy, inefficiency, and substandard living conditions. In contrast to their predecessors, the *engagé* writers of the 1920's, they were only mildly interested in peasant women characters, and after lifting the taboo on the discussion of village morals, left the routine imagery otherwise undisturbed.

The conservatives, following the Party line, as always, were concerned above all with gauging correctly the degree and quality of criticism expected in literature within the new trend. Their cast of women characters remained the same as before. The few changes in psychological makeup were minor and superfluous, something like the substitution of a curly wig for one with long braids in an actress's costume. One *faux pas* on the part of a character was evidently considered a sufficient concession to the "un-varnishing" vogue. It may be entirely out of keeping with the heroine's personality, as in the case of

Zhuravushka (in M. Alekseev's *Bread Is a Noun*, 1964), a middle-aged
widow deservedly respected for her blameless comportment and her
skill as a cowbarn worker *(teljatnica)*. Forced by the author to drink
too much at a wedding reception, she for once forgets her principles
with an old admirer, appropriately named Apollo[n]. Rejecting his
offer of marriage, she has an abortion and resumes her old life and
character at the very point at which she had left them. Her innocence
is so apparent that her status as a positive Soviet character remains
unimpaired in the eyes of the critics.[26]

Yet, peasant Sovietland was no longer the same. Once the coat of
varnish was removed, it looked drab. Living conditions, people, their
morals and attitudes—all appeared different, and women characters
were no exception. On the surface, little had changed in their characterization—and yet something was missing. The Heroine still was her
loyal and efficient self, but the colors had paled and her stature diminished. Post-Stalinist trends provided no new typical models, and the
mass-produced characters still coming from the postwar mold were
now slightly shopworn and out of fashion. The kolkhoz chairwoman
was no longer lionized. A woman's holding that job had become
routine, and the job itself, heroic during World War II and the
subsequent reconstruction, was now dull and frustrating. The Heroine
as innovator still happily combined marriage, motherhood, and Stakhanovite production, as does, for example, Raya in I. Zverev's *She and
He* (1964). But even though she is, as before, decorated, elected delegate to sundry councils and conferences, and received in the Kremlin
by Khrushchev, her mood is less enthusiastic than that of her predecessors. Raya herself shows this by refusing to frame a souvenir photograph of her meeting with Khrushchev; Steshka or Grunya would have
treasured a picture taken with Stalin.

Moreover, by the side of model kolkhoz women, there emerged in
fiction their less attractive sisters: merry divorcees *(veselye razve-
denki)*, thieving slatterns with several illegitimate children, and impu-
dent *(ozornye, razbitnye)* widows who made the most of their independent status. In fact, by the end of the post-Stalinist decade, even an unwed mother in the role of a kolkhoz chairman became possible though,
of course, Aleksandra in L. Mishchenko, *A Visit* (1963) is a maverick.
She has some formal education, drives a car, wears sleeveless summer
dresses, and has no claims to being really typical.

If glamor had gone out of virtues like overfulfilling production
norms, so did excitement out of sins such as evading communal owner-

ship rules. Selling produce from one's back yard on the market, for instance, was no longer shocking though, unfortunately, not to be entrusted to husbands. As the new generation of peasant writers—Antonov, Zhestev, Dorosh, Yashin, among others—testify, husbands still drink. And women have other reasons for dissatisfaction. They enjoy equal rights with men, but work with rakes and sickles while men drive tractors. And men, as Party members, hold the positions of real responsibility, while women, what with kolkhoz work and home chores, get old before their time and forget how to read.[27]

This is not to say that the kolkhoz woman has reverted to the baba's status. Wife-beating has been recognized as a criminal offense, and most importantly, women earn their keep and do not let their husbands forget it. Gala, the bride in A. Yashin's *The Wedding in Vologda* (1962), dismisses her drunken groom's claims to superiority by reminding him that her earnings are higher. Perhaps the best way to sum up the condition of the fictional kolkhoz woman after the thaw is to say that, while continuing as a typical character, she is no longer a Heroine.

THE OLDER GENERATION

Under Socialist Realism, older women in kolkhoz fiction, though cast in minor roles only, developed into several typical characters. Of these, the kindly old grannies are identical except in their names; their main features are enjoyment of happy old age under the Soviet regime and surprised admiration at their married daughters' fortunate lot, so unlike their own used to be. The two types which deserve more notice are the spry oldsters who had actively joined the Soviet society and those who had never broken with the past.

Women of the first type have identical backgrounds, differing mainly in the form of their adjustment to the new conditions. Born during the previous century into a family of landless peasants, they had spent a joyless childhood, nursing babies—siblings at home—or working as servants at a wicked priest's; they were married very young into a loveless union, usually with a domestic tyrant or a drunkard, had numerous children, buried several of them, lived a life of drudgery until the Revolution. After that, everything changed for the better.

When the reader meets them, they are widows in their sixties. There is, for instance, Grandma Katerina (in Medynsky's *Marya*), who had participated in the village government since the Revolution and is now ready for a political career. Avdotya (in N. Chertova, *The Magic Herb*, 1939) is loved and respected by the whole kolkhoz, and is completely dedicated to it in principle and in practice. She had learned to read after listening to Stalin's article "Dizzy with Success,"* so as to enjoy it at first hand. There is Anna (in V. Smirnov's *The Sons*, 1928–37), who brings up her twins to be good Soviet citizens, becomes a Stakhanovite in flax production, and as a kolkhoz delegate, is praised by Stalin. Nastasya (in Yu. Kapusto, *The Bread Growers*, 1950) is decorated four times for outstanding kolkhoz work and rules her household with a firm hand. Another Nastasya (in V. Panova's *The Bright Shore*, 1949), a Heroine of Labor and cowbarn manager, has raised thousands of calves, leaving her home (and, years before, her young son) to the care of a grandmother. This grandmother still defies old age by attending to the chores, the cow, and the vegetable garden. Illiterate before the Revolution, she now enjoys popular books on astronomy and medicine. Other oldsters, such as Grandma Nadezha in *Marya*, simply serve as a chorus to the plot's tragedy: they work hard and have an indestructible faith in Stalin.

The post-thaw period, it is true, offers on occasion a less peaceful picture of the sunset of a good woman's life. Solzhenitsyn's Matryona is hardworking and kindly to the point of holiness—and yet stays destitute. And Avdotya, in F. Abramov's *This and That* (1963), a retired kolkhoz nurse, goes from hut to hut begging for alms. But even so, women like Auntie Dove, another famed cowbarn worker in S. Babaevsky's *The Beloved Land* (1964), carry on their traditional enjoyment of life's harvest. And, as ever, they purport to be the rule which disproves exceptions.

The second type represents the spirit of the reactionary past still lingering in the peasant byt. These women, also in their sixties, with a few exceptions come from moneyed peasant stock. They do not actively oppose Soviet practices, but they keep old attitudes alive and surreptitiously try to pass them on to the younger generation. They are grasping and conservative and sometimes have a shady personal past. Such is Alevtina, in S. Antonov's *It Happened at Penkovo* (1956). A dissolute bootlegger in her youth, she is now a matchmaker and fortune-teller, and on occasion may even supply a jealous wife with poisonous herbs to put into a rival's tea. Another Alevtina (in Tendryakov's *Outsider*), though a respectable matron, uses poison of a differ-

* In this article (2 March 1930) Stalin called for a softening of the drastic methods used in the enforcement of collectivization.

ent kind: nagging and slander. She wrecks her daughter's marriage because her son-in-law, an honest Soviet youth, values kolkhoz property over his own. It is also love of property that makes Stepanida, in *The Harvest*, an outcast in her happy community. She gets a new lease on life, however, by sublimating her desire of personal gain into salesmanship in a kolkhoz-owned booth in the town market.

Conservatism has always been a standard attribute of negative characters in Soviet fiction, but nice old women are also occasionally affected with it. It is, for example, the undoing of Marfa, in L. Voronkova's *The Restless Person* (1953), and it prompts Elizaveta, in *Under the Sky of the Fatherland*, to cheat. Both women are dedicated cowbarn managers, but obstinately obstruct innovations in cattle-raising, being reluctant to relinquish the time-honored ways. For the same reason nice older women do not remove icons from the "honor corner" of their huts, and make the sign of the cross even when they profess to be no longer believers. Vasilisa (in S. Antonov's *Alyonka*, 1960) may have forgotten her prayers, but she is still afraid she may offend God and be stricken by lightning.

> "Don't worry, Aunt Vasilisa," said [the nine-year-old] Alyonka, "There is no God."
> "May God grant it be so! What with my sins, it would be better if there weren't."[28]

Confusion in religious matters is not limited to old women. On church holidays, members of the kolkhoz will not attend services, but they do celebrate the day by getting drunk and refusing to work.[29] Nor will they give up scheduling most village weddings for October, the month of the Holy Virgin's Intercession, in spite of the fact that the religious origin of this tradition has been all but forgotten.* And they still walk about the village as mummers, though no longer in the Christmas and Carnival seasons. Instead, the reveling takes place on the anniversary of the October Revolution and on March 8, the International Women's Day.[30] And while following the agricultural timetable prescribed by the government, peasants nevertheless trust their old weather calendar: hay should be in by the day of Saints Peter and Paul, for such has been the custom for as long as anyone can remember.

---

* The name of the holiday honors the miracle of the Virgin's veil (*pokrov*), which concealed the besieged city of Ustyug from the Tartars; but according to Dorosh (*Village Diary*, p. 238), the village today thinks it refers to the first snow of the season.

Many old customs survive in the form of superstitions. These range from the dispensing of love potions by "witches," to luring rain clouds with a loaf of bread during a drought.[31] Again, positive old women characters are not immune. Stalin's admirer, the grandmother in *The Bright Shore*, would not allow a loaf to be turned upside down and worried when a mirror broke, both, bad omens. Even Marya stealthily consulted a fortune-teller—and was reprimanded by a reviewer.[32]

If superstitions meet with ridicule or at most with amused tolerance, old peasant customs have been of late recognized as folklore and part of the national heritage. Costumes, songs, and the complicated ceremonial of peasant weddings and funerals, all of which had been denounced as barbarous in the 1920's and banned from post-World War II fiction, reappeared after the thaw. They are described in detail, realistically, in a manner not necessarily flattering but without indignation over rustic coarseness. Nor do old customs clash with the new; they are simply kept separate, as belonging to different categories. Civil marriages, for instance, are legal formalities, indispensable but unexciting. " 'Sure,' " a bride's mother explains, " 'the young couple has been at the village council's office; everything was done properly. But what kind of ceremony is to be had at the village council? They signed their names in the register and that was that. No beauty in it.' "[33] "Beauty," then, is supplied by the wedding ceremonial, under the supervision of the matchmaker, who, even in the 1960's, forces the bride to wail— something fictional brides had refused to do in the two preceding decades. As of old, the guests shout "bitter!" and the newlyweds kiss to sweeten the wine. The bridesmaids bring in the "maidenly loveliness," a little tree decorated with ribbons and lighted candles which the groom blows out. Pots and plates are smashed, and the young house- wife sweeps up the shards and the money thrown on them by the guests.[34] Songs—special ones designed for every stage of the wed- ding—are the most important part of the ceremony, and the old women who know and perform them are in great esteem, like Natalya Semyonovna in A. Yashin's *The Wedding in Vologda*. Of similar impor- tance are the women who sing and wail at funerals (*voplenicy*): Avdotya in *The Magic Herb* is a good example.

However confusing postrevolutionary changes were to them, older women, used to a passive acceptance of life, made the few needed adjustments with relative ease. But their granddaughters, facing a whole new way of life from the outset, were to undergo dramatic experiences.

4

The Girls

THE PROBLEMS OF EMANCIPATION

Early marriages being the rule among peasants, a young girl ("wench" [*devka*] in the village vocabulary) had but a short existence socially before becoming permanently classified as a baba. Not only was the period of girlhood short-lived, but it was also hedged in by the restrictions placed on courtship, even though women were traditionally allowed considerable freedom of association with men before marriage. There was open-air dancing and courting on summer nights; and there were long nights in the winter when girls would gather in their parents' huts, dimly lighted with resin-sputtering chips, to spin and gossip and exchange banter with young men visitors. And of course, there were plenty of other opportunities for the young people to get together, all of which village opinion tolerated as customary.

In a way, this comparative freedom was another form of victimizing women. A girl had no other incentive to behave virtuously than threats of beating if she failed to do so; she was permitted to "get acquainted" with a good marital prospect, and the term included a sharing of a bed with him, though fully clothed. Yet, this same girl was expected to withstand a lover's request, a seducer's blandishments, and to show the modesty, self-control, and good judgment of which, as a mere female, she was considered incapable.

In prerevolutionary Russian literature, nice peasant girls did occa-

sionally fall in love but married, obediently and tearfully, their parents'
choice, while naughty girls fell victim to seducers and ended tragically
either as suicides or as prostitutes. A love affair, then, meant ruin. A
good, stern mother (synonymous adjectives in Russian byt) would
protect her girl by forbidding her to stay out late and by endless
scoldings; a good father would find her a husband. This achieved, they
could sigh with relief: the danger of her "bringing a baby home in her
apron" would be over. If, instead, they were to wake up one morning
and find their gate tarred in token of dishonor, the whole family would
turn against the wretched girl.

In the postrevolutionary period this situation, inherited by both the
real and the fictional village, became further aggravated by additional
problems. Among these, the steady drain on manpower caused over ten
years by World War I and by the Civil War ranked high. Wars had
not only brought about economic ruin—land lying fallow, buildings
and farm equipment falling into disrepair—but when the fighting was
over, women found themselves in a special predicament: they were just
too many, in comparison to the number of men. Thus, the returning
veterans found lonely women only too ready to compete for their
attentions. Young girls were desperate in their efforts to find husbands.

The times being unpropitious for social life and most parents old-
fashioned, girls had to fend for themselves. Pooling their resources,
they would hire a hut for the special purpose of entertaining. Some
would even form associations (*arteli*) and live apart from their families,
so as to have more personal freedom. Their gatherings (*posidelki*)
professed to be purely social events—spinning bees dedicated, as of old,
to spinning and visiting. There was also, supposedly, safety for the
participating girls in their numbers, but this assumption often proved
erroneous. Samogon vodka, contributed by the men, flowed freely at
the meetings, and the gatherings easily slipped into orgies.[1] The resulting tragedies usually struck the poorer girls, often war orphans. Rich
girls were seldom permitted by their parents to participate in the
spinning bees, and these were the brides—virtuous and with a
dowry—who were sought out by the few marriageable men.

These much prized men, however, roughened by years of homeless-
ness and slaughter, brought to their native villages the usual heritage of
war: a greed for drink, sex, and gambling; brutality; and diseases. In
addition, boys who had been too young to participate in the wars were
now quick to learn from veterans how to make themselves important in

the village, particularly with the foolish, gullible girls. They jeered at the old-fashioned ones who insisted on marriage and favored those who did not, loudly proclaiming the right of the newly emancipated woman to "free love," the only new idea they welcomed. Meanwhile, parents and future parents-in-law watched a girl's behavior closely, ready to bear down on any immoral actions. Of these, joining the Komsomol was number one, being considered the first step along the path to ruin. Altogether, life was hard for a peasant girl after the Revolution as well.[2]

REBELS AND WEAKLINGS

Fiction, reflecting the Party's growing concern over the deterioration of morals and its stress on Komsomol activities as a remedy, first became interested in younger heroines in the late 1920's; the baba, it will be remembered, had already made her entrance into Soviet literature as early as 1921. The reason for this discrimination might simply have been contemporary reality. However lowly a baba's position was, marriage and particularly motherhood, gave her a certain status; but a slip of a girl was credited with no more sense, and could aspire to no more civic rights, than the calves she was tending. Consequently, the first pioneers of the peasant woman's emancipation could hardly have been recruited among young girls. The first younger heroine typical enough to keep the book on the publisher's lists in later years was Anka in K. Gorbunov's *The Ice Is Breaking* (1927), to be followed in 1928 by Parunka in N. Kochin's *The Girls*.

Anka is an orphan and a pauper, characteristics which were becoming standard for a progressive peasant heroine. After she is seduced by Yashka, a kulak's son, she finds her gate tarred, but this only serves to awaken in her a militant spirit. She joins the Komsomol, is promptly elected delegate to the district Soviet, decides not to marry Yashka, now cringing in the face of her success, and to bring up their unbaptized baby all by herself. She finally marries a worthy Party member, having made sure that he considers her baby a badge of progress rather than of dishonor. *The Ice Is Breaking* was hailed by Soviet critics, Gorky among them, as a "truly proletarian novel." It was adapted for the stage in 1930, and recommended for performances on International Woman's Day as "good propaganda material,"[3] an apt definition which was confirmed by the book's revival in 1953, at the peak of Socialist Realism, with only minor stylistic revisions.

The story of *The Girls*, however, is significantly different. Kochin, a self-educated peasant writer and journalist, had an intimate knowledge of the village milieu, and the novel, dedicated "to the memory of my sister Katya, martyred by her husband and her mother-in-law," is almost a documentary. Its first appearance (in installments in *Oktjabr'*, Nos. 11–12 [1928] and in book form [1929]), was cautiously welcomed by reviewers, but the publishers found it necessary to dissociate themselves from its bitter social criticism.[4] The first two parts published deal exclusively with unfortunate "wenches"; Part III, added to the book edition, with the village Komsomol in general. In 1935, a revised second edition added three more parts reintroducing the two protagonists—the pioneer Parunka and the timid Marka—this time as efficient Party worker and kolkhoz organizer, respectively. In spite of this conformity to current political trends, the author was arrested and disappeared from the literary scene until 1956, when he was rehabilitated,[5] and *The Girls* went into a third edition, unrevised, in 1962.

The original, and by far the best, version of the novel presents a portrait gallery of peasant girls. Many remain nameless, like members of a chorus mourning the tragedy of the protagonists. They participate in the posidelki and arteli, hunt down the rebel Parunka, sing sad wedding songs for one timid victim, and weep when another dies after drinking lye to bring about an abortion. The book's artistic value is in its vivid picture of reality; otherwise, psychological insight is nonexistent and the plot is standard: a Komsomol youth loses his girl to a kulak's son and is murdered by the rival's hireling. The key figure is the orphan Parunka, hired help exploited by kulak employers who joins the Komsomol. She learns to read and realizes that her only chance of a better life lies in escaping the village. Cheated by two villains who had promised her a job in the city, she makes the journey on her own, after having set fire to her hut. In the 1920's, this was evidently considered, if not exactly a happy ending, at least an adequate solution: Glafira, in Karavaeva's *The Village Medvezhatnoe* (1925), did the same.

The main block on a peasant girl's road to emancipation (as heroines realized) was her ignorance and the shyness it bred; otherwise her opportunities could have been better than older women's. Her vitality was as yet untaxed, her looks at their best; being unattached, she could choose her future. If a woman could now escape a lifetime of misery by divorcing an unloved husband, a spirited girl could refuse to marry one in the first place. " 'They forced me!' " says Marka in explanation of her disastrous marriage. " 'Nobody can force you nowadays,' " retorts her equally disappointed husband. " 'A guy can't even beat his woman, nor make her work—not even argue with her. They've made up special laws for women in Moscow.' "[6]

The law alone, however, offered little help. It took real courage for a girl to challenge the whole awesome apparatus of the byt and incur the displeasure of its custodians, who were apt to react in no uncertain manner. Once a girl had opted for the Soviet regime—for instance, by insisting on her right to speak at a village meeting—her punishment could range from the heckling which Anka received, to being walked home by a jeering crowd with a noose around her neck, as was Parunka. Since fiction furnishes no examples of such extreme measures being applied to women, evidently public opinion gave quarter to their pretensions, but did not extend this tolerance to girls. And, of course, if the village ostracized a girl who was virtuous, though too bold, it proved utterly ruthless to one who was moreover guilty of an illicit affair, an old sin which was nevertheless blamed on newfangled ideas.

The girls retaliated after a fashion by actually inviting censure as a matter of principle, reasoning that if their behavior shocked the reactionaries, it was progressive and ideologically correct. Hence, Anka's refusal to let her seducer make an honest woman of her became standard in Soviet fiction, and Natalya in F. Gladkov's *New Land* even refuses to marry a worthy comrade and a loving mate, simply because she wants their child to be illegitimate and exclusively hers. It is interesting to note that at the time certain fictional heroines in the West—Annique, in Victor Margueritte's *Le Compagnon* (1924), and Annette, in Romain Rolland's *L'âme enchantée* (1922–33), for example—held the same views.

Beyond this extreme form of emancipation from the Old, the early girl pioneers in Soviet fiction have little to contribute. Unschooled, they are unable to promote the Komsomol cultural and political activities, even at the modest level of the period. Young and inexperienced, they are of little use to the Zhenotdel, which concentrates on nurseries, midwifery, assisting in divorce and alimony suits, and fighting husbands' tyranny. And they evidently are considered incapable as yet of leadership, a quality which progressive babas miraculously develop on being elected to the village councils.

In later fiction, most peasant girls of the 1920's follow the pattern of the awakened woman; contemporary writers, however, use girl characters primarily to illustrate the "power of darkness" lingering in the Russian village, so that the pioneers and the old-fashioned girls are about equally represented. Unlike the conservative baba, who is reluctant to relinquish the familiar *status quo*, however unsatisfactory, young girls are malleable and ready for any change: they have had no time as yet to become firmly rooted in traditional values. As the proverb says, they are like "a piece of wood out of which an icon can be made as easily as a spade." But whether these girls become pioneers or remain old-fashioned depends not so much on ideology as on individual temperament: old-fashioned girls simply lack civic courage. Moreover, marriage is likely to be important in determining the course a girl takes, for young, timid brides are assumed to be easily swung in either direction.

For example, young Zinka, in Part I of Panfyorov's *Village Bruski*, is heartbroken when Zhdarkin, her Communist husband, draws a pig's head on an icon, a scene omitted in subsequent editions. When, however, he divorces her (primarily for her religiosity), and on remarrying, she finds that her second husband is also against religious practices, she promptly relegates all her icons to a shed. " 'A wife,' " she says, " 'must follow her husband, as the thread follows the needle.' " It is no wonder that the partorgs in Soviet fiction hold husbands responsible for their wives' ideological education. Zinka, left to herself by both her busy husbands, ended a villainess, as did Ula, Zhdarkin's second wife.

Thus, for the old-fashioned girls too weak to demand women's newly acquired rights, the Revolution might not have taken place at all. As before, their parents "sell them for a drink" into marriage, and readers are treated to pictures of the brutalities of wedding nights and the detailed coarseness of nuptial festivities. As before, if the girl is rich some kulak will marry her for her money, and if poor, seduce and desert her. Docile and lachrymose, so alike they are practically indistinguishable, old-fashioned girls did not survive for long in Soviet literature. A new generation of girls was growing up and following the path cleared for them by their valiant pioneering predecessors.

In the village fiction of the period, the beneficial influence radiating from the city is taken for granted, but seldom shown. A few red-kerchiefed lecturers sent by the Zhenotdel encourage women to fight for their rights: Katya Dolga and Praskovya (in *The Bast Shoes*) owe part of their success to these helpful comrades. Occasionally, a returned native promotes novelties she had learned in the city, ranging from humane family relationships to the liberal use of soap, or even to making wild-flower posies, as does Lipa in A. Karavaeva's *The Home-stead* (1926). But generally, the city is distant and rather sinister. Crafty city women wreck peasant homes, and simple girls who leave their village for the city (married women never do) are ruined. Such is, for instance, the fate of Tanya in S. Malashkin's *The Moon from the Right* (1926) and of Sanya in N. Bogdanov's *The First Girl* (1928), heroines of the period's most discussed novels. What is more, the dissolute environment which corrupts them is the city Komsomol. Tanya, after attempting suicide, is rescued by a marriage to an honest comrade from home: but Sanya, formerly the pride of her village Komsomol, is killed by a lover who seeks to save her from complete degradation.

An amusing—and unique—example of a peasant girl who made good in the city is the heroine of G. Alekseev's "Dunka's Luck" (1926). When her seducer refuses to marry her because she is a pauper, she finds a job in the city and promptly denounces her employers as exploiters. With the Zhenotdel's support, she has them dispatched to a labor camp, is awarded their apartment and personal property by the court for damages, marries the father of her future baby, and lives happily ever after.

As a rule, however, writers are chivalrous and avoid portraying the misuse of new laws by scheming women; even the notorious "alimony seekers" (*alimentščicy*), claimants in contested paternity suits, are rare in the fiction of the 1920's. And peasant girls continued to invite the reader's sympathy until, with fanfare, they mounted the driver's seat of the tractors in the newly established kolkhozes. From then on, unless the challenges of socialist competition be considered obstacles, their path is smooth and their happy lives dedicated to the tractors, the Komsomol, and the Party, provider of it all.

Feshka, in I. Shukhov's *Hatred* (1931), could be these emancipated girls' standard-bearer. She is an illiterate, destitute waif who, after a course in tractor driving, becomes a leader and organizer adept in "holy class-hatred." She defeats the scheming kulaks, improves the kolkhoz management, and dispenses excellent advice on everything from sex to politics. Lovely, proud, and chaste, like Diana, she is finally rewarded by the respectful love of a worthy Komsomolets—as, indeed, have all her successors been.

Feshka's career, however, was not to be duplicated. The peasant girl played practically no role in the fiction of the 1930's, and when during the next decade she came into her own, she still was not allowed Feshka's position of importance. Yet Feshka's wealth of personal excellency proved, it would seem, sufficient to endow her two typical successors—the pert girl and the Soviet ingenue of the postwar period.

THE KOLKHOZ GIRLS

While one and often both of the two types of girls mentioned above appear in every work of kolkhoz fiction, they are cast in supporting roles, usually as assistants to the Heroine. This fact probably accounts for the sameness, that distinctive feature of Soviet typical characters, which is so prominent in these girls. Matrons like Avdotya and Grunya, however alike, can still be considered individual prima donnas, but young girls are like members of the *corps de ballet*: within their respective groups all ingenues and all pert girls are interchangeable.

They are as cheerful as the stylized peasant dancers and singers of eighteenth-century fiction, and like them, appear mostly in groups. But the resemblance ends there because, unlike their forebears, kolkhoz girls are blissfully happy, know it, and want the whole world to know it too. They are, in animated form, the *pointe* of Mayakovsky's poem about the Soviet passport: "Look at me, envy me; I am a citizen of the Soviet Union!" They are, indeed, already products of Soviet society, for they are the daughters of the struggling pioneers and of the lachrymose brides in the fiction of the 1920's. They have never been exploited by a kulak—perhaps have never even met one—and take the kolkhoz community for granted; there they attended grade school, and after marrying the boy next door, there they may expect to stay their entire lives. As to Communism, they were born into its creed and therefore join the Komsomol at the age and in the spirit of Christian girls' confirmation.

Content with their lot and immune to frustrations (as, indeed, all Soviet fictional heroines have been) they lead happy, useful lives. Like the Beta children in Huxley's *Brave New World*, they are glad to be what they are and do not envy the bright Alfa children who have to learn so many difficult things. And, in any case, there are no Alfa children around: these (mostly boys) have left for the city; if they ever return, it is to serve as veterinarians, agronomists, and technicians—members of a different social group, the new Soviet intelligentsia. A few come back in the late 1950's in answer to Khrushchev's call for the development of the virgin lands. These characters—Tonya, for example, in S. Antonov's *It Happened at Penkovo*—find adjustment to local conditions difficult and behave more like missionaries than like returned natives.

The natives, on the other hand, identify their lives with kolkhoz work, in harmony with the plot. For instance, the plot of Panova's novel, *The Bright Shore*, dramatizes the crime of and the punishment for selling a pedigree cow to another kolkhoz without previous Party clearance. S. Krutilin's *Fountain Springs* (1953) revolves around the choice of planting methods; L. Voronkova's *The Restless Person* (1953), around that of barn temperatures most suitable for raising calves; and V. Kochetov's *Under the Sky of the Fatherland* is dedicated to both.

Naturally, youthful characters take part in these controversies and are affected by the passions unleashed. In fact, they occasionally receive more than their rightful share of excitement, because while matching the Heroine's dedication to kolkhoz welfare, young girls surpass her in enthusiasm. This is not to imply that the older woman's performance, while efficient, is emotionally lukewarm. On the contrary. But the girl, as is proper for youth, approaches hers in a more romantic spirit. Therefore, high-pitched enthusiasm is a distinctive feature of both the ingenue and the pert girl, although they differ in temperament, appearance, and manner.

The ingenue is shy and retiring; she is slight, not necessarily pretty, but has large, soulful eyes. For some reason, she is usually cast as a dairymaid, perhaps because the barn with its peacefully ruminating cows provides a suitably sheltered background. She keeps the barn immaculate, hangs white, starched curtains on its windows, dreams of a future when milking will be done to music,[7] and feeds her favorite cow into yielding fabulous amounts of milk. She anxiously watches increases in the cow's appetite and weight, while losing her own, and lavishes boundless care on her charges. The local recognition and national fame which she achieves surprise her, but these are only unimportant by-products of her devotion, because hers is a labor of love. The writers' favorite device is contrasting the ingenue with learned and important men, who bow before her simple wisdom. "She sat and milked the cow," the author intones, "a small girl with red earrings like berries; and members of the Academy, Ministry officials, and Party representatives stood respectfully by and looked at her milking."[8]

Calving is a major event in a kolkhoz novel: "'We seem to be delivering a crown prince today!'" grumbles an old-fashioned dairy-maid at the elaborate hygienic preparations. The birth is described in naturalistic detail, and the ingenue vibrates under its emotional impact. The sight of Nastenka with a newborn calf makes a seasoned (and not too sober) kolkhoz manager forget his many worries: "the look of this nineteen-year-old girl was gentle and blissful, almost a mother's look."[9] And Nyusha in *The Bright Shore* "says with pale lips: 'If anything happens to the cow, I won't survive it!' "[10]

In the course of the novel, the ingenue inevitably falls in love. It is either an innocent romance with a nice boy which culminates in marriage or a naïve infatuation with an unsuspecting expert in animal husbandry considerably her senior. But above any other emotions, she radiates, all blushes and shining eyes, an intense, almost fierce dedication to her dream barn and to its inmates.

The pert girl is freckled, snub-nosed, fond of colorful blouses and kerchiefs, and something of a coquette. She squeals with laughter at the slightest opportunity, weeps stormily over kolkhoz mishaps, though seldom over her own, contradicts her elders, and speaks up fearlessly at public meetings. Invariably, it is she who, as leader of her working group (*brigada*) and Komsomol secretary, promises Stalin to overfulfill the norms of kolkhoz production, she who experiments with new agricultural methods—under adult supervision, but with an efficiency and zeal all her own. Finally, it is she who answers first the Komsomol calls for emergency work: snow-shoveling, ditch-digging, or organizing "an evening of culture," the last of these usually including washing the club hut's floor and repairing the stove.

Her element is the outdoors, and reckless courage is her trademark, just as patience is the ingenue's. Above all, she is passionately dedicated to the country's welfare, to the exclusion of any other feeling or desire. A widowed mother in S. Antonov's *Lena* (1948), watching her daughter sleep after a hard day, is worried and puzzled:

Lena, even sleeping, seems to be on the alert. Her eyelids are only half-closed, as if she were peeking from under them, her fingers are curled, ready to grasp a spade or a pitchfork . . . she has lost weight lately, dark shadows have ringed her eyes. . . .

"My darling daughter! . . . What are you seeing in your dreams, what makes you choose the unfamiliar, the most difficult tasks? What wave is sweeping you up so high, beyond your own mother's reach and understanding?"[11]

Sometimes an ambitious girl joins the kolkhoz aristocracy by becoming a technician in the MTS. This job has been considered glamorous ever since the days of the first Five-Year Plan, and the first female tractor drivers were even singled out by Stalin in an early apocryphal story in *The Village Bruski*: "Stalin, merrymaking in the company of writers and painters, sang ditties about the girl who had climbed into the tractor driver's seat, and he kept repeating, 'And just you try to chase her down from there! She'll dare anyone to do that!' "[12]

Certainly, no one tries to chase down Froska, in *The Harvest*, the daring representative of the pert girls. She achieves status by sublimating her fiery temperament into work, though literary critics give the credit to the wholesomeness of the kolkhoz environment. She overcomes many handicaps: she was brought up by a petty-minded mother, a small property owner before collectivization (*podkulačnica*), and she has at first no discipline or sense of social duty. Robust, sensual, and sharp-tongued, Froska is probably the only girl in kolkhoz fiction before the 1960's who contracts an illicit liaison—just one, of course, which ends in marriage. Evidently because her misconduct was a shock to herself (and certainly to literary critics), she reforms and becomes a *Komsomolka*, a combine driver, and a Stakhanovite, in that order. She still remains impulsive and shrewish, but, as her husband comes to realize, the way to tame Froska is to surpass her in excellency of kolkhoz work—which he does. They are rewarded by marital happiness based on common ideals, work, and love.

" 'Actually, love for us women begins only after marriage,' " a woman partorg reassures a girl who hesitates to marry for fear of killing romance.[13] But romance in kolkhoz fiction differs from the traditional Western concept: farm work takes precedence over it. A girl will break a date in order to be present at a cow's calving or a sow's littering (as does, for example, Katya in Voronkova's *The Restless Person*).

And farm work affects the very language of love. Since Grunya (in Panov's *The Red Grove*, 1940) has been on nightly duty in the pigsty for weeks, her lover ventures to seek her there:

"Grunya, my little one" [he whispered, trying to take her hand].
"Don't you dare interfere with my work! . . . Do you know what? We are going to give a piglet to each kolkhoz member, so you will get one too. You're a piglet yourself!" She pulled his bushy hair. "Don't let your mother slaughter it before it weighs about 300 pounds. Do you love me very much?"
"Very much, Grunya. I dream of you day and night."[14]

AFTER THE THAW

With the coming of the thaw, peasant girls once again faded into the background in Soviet literature. The new trend, which exposed the shortcomings of Soviet conditions, blaming them on the previous administration, affected model peasant girls more than it did women. The fairy-tale kolkhoz of the postwar period vanished, revealing in its place inefficient management, poor work, and lean cattle standing in filthy, dilapidated barns. The golden coach had turned into a pumpkin, the horses into rats, and much of her former finery was also lost by Cinderella.

Klava, the best worker in the kolkhoz in Abramov's *This and That*, is also its first in loose morals—an unthinkable combination in the preceding decade. Moreover, she is slovenly, drinks, and uses coarse language. The author puts the blame on the war, which had cheated so many girls of marriage by killing the boys of their generation. Of the several dairymaids in A. Kuznetsov's *At Home* (1961), Olga is brash and foul-mouthed; and Ludmila, a blowsy, red-cheeked young woman, when accused of taking a man away from his wife, retorts that it is not her fault there aren't enough bachelors.

This is not to say that in post-thaw kolkhozes there are no nice girls, but that they are no longer engagingly modest. The Komsomolka Shurochka in *It Happened at Penkovo*, for instance, does not drink or smoke (indeed, no woman ever smokes in kolkhoz fiction) and has no lovers, but she unblushingly sings obscene songs at a wedding. Furthermore, the enthusiastic drive for raising agricultural standards is no longer spearheaded by artless kolkhoz girls. These girls, like Kapa in Dorosh's *Village Diary* (1954–58), have grown lazy and domesticated in a way, the author remarks, incompatible with their membership in the Komsomol. Or, like Valyusha in M. Shitov's "Turn at Berezov" (1963), they refuse farm jobs because they have finished high school and stay at home waiting for husbands.

The young zealots who still live up to the image of the kolkhoz Heroine of Labor come from the city. They too are high school graduates, but education only makes them the more aware of their civic responsibilities. Such is Lizaveta in Antonov's *Alyonka*, who insists on taking a herdsman's job and loses her life on it. And such is Galya in Kuznetsov's *At Home*, who wants to follow in the footsteps of her late mother, once the famed (*znatnaja*) milkmaid of the district. Galya improves sanitary conditions of milk delivery and increases the daily yield of a favorite cow to record heights in the fine tradition of Nyusha in *The Bright Shore*. Unfortunately, she has an affair with the local Don Juan, a no-good stable boy, and is, in fact, so different from her charming fictional predecessors that she embarrasses a reporter who is interviewing her for a magazine story:

> The reporter wrote unhesitatingly: "She makes every cow yield eighteen liters of milk daily, this small, merry, suntanned girl with saucy eyes. And as she tells us all about it, her laughter is infectious!" He glanced at Galya and felt a twinge of remorse, but he had a long-established image of the dairymaid which he could not change now.[15]

Could it be that these unprepossessing portrayals, besides, of course, being truer to reality, try to convey the idea that beneath coarseness beat hearts of gold? Hardly, because a heart of gold alone would not suffice to make a heroine typical, a goal which Soviet fiction after the thaw still continues to pursue. Needed are excellency of morals, of manners, and above all, of working performance. Beauty matters least: as the following quotation shows, Soviet writers take the old adage "handsome is as handsome does" literally. Vasily (in *The Harvest*) inspects a field which Nastya the tractorist has just finished sowing: "As a pretty dress worn by a girl sometimes seems a component of her prettiness and it is difficult to tell the two kinds of loveliness apart, so this evenly plowed soil seemed to be one with Nastya. And Vasily did not know whether he meant Nastya or the soil when he inwardly exclaimed, 'Oh, what a beauty!' "[16] Nastya, in fact, is not pretty, but she is a good girl, the best specialist in her MTS, and completely dedicated to her work. Certainly, Klava and Kapa and even Galya for one reason or another fall short of the mark.

There is a connection between the tarnished image of the youthful Heroine and the deterioration of the village Komsomol. The institution seems no longer to attract the young, progressive, heroic elements, as it had done since the beginnings of the Soviet fiction; and most post-thaw writers reveal its declining influence. Understandably, in the village the Komsomol's possibilities have always been limited compared to those in the city. Yet, in spite—or perhaps because—of that, the village Komsomol took pride in its role as the representative of progress and the promoter of culture. It supported the first heroines in their struggles for emancipation and literacy in the 1920's. During World War II, its membership was first in fighting the invader, and in the postwar decade, in Stakhanovite competitions and cultural activities. In fiction of the 1950's, dilapidated huts were converted into clubs by eager young hands, scrubbed, and adorned with paper garlands and portraits of Stalin. Dancing and singing, amateur theatricals, lecturers' visits, and tumultuous political meetings took place there, the latter ending in resolutions to raise better crops for the State; a lending library would be run in the evenings by some famed and dedicated milkmaid (for example, Nadya in S. Antonov's "The Librarian," 1950).

All these enterprises seem to have melted in the thaw. Young people revel for a week in Yashin's *The Wedding in Vologda,* because "their enormous village still has no electricity, no radio, no library, no club; no movie truck has been seen here for the last six months—and yet, youth does need entertainment!"[17] Dorosh's *Village Diary* notes hooliganism at a lecture in the local club and much brawling "in the Old Russia style." In Antonov's *It Happened at Penkovo,* an effort is made to revive the abandoned club activities. The initiative, however, comes from Tonya, the agronomist, not from the local Komsomol youth, and her efforts and those of a few members are wasted in the stolid atmosphere of kolkhoz daily routine. These "slices of life" have been particularly resented by Soviet literary critics.

Village life, then, has little to offer a girl in the post-thaw period. Like the matron Heroines, she cannot complain of being maltreated, and there is plenty for her to do if she wants to work—but she does not, except for a living and to buy (according to Dorosh) lipstick, perfume, and high-heeled shoes to wear on Sundays.[18] Milking has lost its glamour, raising vegetables no longer opens the road to success.

The kolkhoz is dull. Young people have left, the energetic ones to work on the gigantic new constructions beyond the Urals, the bright ones, to study in the cities. Those left behind are neither energetic, nor bright, nor ambitious. Men are few and unwilling to marry, judging by the return of the seduction topic, which had been absent from fiction since the early 1930's. The frustrated, unattractive girls are left with no other company than colorless grandmothers busy with household chores and babysitting, and aging former innovators and managers who reminisce, perhaps, about the days when kolkhoz life was full of challenge and adventure and when women were cast in the roles of Heroines.

II

THE PROLETARIANS

5

The New Proletarian Woman

It is hardly necessary to point out the paucity of works representing the proletarian milieu in prerevolutionary Russian literature. Workers were too insignificant numerically and politically to play an important role in Russian society, and consequently, in fiction. There were a few short stories which dealt with the proletariat—for example, Veresaev's *The Two Ends* (1898–1903)—but generally fiction concentrated on portraying the bourgeois milieu and offered only glimpses of the hard working conditions, low pay, and poverty among workers as background details. Gorky's *Mother* (1906), a *roman à thèse*, is of course a notable exception.

Women characters were especially insignificant; in fact, they hardly existed as persons. If the much-enduring baba was practically an animated pattern in Russian fiction, the working man's wife (usually nameless) was not even that; she did not have spoken lines. She merely waited, surrounded by starving children, for a factory strike to end, or was brutalized by her drunken husband while trying to salvage the remnants of his pay. However miserable her home, she never worked outside it: it still was a haven compared to a factory, where women were not only overworked and underpaid, but also molested by foremen. Veresaev's Sasha, a young widow who tries for a few months to support her child by working in a factory, considers herself lucky to escape into a loveless marriage. Pelageya, in *Mother*, never thinks of leaving her brutal husband in order to become economically independent. The proletarian woman, just like her peasant and middle-class sisters, had only one career, that of a housewife, and beyond her home had neither rights nor duties.

During the early stages of Soviet literature, works featuring the proletarian milieu remain surprisingly few in contrast with peasant fiction. This fact is made less conspicuous by the popularity of Gladkov's *Cement* (1925) and two other equally mediocre novels, *The Blast Furnace* (1925) by N. Lyashko and *Natalya Tarpova* (1927) by S. Semyonov. Soviet critics, eager to promote a new proletarian literature, greeted every publication to which this term could be applied, no matter how artistically poor. Yet the output remained low, the reason, apparently, being both the authors and the subject matter.

The authors, understandably, wrote about the milieu which they knew best, and peasant writers being more numerous than proletarians (though just as undistinguished), they published more. The Fellow Travelers, the largest and most talented group of writers, though primarily concerned with the intelligentsia, would portray the village—pre-Petrine or newly Soviet as the case might be—but found no fascination in the problems of postrevolutionary industry. Moreover, proletarian and peasant fiction differed in the presentation of their basic subject—revolutionary change. In the village, the process was shown as the breaking up of the Old, while in the the city, as the establishment of the New. Possibly, this divergence also affected the ratio of works published: the crumbling bastions of the past might have offered more drama than the rising strongholds of the new Soviet society.

The peasant family's patriarchal structure and its common ownership of the land provided fiction writers with material rich in human relationships. Peasant women, conservative and progressive alike, were in the thick of events. Requisitions of grain by the government, allocation of the land to individual farmers, mergers into communes and kolkhozes—all these events beyond the threshold of the hut affected the way of life inside it. They contributed to the plot and to the Heroine's characterization as much as did her reactions to the removal of icons, civil marriages, or the activities of the Zhenotdel. The huge, notoriously backward peasantry had to abdicate centuries of traditions before accepting new forms. This, and the task of clearing the site for the new village byt was portrayed within the context of the family.

With proletarian fiction it was different. The small and recent city proletariat, unencumbered by ancient tradition, was free to make immediate adjustments to the new order. Fictional plots centered on postrevolutionary industrial reconstruction, and the home life of the characters remained on its periphery. The male protagonist, absorbed with the affairs of the factory, was shown almost exclusively within its walls, and the reader had only occasional glimpses of the apartment in a workers' settlement where his family lived. His wife, if she stayed at home, was as impersonal as she had been in prerevolutionary fiction, and her role just as insignificant, because she was outside the mainstream of the plot. Only if she joined the factory—and so the mainstream—did she acquire a personality, a name, and the ideological responsibilities of building the new society. A baba could become a pioneer of progress simply by breaking the traditional bonds of her dependence, but her proletarian counterpart was expected to become a class-conscious New Woman.

Living up to this ideal proved no mean task. Aleksandra Kollontay, the ardent pioneer of the New Woman's rights, painted a vision of her, self-supporting, living alone, doing social and political work, and "wrestling from life the small earthly joys of physical love."[1] This any woman could do tolerably well. But Kollontay also showed her eating her meals at the communal kitchen, her children happy in State nurseries, her home tidied, her laundry done, and her clothes mended by special, State-provided workers.[2] And none of these conveniences, needless to say, were available.

Theoretical advice was plentiful. That the bourgeois form of family life was to be abolished simultaneously with capitalism was plainly stated in *The Communist Manifesto*. That the domination of man in marriage would vanish once woman began to earn her living was guaranteed by Engels. That merely legal measures would not assure women real freedom as long as they continue to be "slaves . . . stultified by petty housework in the kitchen and in the nursery" was recognized by Lenin.[3] But the practical realization of all these principles amid the political turmoil and economic hardships of the New Economic Policy period were beyond the capacities of fictional heroines and their living prototypes. This too may have been in part responsible for the small number and unconvincing characterization of proletarian women in the fiction of the period.

Still, the transition from the status of a housewife to that of a citizeness is easier for a proletarian woman than for a peasant. She need not concern herself with the disapproval of in-laws, who in her case live elsewhere, nor with that of neighbors, because unlike her village sister, she has not known them all her life. And the wages and the ration cards she gets at the factory, however meager, give her financial independence, something a peasant woman would achieve only eventually in a kolkhoz. Once she has obtained independence, she does not meet in the world outside the hostility which taxes the courage of peasant heroines. These peasant women are rebels destroying the traditional order of their village community, while the New Woman's participation in establishing the Soviet regime is treated by her proletarian environment as proper and desirable. Party guidance is readily available; helping in the Zhenotdel activities and speaking up at factory meetings are encouraged, indeed appreciated.

In spite of this, the New Woman has her full share of emotional hardships. It is true, her husband is not a domestic tyrant like the husband of Marya the Bolshevik or of Katya Dolga, and he does not object to her political activities. He is a class-conscious, hard-working man, usually a Party member, and he readily recognizes women's equal rights—at least in theory. Unfortunately, however, he still occasionally deserts his wife for other women, drinks, or has inadequate standards of work and Party discipline. And because the Heroine's performance at work and her Party loyalty are so much higher, the ensuing marital conflicts assume ideological aspects, with the husband clearly in the wrong.

In such cases, the Heroine will leave him. She may find a worthier comrade, as did Varya in D. Chetverikov's *Atava* (1924) and Liza in M. Platoshkin's "The New Way" (1924). Or she may decide to live a stern life of social usefulness alone, like Nadya in M. Chumandrin's *The Former Hero* (1929). Often she vows to raise the expected baby away from its father's influence, as do, for example, Vasilisa in A. Kollontay's *Vasilisa Malygina* (1923) and Varya in Chumandrin's *Factory Rablé* (1928). But whatever the denouement of the plot, the woman proves spiritually superior to the man.

When the opposite is true, he fares no better, because he is still responsible for whatever goes wrong with his family life: it is his duty to educate his wife in class-consciousness. If persuasion fails, he is to use drastic measures. Thus Vasily in Lyashko's *Blast Furnace*, a pale carbon copy of Gladkov's *Cement*, refuses to support his wife (she stays nameless throughout the novel) and kidnaps his children to remove them from their mother's disastrous influence (she teaches them prayers). In order to survive, the wife goes to work in the factory, and once a proletarian in her own right, develops class-consciousness; as a result, harmonious family life is restored. In spite of the smallness of her role in the novel, this wife may well be considered the progenitor of the countless women reformed by factory work in Soviet literature.

The real marital conflict, however, arises when both parties have an equally distinguished ideological level, as do Gleb and Dasha Chumalov, the protagonists of Gladkov's *Cement*. It would seem that, on the contrary, such a setup should guarantee perfect harmony—and it has in Soviet fiction under Socialist Realism, especially in partorgs' families in the 1950's. But *Cement*, in spite of its grievous artistic shortcomings, is to be credited with the one heroine whose repudiation of basic feminine emotions was not automatic. Dasha lived her Marxist principles as martyrs or revolutionaries live theirs, to a degree unmatched by any other Soviet heroine. But while unflinchingly accepting the hardships of such complete dedication, she suffers, and suffering enhances her sacrifice in the eyes of the reader.

Cement, written in the eventful years 1922–24, is a Soviet classic. It has the distinction of being the first novel dealing with the task of "socialist reconstruction," of introducing a true proletarian hero and heroine, and of stating the problems of the newly emancipated Russian women.

Gleb and Dasha are model Communists, at least according to the standards of the 1920's: in the novel they pass with flying colors the test of a drastic Party purge. Gleb's efforts to rebuild the cement factory after his return from the Civil War constitute one of the twin plots; the other features the couple's difficulties resulting from Dasha's emancipation. Estrangement follows, and finally Dasha moves out of her ruined home to dedicate her life to serving the new society. She leaves behind her baffled and sorrowful husband and the grave of their little daughter, Nyurka, who died at an orphanage where she had been put by her mother at the start of the latter's break with the old order.

The sympathies of the critics were on Dasha's side. Dismissing in a few reluctant remarks her extra-marital affairs and the death of her abandoned Nyurka, they blamed the Chumalovs' differences on Gleb's "possessive attitude toward the woman" and his painful slowness in "shedding the ancient Adam lingering in his soul."[4] Yet, there was much he could complain about:

Gleb never came home during the day: this desolate room with its dusty windows—not even flies ever buzzed against the panes—its unwashed floor and the heap of ragged clothing, was unfamiliar and stuffy; the walls seemed to close on him. . . . He would return home by night but Dasha was not there to meet him on the threshold as she did three years ago. . . . She came after midnight . . . not the former Dasha, that one was dead . . . undressed standing by the table, munching a crust of the rationed bread, not looking in his direction. Her face was tired and stern.[5]

And, even worse:

The children's home was there in the mountain gorge among clumps of trees. . . . Among the bushes . . . Gleb saw children . . . prowling, digging hurriedly, greedily, watchful as thieves . . . snatching their "finds" from each other . . . digging in the manure. . . .
"But these poor brats are starving, Dasha! . . . Is Nyurka—does our Nyurka, too?" . . .
[Dasha shrugged] "Why should Nyurka be any different? She has her rough times too. If it were not for our women, kids would have perished from lice and disease and starvation."[6]

Unquestionably, whatever her shortcomings, Dasha is a pioneer. She is given to drastic measures, she shows off, but much of it stems from the desire to prove to herself, more than to the others, that she really is the New Woman. She is not callous. It hurt to let her geraniums wither unwatered on a dusty window sill, to see her child die for want of love and care, to repulse Gleb, whom she had never ceased to love. Even her promiscuity, like Virineya's, is a form of defiance, of breaking established norms. She plunges into exhausting, unpaid work with the fervor of a settler felling the forest for his future home. She is the best worker of the Zhenotdel; she speaks at meetings, organizes children's homes and community kitchens, and risks her life foraging in the villages for food for these institutions.

In spite of all these merits, Dasha has no issue in Soviet literature comparable to that of Katya Dolga: she was not typical enough to become a pattern. Perhaps Korobov had kept closer to reality in the characterization of his heroine, while Gladkov, as a critic put it, "insisted on creating a hundred percent proletarian heroine, a Joan of Arc."[7] Perhaps the slower tempo of change in the village byt kept alive the fighting spirit of peasant women after it was no longer needed in the city. The peasant Heroine—Marya, Avdotya, Grunya—still had to assert her independence at home in the 1950's. When Dasha, on the

other hand, reappears in *Energy* in 1938, she is already a maverick, and
not just because she is a female commissar in the Red Army. Morose,
uncompromising, and ideologically as righteous as ever, she is now
alien to the new proletarian women, who are contented housewives and
wage earners.

Dasha and her lesser comrades, such as Chumandrin's two heroines
and Kollontay's Vasilisa, represented the spiritual elite of the new
ruling class. Stern in their hatred of the bourgeois way of life, demanding towards themselves and others, these women sincerely tried to
build their lives on what they considered pure Marxist ethics. They
were proletarian aristocrats, and Varya's husband in Chumandrin's
Factory Rablé called her just that, though he had primarily appearances in mind: Varya's tidy clothes, dignified bearing, and even the
two gold teeth gleaming daintily when she smiled. Gold teeth, incidentally, have been a recognized symbol of refinement in Soviet literature,
whether used ironically, as in Zoshchenko's "The Aristocrat" (1923),
or in apparent earnest, as in Panova's *The Train* (1946). When clothes,
manners, and principles became standardized in Soviet fiction under
Socialist Realism, spiritual refinement became the staple attribute of
positive characters, while negative characters have been wont to over-
emphasize elegance and comfort.

Another type of proletarian elite—what might be termed an uncut
diamond—is represented by Nogayko in Semyonov's *Natalya Tarpova*
(1927). A veteran factory worker, unattractive, carelessly dressed, she
dispenses loud-voiced advice on everything from free love to factory
management, chain-smokes, and is elected by acclamation to any committee which needs a truly class-conscious Party member—and what
committee does not? This type, unlike Dasha's, survived practically
unchanged over a quarter of a century. They are "distinguished working women" (*znatnye rabotnicy*), like Vlasovna in Gladkov's *Lyubasha's Tragedy* (1935), Kartasheva in E. Katerli's *The Bronze Spinning
Wheel* (1950), and Ermolova in A. Rybakov's *Ekaterina Voronina*
(1955); or, retired, they have become sage old matriarchs and oracles,
like Grandma Lesnyak in B. Gorbatov's *Donbass* (1951) and Trubni-
kova in Rybakov's *The Truck Drivers* (1950). But they all have
preserved their bluntness and sterling Communist qualities, and
proudly reminiscing about their days of toil and glory, wear their
revolutionary past like a halo. Yet, even so, they remain secondary
characters for reasons that will be discussed in the following chapter.

6

Proletarian Women
Under Socialist Realism

THE INDUSTRIAL NOVEL

The role of the proletarian woman, insignificant in postrevolutionary fiction of the 1920's, became even more so during the next decade. The Zhenotdel, the main field of Dasha's and Vasilisa's activities, was abolished in 1929. During the period of the first Five-Year Plan, dedicated to the urgencies of Russia's industrialization, fiction portrayed intense physical effort in which women participated only as faceless crowds, digging ditches and paving roads. Kataev's Fenya in *Time Forward!* (1932), who hauls logs till the last day of pregnancy, was emulated as late as 1938 by Ketlinskaya's Sonya in *Courage*, but such feats were subsequently discontinued. And in the industrial novels which have flooded Russian literature since, women workers are never protagonists. From the start, the genre established a type of female proletarian who was distressingly lifeless, worse, if possible, than the "dozen-in-the-box" pattern featured by kolkhoz fiction. The mediocrity of the industrial novels and the unrelieved boredom they radiate are sufficient explanation for their dearth of credible characters of either sex: no breathing creature could survive in that vapid atmosphere of technical details and harangues on loyalty to the regime. Somehow, the best among the kolkhoz novels, while carrying their full share of ideological pomposity, manage to convey glimpses of normal, if trivial, human feelings and existence. Peasant writers meeting Socialist Realism's requirement of showing the characters in their daily work interpolate naïve descriptions of nature into those of electrified barns, and in the post-thaw period, even a few colorful scenes, such as weddings or hunting. But the same requirement fills endless pages of industrial novels with descriptions of production techniques—welding, weaving, machine assembling, as the case may be—which nobody except specialists can, or cares to, understand.

Moving among the machinery are men and women seemingly immune to sensations or thoughts beyond those connected with efficient production. The factory's reputation, endangered by villains (or simply by non–class-conscious loafers), is finally rescued by positive characters in an apotheosis in which norms are raised to record heights and—perhaps as a concession to the romantic reader—all the younger workers are paired off in marriage. Couples already married (always happily) are usually rewarded with another baby: fat, blond, exactly like the one in the kolkhoz novels; in fact, one suspects, the very same.

The real protagonists of industrial novels are work and the guiding hand of the Party; characters are only the means by which these factors can be shown. Hence, the key characters in the plot are partorgs, the custodians of the institution's efficiency and morale, and innovators, the inventors of laborsaving devices. These elite, it should be stressed, are members of the Soviet intelligentsia who had risen from the ranks of working masses, but having done so, no longer belong there. And, while the intelligentsia does include career women, innovators among the proletariat are an all-male cast, and women workers are not shown in positions of responsibility.

A lonely exception—and one that seems to prove the rule—is the heroine of *Lyubasha's Tragedy* by F. Gladkov. The novel is, of course, of very inferior artistic quality, but this could hardly have been the reason for its exclusion from Gladkov's *Collected Works* (1958–59). More probably, it was the unpleasantly realistic picture of a factory community: unprepossessing-looking proletarians who "howl, yell, swear, engage in slander and gossip, and gloat over each other's misfortunes,"[1] particularly over those of poor Lyubasha.

And yet Lyubasha possesses all the prerequisites for a responsible role: active membership in the Komsomol; happy motherhood (her little daughter, unlike Dasha's Nyurka, thrives in a model day nursery);

marital life based on love, mutual appreciation of efficient factory work, and dedication to that work. But she lacks stamina, proves too emotional, sensitive—too feminine, perhaps—to withstand unjust criticism and to master the unruly work brigade of which she is in charge. She breaks down as a result of malicious intrigues of her co-workers and the unreasonable demands of the management, and so disqualifies herself as a positive protagonist in an industrial novel, where the plot is routinely based on just such an ordeal. Evidently, men are made of tougher moral fiber than women and are rightly given priority.

This does not mean that the promises of the Revolution to women have been forgotten. On the contrary, no industrial novel is complete without a director's laudatory speech on Soviet womanhood, and partorgs will seek out among the rank and file a quiet, middle-aged "Auntie" Dunya or Pasha to ask her opinion on current factory affairs. Still, women are lost in the crowd of extras on the factory stage. At a mass meeting, an Auntie may embarrass a bureaucrat by a shrewd question on his managerial policies; a younger woman on the same occasion may move to wire a message of thanks to "our own Stalin"; excellent, hard-working women abound in every plant, building construction, or mine. But there are no women protagonists: they just do not quite make the grade.

The thaw had little effect on the industrial novels, except perhaps that fewer have been published. Portraits of Stalin, to be sure, disappeared; new babies were no longer named after him "because Joseph is not really a Russian name";[2] and thanks for the greatness of the Soviet Union went, for several years at least, to Comrade Khrushchev. In addition, fewer technical details of production were given, and bureaucrats were denounced for putting production quotas over workmen's welfare. But plot and characters remained practically unchanged, particularly female characters, who, within the bounds of their common insignificance, had already diversified into several basic types.

THE TYPICAL WORKING WOMAN

The characterization of a typical proletarian woman in the years 1935–55 was determined by the two main socio-political factors of that period: Stakhanovite working methods and the newly stabilized code of Soviet ethics. Between the call for heroic labor and eulogies for family happiness and motherhood, the pattern of a young proletarian matron took shape independently of her predecessors. In kolkhoz fiction Avdotya or Grunya, with minor changes, followed the Katya Dolga blueprint, but the housewife doubling as industrial worker has scant resemblance to the new proletarian woman of the 1920's.

Her outstanding feature is femininity, though she holds rough and physically demanding jobs. She is gentle, soft-voiced, friendly toward her fellow workers and well liked by them. The reader has glimpses of her at work: Dunyasha (in V. Kochetov's *The Zhurbins*, 1952) in a shipyard, her new baby left in grandma's care; Sonya (in A. Rybakov's *Ekaterina Voronina*, 1955) in the cabin of a huge crane, next to the one manned by her husband. But she is also a homemaker, cooking special treats for her family on a free evening, sewing white window curtains. And she is a tender mother. If she happily leaves her children to be raised by nurseries, kindergartens, and schools, this is because she is confident that these Soviet institutions will do it better than she herself could have done.

Finally, these women are excellent wives—to deserving husbands. In the rare and unfortunate cases of a spiritual misalliance, a wife spares no efforts to improve her mate's class-consciousness or morals. But if she fails, she leaves him, and the children take her side. Usually, however, he is a Stakhanovite and an innovator, and she can safely respect his judgment whether on production problems or at home. Theirs is the same happy home, the bedrock of Soviet society, which the reader finds in kolkhoz fiction, though with more authority vested in the master of the house. It is he who disciplines the children, settles their arguments, and checks their school work, always calmly without a trace of despotism. But in practically every industrial novel, he is also seen feeding and even diapering babies (an unusual thing for European fathers), or pacing the floor of maternity wards, or proudly carrying the new baby home from the hospital.

Between the proletarian man and wife there is no professional envy or even competition, although these often serve as a fulcrum for the plot in works featuring the Soviet intelligentsia. The couple assume their rights to be equal, and the matter is not discussed or disputed— but neither is the husband's authority ever questioned in any matter or at any time. He is the senior partner (*staršij*), with all the duties and privileges the position entails.

Both spouses are faithful and loving. Sex scenes are never shown within the proletarian milieu, but couples often discuss current matters in bed, their favorite topic being, it seems, the factory's efficiency. This habit, questioned during the thaw by some critics, was heatedly defended as proof of Soviet moral superiority by Kochetov, the die-hard supporter of Socialist Realism.[3]

Writers are not generous to working matrons. They are plain; they wear old slippers and aprons at home, rough boots and overalls at work, and kerchiefs on their heads most of the time. Inconspicuous in attire, they are even so at work: efficient, but without that "seething energy" which is characteristic of young Stakhanovites—a separate type in proletarian womanhood. Unsophisticated, they trust and respect the Party, but are not shown playing any role in its policies, even at the lowest local level. They never open a book, seldom read a paper, and unlike kolkhoz women, do not try to improve either their education or their professional skills. In short, they are in every respect consummate secondary characters.

Theoretically, "a Soviet woman realizes that she may not immure herself within the narrow space of household duties,"[4] that she should find time for some social work, such as organizing a committee to improve the quality of food served by the factory cafeteria. But the principle is seldom rigidly enforced by authors in the case of proletarian and kolkhoz women, though they are less lenient with the intelligentsia. A paragon like Katyusha in S. Sartakov's *Bedrock Foundations* (1950) may occasionally combine the duties of a housewife and mother with those of factory nurse, bulletin editor, and representative to the Workers' Soviet. But even she undertook factory work only as wartime replacement for her soldier husband; and generally women in industrial novels are allowed to divide their time and energy between work in the factory and work at home. They do not go to the movies or to dances; such frivolities are for girls. Nor do they eat out: restaurants are frequented only by the intelligentsia. Prolific mothers in their forties and up are excused from any duties except homemaking, with the Party's blessing, it may be assumed, because they always are positive characters. Such a homemaker has no claims to being anything else: placid, neat, her face innocent of cosmetics, her hair parted and gathered into a bun, she prepares excellent food, shakes her head in sympathy when her husband has difficulties on his job, and sighs, " 'It's hard, oh how hard it is to raise a child, to bring up a human being!' "[5] while perhaps half a dozen of the objects of her solicitude are cavorting around. Moreover, she is not simply a housewife, but the continuator of a noble tradition, mother of still another generation of an established proletarian family. "Illustrious workmen's houses" have become quite fashionable in Soviet fiction since the early 1950's. There are "distinguished houses" of miners in B. Gorbatov's *Donbass* and V. Ketlinskaya's *No Sense in Living Otherwise* (1960); of the Volga river navigators in Rybakov's *Ekaterina Voronina;* of shipbuilders in Kochetov's *The Zhurbins;* and of steelworkers in Kochetov's *The Brothers Ershov* (1958). Members of these sprawling families are proud of their names, professional reputations, and of their geneological trees, which they discuss as often and as willingly as any nobleman in Sir Walter Scott's novels.

Proletarian women are happier than their counterparts in kolkhoz fiction and among the Soviet intelligentsia. It is true that, not being innovators, they cannot achieve fame, but then they are spared the double anxieties of a demanding career and a home neglected for its sake. If life is uneventful, it is active and secure, and on the whole, satisfying for these well-meaning, respectable, uneducated women. There are exceptions—women who have had no luck in love—but even these, sometimes after many years of loneliness, get happily married. It is as if Soviet writers could not bear to punish cruelly a girl who erred just once.

Moreover, these girls are always nice, even if gullible and seduced by men unworthy of their love. They are not, however, meant to arouse the reader's sympathy; in fact, it is usually the seducer who, having belatedly realized the girl's sterling qualities, is left lamenting at the end of the story. A Soviet working girl is quite capable of managing alone. " 'Literature portrays unfortunate girls abandoned by vile seducers,' " muses Varvara, in Nilin's "The Beloved Girl" (1936). " 'But I am not an unfortunate girl, and nobody yet has, or could have, abandoned me or seduced me. I'm the one who'll do the abandoning, and if necessary, the seducing—and will also pay, all by myself, for my own mistakes!' " As for the baby's illegitimacy, he can use his mother's name in the place of a patronymic: let him be "son of Varvara" (*Varvarovič*).[6]

So, instead of being driven to suicide or prostitution as in prerevolutionary fiction, or to an abortion as in that of the 1920's, seduction victims thrive under Socialist Realism—hurt, of course, and lonely, but granted their second chance. Until the right man appears on the scene, they dedicate their lives to work. They earn their own living and the child's by excellent performance in the factory; they are given un-glamorous and demanding assignments by the Komsomol cell; and they spend long evenings studying for a correspondence course. The baby, home from the model factory nursery, is peacefully asleep by their sides in a neat, cosy room, and true love is discreetly knocking at the door (for instance that of Nastya, the famed steelworker in B. Pole-voy's *The Active Workshop*, 1939).

Even these deserving women were seldom allowed to mix with the inhabitants of the Soviet fictional world during the prim postwar decade. In the 1960's, however, they were joined by a risqué character extinct for nearly thirty years: a young woman with a questionable past, and in a few cases, even a questionable present. Such wanton females serve as foils to the virtuous. They recognize with bitterness and humility their low status within society. " 'One doesn't marry the likes of me,' " says Anfisa to Ilya, who offers to make an honest woman of her in Bedny's *The Girls* (1961). " 'If it's a bit of fun you are after, that's fine, but if it's marriage, there are girls of a different kind, the ones with good moral principles.' " And the author, to make his posi-tion unmistakably clear, closes the incident with this symbolic scene: "Across the floor fell the shadow of Ilya embracing Anfisa. The shad-ows' heads merged in a kiss and their lips met at the spot where a twisted cigarette butt was lying by the stove on a dirty sheet of tin."[7] Finally, in 1963 Katya in V. Voevodin's, *The Daredevil*, as good-hearted a soul as Nancy in *Oliver Twist*, became the first shocking instance of a prostitute in Socialist Realism fiction. But she too ends by being happily married and employed as salesgirl in a creamery.

Nevertheless, these girls are still basically good, even if they do stray from the path of virtue, use strong language, and drink—a combination of failings inseparable in Soviet fiction. And there always are extenuat-ing circumstances. Lyolka (in Ketlinskaya's *No Sense in Living Other-wise*) grew up in the streets, a homeless waif (*besprizornica*); her namesake (in Kochetov's *The Brothers Ershov*) had been disfigured through torture by the Gestapo. They also have redeeming qualities, being courageous, kind, and above all, capable of true love and of finding their salvation in work, like Dusya in Rybakov's *Ekaterina Voronina*. Thus, work and love, the essential plot elements of Soviet fiction, prevent these young women from becoming negative charac-ters.

THE YOUNG STAKHANOVITE

In kolkhoz fiction, women characters are drawn with more attention to detail than are girls. In industrial novels the reverse is true, and young proletarian girls are nearer to being three-dimensional characters. Irrespective of their age they are not cast as protagonists, but a pattern does exist for a young proletarian Heroine. Although the type does not present enough variety in psychological and physical makeup to justify subdivisions, it is possible to distinguish within it a group of rather noisy extroverts and another group who manifest their emotions in a more subdued and refined manner. In every case the emotions—and so the means of characterization—are concerned with work and love.

In industrial novels working girls are not innovators; this role is reserved for their lovers, and very infrequently, for young career women. But they are Stakhanovites in that they are completely dedicated to the efficiency of their performance and are ambitious to prove themselves in jobs normally considered suitable only for men. They thirst for occupations which are dangerous or demand physical strength or special technical skill; they want to be miners, stevedores, locomotive engineers, sailors, parachutists, and truck drivers. What makes their work unusual is not their enthusiasm alone—milkmaids in kolkhoz novels are enthusiastic too—but its quality of harshness, of backbreaking physical effort.

Girls work in coal mines, sometimes having purposely switched from easier jobs, such as a postman's; overfulfill the special female norms of production; and if barred from taking extra risks, protest violently: " 'Why can't Sima work in the detonation brigade? Is it her braids that are in the way? Or did Nature specially equip men for igniting explosives?' "[8] They also overfulfill norms set for men in digging canals and in removing rubble and carrying bricks on postwar reconstruction sites; weeping, but undeterred, they glaze windows with bleeding, gloveless fingers in sub-zero temperatures.[9] They wield axes felling trees in logging camps and pan gold in Siberia—with proper tools when available, otherwise with just their bare hands.[10] If they ever complain, it is when primitive equipment is detrimental to the results they are trying to achieve. " 'How much can you do with mesh wire and a spade?' " a road worker queries bitterly. " 'And it is all we have for putting on the concrete at a time when atoms are being split and rockets are launched.' "[11]

In the 1950's, voices were raised among critics wondering whether "this poetizing of women's labor in mines is really necessary . . . whether strong men cannot manage without help from these girlish hands?" The main argument was that this type of work jeopardized femininity and that "girls doing men's work sometimes also try to emulate them in other things, learn to smoke, don't even mind drinking."[12] Actually, these fears were unfounded, at least as far as fictional heroines were concerned, because a Soviet working girl's duty, according to fiction, is to combine sturdy efficiency with exquisite femininity.

As a rule, she does not drink, swear, smoke, or dress provocatively. A few exceptions (like Katya in E. Vorobyov's *The Heights,* 1951) are promptly cured of such extravagances by a good man's love. She wears her hair in a long braid and fidgets with it to convey her emotions to the reader—when listening to a declaration of love, for instance, or reporting to a Party secretary on her brigade's achievements. That her hands are rough and calloused is taken for granted, though at least one girl (Klava in L. Solovyov's *High Pressure,* 1938) is reported to have bought hand lotion. And dressed in her worst clothes at work, she understandably looks grubby and unattractive, though even to this there are exceptions. Tanya, in N. Ognyov's "The Contemporaries" (1937), wears a silk dress to work—and ruins it putting out a fire in her workshop at the risk of her life; and Nadya, a house painter, "is a joy to behold when, powdered with chalk and bluing, her overalls gay with multicolored splashes of paint, she wields her magic tools."[13]

But on festive occasions, particularly on International Woman's Day, heroines wear perfume and lovely pastel dresses and radiate feminine charm, delicate or intoxicating, depending on their physiques. These, in turn, depend on whether the author chooses a characterization which can be harmonized with harsh working conditions or one that can be contrasted with them. In the first case, the heroine is either "a thick-set, robust girl, capable of knocking down with a blow of her fist the strongest truck driver in her garage,"[14] like Nyura in Rybakov's *The Truck Drivers,* or a dark, statuesque beauty, tall and proud as Juno, like Katerina in Ketlinskaya's *No Sense in Living Otherwise.* In the second eventuality, she is small and thin, and looks deceptively fragile.

She proves, however, to be very durable, and whether plucky and saucy as is snub-nosed Tosya (in B. Bedny's *The Girls*) or shy and composed as is graceful Yula (in Katerli's *The Bronze Spinning Wheel*), a first-rate worker. They are all popular; in fact, unlike their kolkhoz sisters, working girls never lack beaux, perhaps because there are more young men to be met in the factory than on a collective farm. At any rate, the atmosphere of industrial plants seems favorable to young love, which is combined with heroic work in a kind of osmosis.

"Heroism in the Soviet land," says a critic, "is a mass phenomenon and yet a common, everyday occurrence. Such is the groundwork of the Soviet social system." And, explains a representative hero, a rank-and-file, unsophisticated worker: " 'Our work is everything. In it is the Truth and the Glory and all our joys. Work is a cure for all misfortunes.' "[15] Combined with love, it also apparently provides the formula for happiness.

In an industrial novel boy meets girl at work by a red-hot furnace or in a coal pit; he may ask her for a date in a slaughter house, for instance, while bloody animal skulls are gliding on a conveyor belt under her deft hands;[16] he usually proposes while walking her home after a movie or a lecture. (Needless to say, workers in Soviet fiction do not own cars.) With the help of a kindly partorg or director, the young couple is allotted a room in a communal apartment and henceforth will build their personal life and Socialism (Communism, since the death of Stalin) together.

These two goals are inseparable, and work may determine the course of a romance, as is illustrated by the case of two delegates meeting at a dance at an All-Union Komsomol convention. The girl tells the youth that she is glad to meet him because they are, in a way, acquainted: she works at the factory that makes lamps for the mine where he is employed. Isn't he glad, too? " 'No reason for joy,' " is his answer; " ' they are poor lamps. Improve the quality of your production and then I'll be happy to know you better.' "[17]

Conversely, love may serve as the incentive for better working performance. Here, for example, is a love scene in a moonlit garden:

> The youth put his hand on the girl's shoulder and said hesitatingly: "Annushka, do you know?"
> The girl's answer came, barely audible: "You don't have to say it, I know. . . ."

> With happy laughter, embracing, they went towards the gate, and the youth, suddenly stopping, exclaimed: "Oh, Annushka, you can't imagine how ardently I am going to work from now on!"[18]

For a reader who likes the point to be stated clearly, so as to preclude misunderstanding, there are passages like the following reverie of a young man in love.

> When he thought of the Fatherland he also thought of Dasha—for wasn't it her Fatherland too? Lost in dreams about the future of the coal mine, the town, the State, he again felt he was dreaming of his own future, of Dasha's, and even—here he could not help blushing—of their children's future. Everything became tied together into one firm knot: Dasha, and love, and the mine, and the State.[19]

However high the moral and civic standards of a young hero may be, those of the young heroine are higher. A plot telling the story of a wayward youth reformed by love for a good girl is routine in Soviet fiction, provided both are proletarians. The situation, as will be discussed later, is reversed when the girl is a pampered scion of the "priviligentsia," the new Soviet elite. Another matter, when she is

> a proletarian's daughter who grew up in Soviet era, has been since her childhood accustomed to respect and value labor, and to consider it the basis, the natural and necessary requisite of life. . . . [She is] not an artist's dream, but the heroine of our time, one of the millions of girls just like her who are inhabiting the happy Soviet land.[20]

Naturally, such girls would not fall in love with a villain, but their lovers may be just imperfect enough to present a challenge to the reforming power of love and to revitalize the anemic plot. Their most common failing is conceit: these handsome men have been spoiled by success with women. When, however, Ilya (in Bedny's *The Girls*) recognizes the sterling goodness of that "green, unkissed innocent" Tosya, he is ashamed of his former love affairs and will make Tosya a devoted husband. Similarly, when Sergey (in N. Nikolaeva's *The Battle on the Way*, 1957) realizes that Dasha considers them engaged because she had let him hold her hand in a movie theater, he is at first astounded by her naïveté, then touched, and finally, actually proposes. Perhaps the best testimony to the purity of morals in industrial novels is provided by the story in *The Truck Drivers* of a midsummer night spent in the meadows by Nyura and Pavel, crack truck drivers engaged in socialist competition. He helps her with some emergency repairs; she tells him what she understands by true love; and after discussing methods of saving time and gas for their State-run garage, they prepare two beds with seats from their trucks' cabins, and fall peacefully asleep. "At the edge of the misty morning sky appeared the sun. Its first radiant ray slid over the earth and came to rest on the haystack by which the youth and the girl were sleeping. A strand of her bright hair, slipping off the black leather cushion had fallen on his curly head."[21] Nyura, incidentally, is the very same girl who could have knocked down any truck driver with a blow of her fist.

Finally, a young proletarian heroine can stand what any woman would recognize as love's acid test: she is ready to take second place in the life of her beloved, yielding the first to his work. What is more, she holds that work so sacred that she will not hesitate to hurt him for its sake. Natasha (in N. Evdokimov's *The High Position*, 1950) has a date with Sergey after work at the gate of their factory. During the day, as a member of the Komsomol controlling committee, she notices some faulty work by Sergey, makes out her damaging and financially calamitous report—and meets him at the appointed hour and place. " 'I thought you would understand!' " she says, hurt and surprised by his reproaches. Then he does understand and bows before her higher ethical standards, and the experience makes their romance even more wonderful.

Whatever changes have been brought to industrial novels by the thaw have affected the intelligentsia without disturbing the life rhythm of proletarian characters. Consequently, proletarian heroines are happier than women of the intelligentsia. The former continue to be virtuous and deserving, and earn by hard work the right to their modest personal happiness. They are secure in the sense of righteousness, in the absence of any doubts that cannot be resolved by consulting the partorg. Their factory is pulsing with efficient work, their Komsomol, with cultural activities; the skies over the Soviet Union are blue; and the Party is keeping watch in Moscow.

7

The Komsomol

🌿

THE CRACK GROUP

The role of the Komsomol in Soviet fiction can be summed up in a quotation from Lenin's speech at the Third Congress of that institution in October, 1920: "The Young Communist League should be a crack group which, in every job that has to be done, gives a hand, displays initiative, makes a start."[1]

At that time the membership in the Komsomol, in its third year of existence, was 400,000, as compared to the original 22,000 in 1918. Within a decade, when Stalin reinforced his first Five-Year Plan by putting Lenin's slogan into practice, the membership had grown to 2 million, and volunteers answered the call for building socialism 350,000 strong. It was they who built the town (named after them) in the impassable tundra on the Amur River, and in 1935, the Moscow Metro. The Don Basin miner Stakhanov was a Komsomolets, as were the youthful heroes of the underground in World War II, whose story was told in Fadeev's novel *The Young Guard* (1945), and so were the boys and girls who helped raise the country from ruins in the postwar period and went to cultivate the Siberian virgin lands in the 1950's. By 1958 the membership was 18 million. Wherever reckless courage, strenuous effort, and passionate enthusiasm were needed, the Komsomol has been traditionally first.[2]

Fiction has taken full advantage of the dramatic possibilities offered by this enthusiasm, and no prose work since the early 1930's has been without its dedicated *Komsomoltsy*, the doers, the dreamers, the romantic faithful of Communism. They have been shown in dangerous encounters with desperate kulaks while requisitioning food or promoting collectivization in villages. They have been portrayed felling Siberian forests, damming rivers, raising cities and gigantic industrial centers in the frozen taiga and in blistering deserts. They have worked eighteen hours a day in appalling conditions, living in tents, without adequate food and medical care, plagued with scurvy, mosquitoes, or frostbite. The greater the challenge, the more readily they have risen to it and, accordingly, the greater their merit. It was in this spirit, for example, that Erenburg wrote his *Second Day of Creation* (1933) and Ketlinskaya her *Courage* (1938). In the latter novel, however, the dire working conditions were treated as regrettable, and following the then current political fashion, blamed on saboteurs.

Besides physical hardships, the Komsomolets had to be ready for personal sacrifices: to leave a good job and that prized possession, a room in a communal apartment; to wreck a romance, though love, if true, was guaranteed to survive the ordeal of separation or of hard camp life; to lose health (cases of sickness and accidents are numerous though, to be sure, they usually end in recovery); finally, even to die in the line of duty (funeral orations have been always popular in Soviet fiction). In short, it is an accepted notion that "a Komsomolets should emulate the best [men]: those who develop science, technical skills, music, [great] thoughts; those of lofty spirit who struggle with Nature and defeat Death."[3]

In spite of the exacting demands of his status, a Komsomolets under Socialist Realism is portrayed as a happy person. His youth makes all burdens lighter, his morale is kept high by the sense of duty well done, and his peace of mind is ensured by freedom from doubts and decisions, because the responsibility for these has been taken over by the Party. There was, however, in the late 1920's a period when the Komsomolets, still capable of ideological doubts, was trying on his own to evolve a code of ethics and a way of life befitting a Marxist. And Soviet fiction dedicated more attention to the portrayal of such an effort than it has ever done before or since.

THE CRADLE OF THE
SOVIET INTELLIGENTSIA

In the postrevolutionary period the position occupied by the Komsomol in the city was materially different from that held in the village. Membership in the village Komsomol was small, its relationship with the backward peasant community was based on dislike and distrust, and the Party, locally, could offer but little support. No wonder that in the 1920's the ablest—though not necessarily the most dedicated—youths escaped to the city. There, in case of ideological incompatibility with his parents, a young man could emancipate himself from their authority by becoming self-supporting, and the Party would provide encouragement, and occasionally, some help.

Life was hard under NEP conditions, when even the basic necessities—food, clothing, housing—were scarce and unemployment rampant. Young proletarians worked in mines and factories, the bright and ambitious among them also attending special factory schools (*rabfaki*) to prepare for academic studies. Those fortunate enough to be admitted to the University valiantly fought their way to diplomas, overworked, starving, sleeping in parks, going coatless in winter.[4] Resentful but contemptuous, they tried to ignore the luxuries which were meanwhile enjoyed by the NEPmen and the budding Soviet privilegentsia. The future, they felt sure, belonged to them.

However they imagined that future, all the roads to it led through the Komsomol. It was the headquarters for militant idealists, the hunting ground for careerists, the melting pot for all. Everyone belonged. Factory Komsomols teemed with authentic proletarians doggedly attending their evening schools and with idealists and opportunists with upper- and middle-class backgrounds who tried to merge with the working masses and become proletarians by choice. University Komsomols were full of progressive intelligentsia endeavoring, in the spirit of comradeship, to help educate the masses. Patronage of a specific factory by a college was much in vogue. Young workers who, a 60 percent majority in the student body, were poorly prepared and awkward but strove to become intellectuals at least formally were the main targets.

The heterogeneous membership included former juvenile tramps (*besprizornye*) and the village elite sent by their Komsomols (*vydvižency*). There also were some scions of the former ruling classes (including small tradesmen) who had no right to education, and in order to get in, forged certificates of proletarian descent or obtained, by means foul or fair, the support of an influential Party bureaucrat.[5] And, of course, there were the rank-and-file workers and students.

All these young people had one thing in common: while taking material privations in their stride, they found emotional adjustment to the new order of life difficult. In this respect, too, their problems differed from those of the village. City youth did not have to fight for civil marriages, or divorces, or the removal of icons. These things soon came to be tolerated (however reluctantly) even by the most conservative parents, who, as was indicated, in any case could not exert significant pressure. But the problem was that youth, playing at high stakes the fascinating game of a "New Soviet Life," was confused about its rules—and kept losing.

It was a matter of principles and their practicability. Did social work or baby come first? Should a true Marxist wear a tie, keep his room clean, dance? Was home life a bourgeois prejudice; most particularly, was love? Like Abramchik in V. Kataev's play, *Squaring the Circle* (1928), the well-meaning Komsomolets paused at every action, from stealing a roommate's sausage to divorce, to ask: "Is it ethical or unethical?"

They were eager to choose what was right but had little to guide them. The works of the pundits of Marxism were slow and difficult reading and seldom explicit on matters of ethics; and the contemporary popularizers of the doctrine offered maxims such as "Sex life is an inalienable part of social, i.e., class activity. . . . The collective should attract [a class-conscious proletarian] more joyfully, more strongly than a love partner"; and "One should try to discover through the domain of sexual relationship and the so-called psychological domain of love, the source of the new, inevitable, victorious dawn of proletarian culture."[6]

This is not to say that the Party and its followers advocated sexual licentiousness. On the contrary, with the exception of Kollontay (who was, however, sharply criticized[7]), the consensus of opinion, including Lenin's, was that Communism favors self-discipline, sports, intensive studies and work, and above all, channeling physical and spiritual energy into the service of the revolutionary cause. The call was for a lasting monogamous marriage contracted not too young and for children who would be brought up in Communist ideology. But with religious morality and prerevolutionary ethics denounced as the heritage of reactionary society, with parental authority rejected and teachers' advice discredited as coming from former members of an enemy class, a whole generation of Russian youth was adrift in the dark waters of NEP society. Hooliganism, sexual licentiousness, abortions, cases of nervous breakdowns, and suicides were rampant;[8] and the mirror of contemporary fiction reflects a picture of an unhealthy, graceless, and unrewarding existence.

THE PROBLEM NOVELS

Literary critics of the late twenties admitted that basically contemporary fiction was holding a mirror to reality but protested that the picture, nevertheless, was a distorted one. They accused writers of willfully omitting the bright facets of Soviet life while seeking out occasional dark spots for use in sensational plots and of concentrating on sexual problems in Komsomol life to the exclusion of more important and valuable aspects.[9]

The authors, most of them young men, often writing from first-hand experience, stood their ground. Their characters, they contended, were composite beings who without "actually existing in a chemically pure form"[10] combined the typical features of many real persons. Some of the plots were based on police reports, such as the lurid stories of rape and murder in M. Mirov's "Masha" (1929) and D. Eryomin's "Cloaked with Darkness" (1932). Some closely followed court trials; for example, D. Sverchkov's "Case No. 3576" (1927) is about a working girl turned child murderess and an attempted suicide. Stories by local and special correspondents from provincial industrial towns, articles by journalists visiting university dormitories—all gave credence to the gloomy setting of the Komsomol novels.

Undoubtedly, some authors purposely deepened the gloom in search of sensational effects. Mysteries and crime novels proliferated, not as a cunning detective's exploits, but as tales of violence, rape, and murder. Entire novels—B. Gorbatov's *The Cell* (1928), N. Nikitin's *The Crime of Kirik Rudenko* (1927), L. Gumilevsky's *The Dog's Lane* (1927), to cite a few—were peopled with juvenile gangsters working in mines and factories, attending colleges, active in Party bureaucracy. They used foul language, got drunk on samogon vodka, engaged in brawls often ending in bloodshed, assaulted or seduced girls. If these antiheroes were of bourgeois descent, their vices were stamped with decadence: they substituted wine for vodka and opiate cigarettes for cheap tobacco, and made cynical speeches on free love, speeches larded, moreover, with quotes from Communist authorities. They even staged orgies—as in S. Malashkin's notorious novel *The Moon from the Right* or V. Lidin's *The Renegade* (1927)—which the participants called "Athenian nights" and "in the attic" respectively.

Naturally, there were also nice young people in the Komsomol fiction of the period. In fact, five years after *The Cell* was published, Gorbatov affirmed in a retrospective novel, *My Generation* (1933), that he had never seen a Komsomolets drunk.[11] Be that as it may, hard-working, clean-living youths and girls were to be found even in the most lugubrious novels, and in those less despondent they were numerous. Though their studies or factory work were not yet shown in minute detail as they would be after World War II, their performance was understood to be excellent and therefore beneficial to their morale and morals. It goes without saying that these wholesome Soviet youth are those who survived as typical characters the literary debacle of the subsequent period and have been representing the Komsomol ever since. In this capacity, their salient feature is a talent for finding ideologically correct solutions to ethical problems. But in the 1920's they were less perfect, more human, and like their living prototypes, groping anxiously for a workable code of new Soviet morality.

Yet young readers seemed to identify themselves with these fictional characters, and moreover, assumed that since writers perceived their ethical problems, they also knew the solutions. Authors were besieged by letters, questions from the participants in public literary discussions, and queries from the "readers' tribunes" published in magazines. The discussion of V. Veresaev's "Isanka" (1928) drew an audience which overflowed the theater where it was held. Should the student heroine have risked pregnancy and abortion in premarital relations with her fiancé? Or should they marry and so, under existing conditions, jeopardize their diplomas? Should they continue the halfway status which, the doctor had warned Isanka, is adversely affecting her health? Or should they sacrifice their love and part?

As has been mentioned, fiction made no special effort to portray milieu, except insofar as it helped character drawing. There are de-

scriptions—meant to stress the occupants' contempt for bourgeois notions of comfort—of dingy rooms with filthy, unmade beds and with
naked bulbs swinging from the ceiling. And conversely, bourgeois
inclinations in a character are shown by his possession of a neatly
stacked pyramid of bed pillows or of window curtains, which had
practically been raised to the status of a symbol. But the home, as well
as factory halls and class rooms, is only a stage on which personal
dramas are acted.

In the same way, religion or parent-child relationships mean nothing
in themselves, but serve to classify a character as progressive. Young
people abandon their religion just as easily as they march away from
home into a new life, without a backward glance at their parents. These
parents, it must be said, usually deserve such filial indifference: the
callousness with which, for instance, Soviet fictional mothers treat their
teenage girls who "had got into trouble," makes the Komsomol community seem a haven indeed. Fathers are seldom introduced, except as
confused and pathetic priests.

The spotlight in Komsomol novels is therefore on the characters and
their efforts to coordinate their interpretation of Marxist ethics with
the practical exigencies of life. Not surprisingly, the need for establishing a firm basis for newly emancipated love, marriage, and family life
was acutely felt primarily by young women. It was presumably that
need which in the late 1920's launched the thousand novels on sex
problems.

FACTORY GIRLS

The harbinger of the furore raised in postrevolutionary literature by
the question of a new moral code was Zhenya, the heroine of "The
Love of Three Generations" (1923) by A. Kollontay. Daughter and
granddaughter of strong-willed women who were the avant-garde of
emancipation in their time, Zhenya is a busy Komsomol worker. Aged
eighteen, she lives with two men, one of whom is her young stepfather;
has an abortion without even being sure by which of them she was
pregnant; and is surprised and pained by her mother's grief. Had she
known that her mother would take it so hard, she would had kept her
liaison with the stepfather a secret. As for herself, she feels neither
jealousy nor guilt, because she does not think that either morality or

love is in any way connected with sex. She loves Lenin, she explains, and she loves her mother; but the two men were merely partners in a physical contact as meaningless as drinking a glass of water to quench one's thirst.

No less an authority than Lenin himself denounced the "glass of water" theory. It was, he said, against the interests of the proletarian youth, wasteful of their time as well as disgusting and foolish: "Who would want to drink from a glass greasy with many lips?"[12] Nevertheless, the theory was raised as a banner by self-appointed legislators of Marxist ethics, and it found enough followers to become a social trend, at least among the Komsomol youth as reflected in contemporary fiction.

The theory called for a complete divorce between the physical and emotional aspects of love. Physical love was to be kept casual ("it makes no difference whether it's Masha or Dasha who satisfies your sexual needs"[13]) and was declared infinitely less important than Party work. Romantic love, or rather any feeling beyond physical desire, was declared petty bourgeois, a thing to be ashamed of and capable of branding the culprit as unfit for the Komsomol community. Here is a budding romance A.D. 1928:

> VICTOR (*agitated*): Mayka, do you know that, no matter how ridiculous it may sound, I seem to—that is, I—I love you! (*Recollecting himself.*) That is, I feel for you a strong sexual urge.
> MAYA (*decisively*): Listen, Comrade Victor, the love question has been taken off my agenda for a long time, and as I see it, in earnest. On my agenda is work. We women social workers have no time for all this love stuff. . . . And, at any rate, you are not at all what a hero of our time should be. What you need is to do some routine factory work, inhale a whiff of factory smoke![14]

The degree to which young people accepted these principles was not uniform, and in the fiction of the 1920's, three groups can be differentiated along the lines of education and social background. The earliest and smallest group, of whom Zhenya is the oustanding example, are mostly Party activists who believe that ethics concerns work and politics but does not include sex. Their behavior in matters of sex can therefore be considered amoral. By the same token, the members of the second group, the sophisticates, are immoral, because they raise libertine pursuits to the status of revolutionary ethics by identifying them with the freedom of the individual; these are best represented by the

characters in Malashkin's *Moon from the Right*. The third, and by far
the most numerous, group is composed of the unsophisticated: the
frankly promiscuous, the gullible, and—not to be overlooked—the
sensible.

The fiction of the period shows the Komsomol within two milieux:
factory and university. In the case of girls, the division is also that of
social background, because of the 10 to 20 percent of the student body
who were coeds, practically none were of proletarian descent.[15]

The characters of proletarian girls, then, are to be found in factory
Komsomols; but it does not follow that the intelligentsia and the
bourgeoisie are similarly consigned to the university milieu. Fraterniza-
tion and factory work are sought by daughters of middle-class families,
who are eager to be transformed into proletarians by inhaling that
magic "whiff of smoke." Whether sincere zealots or hypocrites they
are aliens among the factory workers. The great divide is primarily
education, but class differences are also strongly felt, because while
members of the intelligentsia are doing their best to act the part, their
very zeal causes resentment. A class-conscious working girl, by virtue
of her proletarian descent, is superior to any former fine lady and does
not forget it.

This popular idea was clearly spelled in M. Kolosov's short story
"Individual Education" (1929). Komsomol activist Sonya, a student,
sporting the invariable leather jacket and red headkerchief of her kind,
patronizes "those cute factory girls" and especially the stolid, pockmarked Manka. But on the International Woman Day's celebration,
Manka, spurning the speech she was coached to deliver, makes her
own—clumsy, but heartfelt and wise:

> "Women! . . . we've got many sufferings! Many sorrows and wrongs!
> Girls are being jilted, just like in a play! Lockers in public bathhouses
> are not safe—such things don't happen even in Africa! Such a lot of
> money is being spent on students—and yet they are fools! . . . Women,
> avant-gardes of the world! We've got freedom but so far not all women
> have awakened. . . . Still, I assure you: the day will come when the sun
> will shine and we'll all die for this here banner!"[16]

Manka has tears in her eyes and so does the audience, including the
chastened Sonya.

The factory milieu, then, serves as background to its natives and to
outsiders, and typical characters are discernible within each group.

The Natives

With respect to Marxist ethics, all factory "natives" belong to the category of unsophisticates. They do not waste time theorizing; they trust the Party and work hard under its direction, uncomplainingly, however difficult the conditions. But they differ among themselves in the ways of building their personal lives, and even more so, in the reasons which prompt their behavior. There are, therefore, what could be termed the iron proletarians, the sterling kind who denounce decadentism posing as Communism, nice girls whose naïve trust is betrayed, and so-called "Komsomol prostitutes."[17]

The iron proletarians are humorless and uncompromising. Uneducated, they nevertheless choose the right paths with the help of their inborn class-consciousness. Duty to the Party comes first with them, and in discharging it they are not merely ruthless but devoid of any sensitivity. When Ryzhova (in V. Gerasimova's "The Sisters," 1929) ferrets out that Tonya is a priest's daughter, she does not rest until she has her victim expelled from the Komsomol, which, under the existing conditions, entails the loss of the job in the factory. It is not a matter of personal prejudice: Tonya is an excellent worker and has brutally disowned her parents in token of her devotion to the revolutionary cause. But Ryzhova, on her "heavy, strong legs encased in purple stockings," is pursuing the class enemy unrelentingly, big game and small, along every hunting trail.

Iron proletarians have poise. Sima (in G. Nikiforov's *The Woman,* 1929) "makes fast decisions on everything, everywhere; sees all things as plain and simple; is free from complexity of feelings . . . free from the pollution of bourgeois [intellectualism]." But neither does she reduce sex to a mere physical function, as do alien impostors such as Zhenya. Hers is to be a stern life of work until she meets a man whose love she would accept:

> "Do you think I am the sissy kind who's going to hang around his neck and yell 'Kiss me, honey'?"
> "Well, how will it happen, then?"
> "No how. I'll simply say: 'If you want us to live together, let's do that, as real comrades, because that's what we are—comrades and citizens, equal in everything.' There must be no monkey business with us honest workers."[18]

Sima's ideas about marriage based on comradeship have been advocated by proletarian fiction from its beginnings, but its form mellowed considerably, and equal marital rights, as will be shown in discussing those of career women, have since become subject to reservations.

The pattern of an iron Komsomolka like Sima was not continued beyond the 1920's, but that of a sterling proletarian girl has been perpetuated ever since. In fact, it is to her that the standard types subsequently developed in the industrial novels—the Stakhanovite maiden and the young working wife—can be traced. The salient characteristics of the sterling proletarian girl are buoyant spirits and a high degree of dedication to the Cause. She is engulfed by Komsomol work: office chores, membership meetings, organization of youth clubs, anti-religious and cultural propaganda, volunteer group projects (called "workday Sundays" [*voskresniki*]), such as street cleaning. In the words of an antihero, these young enthusiasts "work till their noses scrape the ground," and, it might be added, till they barely have the strength to collapse into bed, till they develop chronic headaches, anemia, and tuberculosis. The effect of these conditions on their personal life is suggested in the following excerpt from the notorious novel *The Leap* (1928) by I. Brazhnin. The scene is introduced as, late in the evening dog-tired Stepka, Zhenka's husband of two years, returns to their cold, untidy room.

> He set the teakettle on the kerosine stove, and settling by the table, spread among the scraps of stale sausage the letter he had received from Zhenka this morning and had had no time to open until now. It was short.
> "Stepka! [wrote Zhenka, away on a Komsomol business trip] Be a dear and answer immediately: do you know the color of my eyes? If I don't get an answer I'll divorce you, you dog! Zhenka."
> Stepka frowned, turned the letter around, deliberated a moment. . . . Finally he gave up, and taking a stump of a pencil, wrote across the bottom corner of the letter, as he did on Komsomol applications, "Can't tell" and signed his initials. With a sigh, he searched for an envelope and finally found one in a wicker suitcase under the bed. He sealed it, and munching a piece of roll, wrote the address.[19]

The sterling Komsomol girls in fiction of the 1920's are free from the wooden cheerfulness which their successors acquired after World War II. They are human: after all, Zhenka did care whether her husband remembered how she looked. And Marusya (in M. Platoshkin's *On the Way*, 1929), worrying about the deteriorating health of her overworked husband, limits her Komsomol activities and cooks and washes evenings instead of in the middle of the night after returning from meetings. She does not, however, curtail factory work as—friends darkly predict—will Lyolka, in the same novel. Lyolka, who candidly states that what she wants for herself and her husband is a home, is not, of course, cast as a sterling character. She serves rather to prove that marriage is a dangerously bourgeois institution. But since the authentic proletarians are sensible, they belong to a different school of thought, and like Zhenka, denounce the detractors of family life at meetings, insisting that it need not impair a woman's social efficiency.

Zhenka (she and Stepka have a baby whom, good Marxists, they name Plekhan*) tries to live what she teaches. Glowing with young motherhood, she works with the Zhenotdel, acts as leader of pioneer groups, and concentrates on nurseries—and not just for Plekhan's sake because, she says, " 'they all are Soviet kids and belong to all of us alike.' " Her namesake and double, Zhenka in V. Ketlinskaya's *Natka Michurina* (1929), even suggests that the family is a Soviet institution. " 'Who is to bring up the new kind of people,' " she queries, " 'if not Communists and Komsomol members? Are they to keep on making abortions and leave the raising of children to the bourgeoisie and the NEPmen?' "[20]

It should be recalled that the characters under discussion are not conceived as those of young matrons; they are girls who fall in love and get married in the course of the plot. They are there to bring up the persistent question of Communist morality and its practicability under existing conditions. Lenin criticized working women for wasting the time they should be dedicating to the Cause on futile discussions of sex and marriage questions. In fiction, secretaries of Komsomol cells upbraided girl members for reducing every discussion on the new Soviet way of life to sexual problems.[21] But in life and fiction alike, women demanded to be told what was right and what wrong, and also how a girl should live and work without having to perform miracles of efficiency in the factory and at home. And fiction writers had no objections to this widespread interest in morals and sex. As always, these questions provided rich material for plots, and authors took full advantage of them.

Necessarily, ideological issues and characters serving to illustrate

* In honor of Georgy Plekhanov (1857–1918), the dean of Russian Marxism.

them were less colorful. For example, Marusya in *Natka Michurina* is a valuable propagandist "in whose head all information seems to have been filed in an orderly fashion."[22] But, except for ideologically correct opinions, she does not contribute to the plot. Amidst the welter of marriages and seductions, Marusya's morals stay very high; she thinks nothing of spending half the night with a comrade in editing the factory bulletin and then sharing his bed, in all chastity, for the other half. In many respects, Marusya's character pattern is reflected in that of the working girl in postwar industrial novels, except that the latter, like Nyura in Rybakov's *Truck Drivers*, knows little beyond the A B C's of Marxism, and so specializes in physical work rather than in propaganda. But modesty, dedication, and efficiency are innate qualities of both types.

It will be recalled that in Komsomol novels all the factory natives belong to the category of the unsophisticated. The most artless among them are the protagonists of best sellers. For example, Panya in Platoshkin's *On the Way*, Ketlinskaya's *Natka Michurina*, and Yulka in Gorbatov's *My Generation* are starry-eyed idealists who end as embittered, worldly-wise women. Even the so-called Komsomol prostitutes (discussed later) insist that their promiscuity is actually the proper way of life for the new woman freed from the fetters of bourgeois morality. But the ingenues join the Komsomol as one would join an order of lofty ideological standards. Full of trust and respect for Party comrades, they fall in love in an old-fashioned way—and in an old-fashioned way get ruined.

It is all very well for the sterling proletarian girls to build their lives on the foundations of Communist morality: they have been lucky in finding the right mates. Both Zhenkas, for example, as well as their respective husbands, take it for granted that they are equals; and so they are, in whatever modest degree of worldliness and education they may possess. Since, moreover, neither of them is flirtatious by disposition, their relationship from the start is based on camaraderie and mutual appreciation, and eventually culminates in a happy marriage. The ingenue, on the other hand, invariably falls victim to violence, or seduction, or both, before she meets the hero.

She does, of course, meet deserving comrades in the Komsomol, but unfortunately they do not act to help her until tragedy strikes. So she has to deal at best with weaklings or poor Communists and at the worst, with hooligans. Weaklings are usually well-meaning and genuinely in love with the ingenue, but they offer no protection. For example, Nyurochka's boyfriend (in Semyonov's *Natalya Tarpova*) tries to prove his love by encouraging her to "live like a free woman" at a Komsomol party. Drunk, Nyurochka becomes pregnant by an unidentified comrade, and ends by dying of an abortion in the arms of her wildly despairing fiancé.

As for bad Communists, the antiheroes of Gorbatov's *The Cell*, Platoshkin's *On the Way*, Ketlinskaya's *Natka Michurina*, Gladkov's *The Tipsy Sun* (1927)—to mention a few—occupy positions of responsibility in the Komsomol hierarchy. Some actually owe their moral depravity to this very fact, because, ignorant and unprincipled, they misunderstand their duties and misuse their authority. These valued activists seduce the ingenue by assuring her that theirs would be a real Communist union and by ridiculing her bourgeois scruples, as in Natka's case. Or, as in the case of Panya, herself an activist, they suggest a "truly free" common-law marriage and later flaunt their infidelities as a matter of course. Both liaisons end by the men's demanding abortions, because a child would interfere with its parents' work. Natka complies, loses her lover notwithstanding, gets into bad company, and is saved from ruin only in the nick of time by the tardy hero. Panya refuses and loses her lover, her reputation, and finally her child. Alone and embittered, she finds solace in work. These liaisons are never graced by the mutual love or real equality that the sterling proletarian couples enjoy.

Even the work of these hapless ingenues goes unappreciated:

> All the executive positions in the Party centers are held by men, but in the local cells all the secretarial work is done by those invariably quiet, unassuming, gentle Komsomol girls. Nobody notices them. They are never elected [to serve on any committees], nobody remembers their last names . . . the awesome, shaggy chairman keeps yelling at them, but without them he is helpless.[23]

Finally, the hoodlums who abound in the factory Komsomol of the period have a special liking for ingenues. Whether the girl wants to engage in an adventure is not her decision. If rebuffed, hoodlums seek revenge using slander or brute force. A group of vacationing Komsomol youths attack Marusya (in Gladkov's *The Tipsy Sun*) while she is walking alone in broad daylight. Komsomol hooligans, led by her seducer, gang up on Katya (in Nikitin's *The Crime of Kirik Rudenko*) when she refuses to abort her child. It is in an escape from Komsomol drunks that Yulka (in Gorbatov's *My Generation*) seeks protection with a noble Party official—only to be slandered by them and so expelled from the cell "for systematic debauchery."

No wonder that in the decades following the twenties and early thirties the bestsellers of the period under discussion were omitted from the collected works of authors who had later adjusted to the demands of Socialist Realism, and that the names of those authors who did not were not mentioned in bibliographical literary encyclopedias. Actually, these notorious bestsellers became tersely summed up—and dismissed—as "works in which the problems of family, love, morality were presented in a way both distorted and superficial."[24]

The most disgraceful type of young woman, deplored by every Party spokesman in fiction, and presumably, by thoughtful readers, is the Komsomol girl who considers emancipation synonymous with promiscuity. In the university Komsomols of the period (to be discussed separately in Part IV) sexual licentiousness is ideologically propounded: in the words of a literary critic "theirs is not just an ordinary debauchery but one with philosophical trimmings."[25] In the factory milieu, however, loose behavior is of an unsophisticated kind. " 'If I like a man, I give myself to him at once, without all that claptrap about love,' " announces Katya cheerfully; and Nina curtly dismisses a naïve gallant: " 'Why did I give myself to you at the party yesterday? Because I happened to want to. Why make such a heck of a ruckus about it? It's such a simple matter.' "[26]

These girls, it should be stressed, are valuable Komsomol activists. If they drink, smoke, and swear, it is as a matter of principle. Red kerchiefs worn over shingled hair, men's red shirts, and leather coats are their badges of progress. And while they are brazen toward men, they are never coquettish—for the same reason. One boy complains: " 'I told Vera once, "You are so attractive, so feminine," and she got mad and yelled at me: "You're scum, scum! I don't wish to be feminine and I won't!" As if a Komsomol girl had no right to be attractive!' "[27]

To apply the term "Komsomol prostitutes" to them therefore, seems unfair, particularly since their behavior is not prompted by any mercenary considerations. Except for a random factory girl getting involved with NEPmen, prostitutes do not roam Soviet fiction even in the daring 1920's, certainly not as Komsomol members, who are merely trying to assert what they understand to be their equality with men. It was also understood—indeed demanded—that girls exercise their equal rights within the confines of the Komsomol. Sanya (in Bogdanov's *The First Girl*) was reprimanded by her cell for having affairs with outsiders: "We are the chosen best of our social class, so let her be satisfied with us." It would almost seem that Sanya's death at the hands of her lover is the punishment for her disregarding her comrades' warning, but her diary reveals a different reason. "Free love!" she writes, "How mistakenly did I interpret the idea, how pettily did others, when we reduced its meaning to freedom of lust!"[28]

Needless to say, these pioneers of women's rights did not survive in Soviet fiction beyond the 1920's. Sanya's case, even at the time, evoked especially bitter remonstrations from the critics. They pointed out that the story told by her peasant lover was biased, her character too flatteringly drawn and unrealistic.[29] Indeed, for a charming peasant girl to be corrupted by the environment of the city Komsomol was doubly insulting to the Komsomol's reputation, because though it did have its shortcomings, everyone knew that the "outside element" (*čužoj element*) should be favorably influenced, indeed reformed, by that salubrious "whiff of the factory smoke." Of course, the natives knew very well that even so the newcomers would remain just that: outsiders.

The Outsiders

Not all outsiders are alike. There are, for instance, important differences in their backgrounds, as they may come from the intelligentsia, or from the lower middle class, or even from priests' families. It must be acknowledged that they are accepted or rejected on their personal merits, at least in fiction. What matters most is not so much their performance at work, because they are always eager to do their best and their best is excellent, as the degree of sincerity in breaking with the past—not their own, for they are teenagers, but that of their parents.

The novel which provides the most insight into the outsider's psychology is *The Sisters* by V. Veresaev (1933). The heroines, Lyolka and Ninka, prefer factory work to studies, as a surer way of merging with the masses. Both girls are dedicated activists, but Ninka caused some embarrassment to the literary critics. As head of a Komsomol dekulakization brigade, she advises humane methods of confiscating kulaks' property (notably, she is against taking overshoes off a child) *before* the appearance of Stalin's famous article "Dizzy with Success." Lyolka, unlike her sister, is not guided in political matters by instinct (an un-Marxian conception), but by Party discipline. She tracks and piti-lessly denounces loafers and saboteurs; rejects a suitor because, like Mayka's, he is not what "a hero of our times," an ideal proletarian, should be; and ruins her health by factory work which involves inhala-tion of poisonous chemicals. She envies a fellow worker's "perfectly democratic, proletarian face, very attractive though angular and snub-nosed,"[30] but in personal life follows the decadent glass of water pattern, like Kollontay's Zhenya, whom she also resembles in other respects. Both sisters treat with contemptuous tolerance their now old-fashioned mother, who before the Revolution belonged to the most progressive intelligentsia circles.

Yet, they never quite arrive. Neither does Favsta, in Nikiforov's *The Woman*, who manifests her repudiation of the intelligentsia by knock-ing her father over the head with an iron bar. She works in railroad construction, driving nails with bleeding hands, but even so, wins but grudging recognition from the iron proletarian Sima, whose friendship she covets. Perhaps the outside elements are too eager to resemble proletarians, and insult the proletarians by exaggeration bordering on caricature. Here is what a Komsomolets thinks of such a female in-truder: " 'A leather jacket. A cigarette. A voice, deliberately loud, and rude speech: "the gang," she says, and "the grub"! She is impersonating us workers, while what is needed is rather for us to drop all these "gang" and "scum" expressions.' "[31]

So it is primarily a matter of not striking a false note, which the proletarians, for all their simplicity, are quick to detect. The least hint at cultural patronizing is irksome to the new ruling class.

When, on the other hand, the social transformation is genuine, even a priest's daughter may be accepted by the proletarian community. Zoya, in Gumilevsky's *The Dog's Lane*, even has the good fortune of mar-rying into the working class. The milieu in the novel is the university, but Zoya's fiancé is of proletarian origin and approves her preferring factory work to studies. He explains Zoya's case by the Marxian theory of environmental influence: she has never really belonged to the camp of outsiders. There, he tells Zoya " 'ninety-nine out of every hundred persons are our enemies. But there are exceptions and you are one . . . very possibly because you grew up with the children in the street, and the street protected you from your father's influence.' " In the same way, Varya, in Erenburg's *Second Day of Creation,* is found deserving of a good comrade's love. Brought up by an aunt, a working woman, she had escaped the tainted atmosphere of the home of her father, a grocer. Generally, the painful question of whether it is permissible to love a class enemy is not raised in proletarian fiction, but it occasionally appears in fiction dealing with the Soviet Amazons and the intelligentsia.

The basic difference between an inveterate outsider and an adopted native is shown in V. Gerasimova's "The Distant Relative" (1931). Masha, a widowed teacher's daughter from the provinces, owes her admission to the university to her influential uncle, a professor. She divides her time between her studies and a maidservant's duties in his home. Her pretty cousin Ada wears a red kerchief, uses the vocabulary deplored by that discriminating Komsomolets in Gorbatov's novel, and puts in a few hours' work in the factory daily—all of which Masha recognizes as a masquerade. Since, moreover, she overhears some anti-Soviet remarks at a party given by her uncle, she reports the whole family to the authorities, even though she now has to leave the university. Befriended by comrades from the Zhenotdel, she becomes a dedicated activist and is henceforth one of them.

It remains to trace the subsequent fate of the outsider's pattern. Its representatives were few. As has already been stated, proletarian girls did not attend the university, and therefore it is they, rather than outsiders, who provided fictional models for the factory Komsomol membership. The type featured by Veresaev in *The Sisters* owed its existence to the galling problem of the 1920's: the adjustment of the prerevolutionary upper and middle classes to the conditions of the Soviet regime. The topic will be discussed in the following chapters, and here it suffices to say that, as time went on, the problem disappeared.

So did, in fiction, the tense, insecure girls who tried, by exaggerated loyalty to the proletariat, to atone for having been born in the enemy camp. On the eve of World War II, a teenager would have no other childhood memories than those of Soviet schools and of a home where prerevolutionary concepts would, at least, be kept from interfering with her Pioneer and Komsomol activities. As for the Ada type, it reappears in postwar Soviet fiction in the guise of a daughter pampered by parents from the Soviet privilegentsia. She brings heartache to many a good working youth and enlivens many an anemic plot. But strictly speaking, the outsiders of the 1920's, both in the factory and the university milieu, are a "lost generation," replaced in the 1930's by the Soviet-educated youth.

III

THE AMAZONS

8

Women on the Battlefield

🌿

Warfare has always been a popular theme in Soviet literature, and numerous works have been dedicated to the portrayal of the Civil War and World War II. The Civil War theme was particularly prominent in the early 1920's, and with some ideological adjustments, it came into vogue again at the end of the 1930's. The popularity of World War II as a topic has lasted, with slight fluctuations, for almost a quarter of a century.

This Soviet fictional world has had numerous inhabitants whose counterparts are seldom met in Western literatures: women who have cast their lot with the Red Army. At different periods, they have participated in actual fighting; have been employed by the *Cheka*,* by the military intelligence agencies, and by the underground organizations; and have worked in auxiliary technical services, besides, of course, nursing the wounded.

The characterization of these heroines has varied, depending on the ideological stand of the authors. In the postrevolutionary decade, the Fellow Travelers saw them as psychological freaks, and the proletarian writers, as citizenesses heroically performing their duty. In the 1930's, the stern amazons of the Revolution, seen in retrospect by the now homogeneous body of Soviet writers, mellowed and assumed the virtues expected of the fictional heroines of the day. And the fictional women

* Extraordinary Commission (1918–22), a police organization famed for its ruthless struggle against counter-revolutionaries.

combatants in World War II, while in uniform, behave modestly and nobly, much as they have been behaving in civil life since the establishment of Socialist Realism. They do occasionally possess less exalted principles (but higher artistic value) in the works of nonconformist writers, especially those of the post-Stalinist era. Accordingly, in each period the treatment of these women's emotional and biological problems—and of the ensuing plot situations—has been different. The focus has always been on love, but unavoidably, attitudes towards motherhood and bloodshed had to be taken into consideration.

Love fears the clamor of arms as much as, allegedly, do the Muses, and violence has always been considered the domain of the males. Still, in the Western tradition of literature and folklore, love and war are by no means mutually exclusive. Political events are set in motion by romance—Helen of Troy's, Isolde's, Guinevere's. Knights and heroes earn as much fame for a romantic affair as for defeating a monster, as did Tristan and Lancelot, Siegfried and Theseus; and even immortal gods endanger their prestige for the sake of a gallant adventure.

Not so in the world of Russian sagas (*byliny*) and fairy tales, ruled by huge, robust males who relish meat, drink, and above all, battle. Ruthless and coarse, they pay no homage to women, and are not easily ruined by love, whether sacred or profane.* Witches busily brew love potions in Russian folklore, where the very word "beloved" (*zaznobuška*) translates as "my darling and my infirmity." A man in full possession of his senses would not, it is implied, willingly accept the bondage of love. Women, on the other hand, are decorous and wily. Their weapons are tears, sex appeal, and ruse. In a medieval saga the Russian Penelope, Olga, devises an arson plot to destroy her suitors and their town.

Some elements of this unromantic tradition are echoed in Soviet fiction after the Revolution, most noticeably in the numerous stories of worthy men destroyed by scheming women; and in a modified, sublimated form in the recurrent phrase, "this is no time for love."

The sentiment has divergent interpretations. Sergey, in A. Yakovlev's "Without Shores" (1924) is a cynical intellectual and does

---

* When, for instance, the knight (*bogatyr'*) Dobrynya was entrusted with the classical medieval errand of escorting his prince's bride to her new country, the hero did not fall in love, as in Western sagas. Instead, he fought and brutally slew the lady's elder sister, who had followed them in a knight's disguise. It might be noted that this amazon princess was a Lithuanian. Russian heroines, as a rule, were not pugnacious, though there are a few amazons, called *polanicy*.

not object to a casual liaison, but considers emotional involvement ill-timed. To the sterling proletarian Emelyanov in A. N. Tolstoy's *The Viper* (1928), on the contrary, the emotional involvement is so essential that he will not accept a wartime liaison as a substitute. But to both commissars, dedication to the cause of winning the Revolution means exclusion of personal happiness.

Women feel different, not because they question the importance of the Cause, but because to them not even the Revolution is important enough to exclude love. They suffer. Sergey's decadent mistress, Nadya, suffers hysterically; Emelyanov's romantic Olga, with tragic resignation; and Anna, the worthy mate of Commissar Bunchuk in Sholokhov's *The Quiet Don*, settles for a brief happiness stolen from fate: " 'I may lose you any day, and I want to love you completely.' She shuddered at her own determination: 'Now!' "[1]

In their carefully edited portrayal of revolutionary events, the 1930's do not raise the question of whether romance in time of military struggle is proper. The impression given is that during the Revolution true love was allowed to flourish but not to interfere with the performance of soldierly duties. Women—for example Agrippina in A. N. Tolstoy's *Bread* (1937)—were shown as accepting this attitude as a matter of course, as did their men.

Love does not flourish in the fiction dedicated to World War II, not because it is sacrificed to some stern principle, but rather because of the awesome scale of the surrounding disaster. This feeling of impending doom is shared by lovers: there is no time, no place for love in such close vicinity to death.

Thus, just as it did in the Russian legendary tales, romance always takes second place in Soviet fiction dealing with time of strife. There, armed contest itself becomes the drama, the setting, and the protagonist; and so, except in a few short stories, whatever happens to characters may be considered actually a subplot.

For women in the armed forces motherhood, understandably, is seen as even less acceptable than romance. It does not offer problems to Civil War amazons (though there are occasional mentions of abortions), while the heroines of World War II are predominantly unmarried and very nice girls. Because of the popularity of motherhood in the fiction of the 1930's in general, a few Civil War heroines during that period do bear posthumous babies to men who had fallen in battle (in Tolstoy's *Bread*; A. Perventsev's *Kochubey*, 1937; and V. Grossman's

"In Berdichev," 1934). Otherwise, the subject is generally glossed over, as is another obvious question, that of a woman's natural aversion to bloodshed.

Here again, fiction's handling of the theme conforms to the overall trends in the respective periods. At the hands of the Fellow Travelers, the amazons adjust to killing to the point of enjoying it: witness Maryutka in B. Lavrenyov's *The Forty-First* (1924). In the 1930's, the authors dodge the issue altogether, or make it impersonal. In later fiction women serve primarily in technical jobs, dangerous to themselves but seldom involving their using arms. Female spies and workers of the underground on occasion have to kill, but do so with utmost reluctance, in sharp contrast to the sadistic practices of their predecessors in the fiction of the 1920's. Often they themselves perish in action. All in all, Soviet heroines, like women anywhere else, prefer to allay suffering rather than to inflict it, and a variety of nurses throng Soviet wartime fiction, particularly that of World War II.

9

The Revolutionary Strife

◤

THE CIVIL WAR IN SOVIET FICTION

The theme of the Revolution and of the Civil War swept Russian literature from the moment the actual fighting was over. It seemed as if all the pent-up emotions and the sufferings undergone by the nation had been waiting for years to be recorded in artistic form. In the literature of the early 1920's, dominated by the Fellow Travelers, the political aspect of the Civil War played a comparatively insignificant role. It was the struggle itself that these works endeavored to portray and not its reasons, Russia torn and bleeding rather than the advent of the dictatorship of the proletariat. Above all, this fiction reflected a romantic fascination with chaos and anarchy, which had been of such magnitude that they acquired the mystical attributes of destiny. Passions unleashed on such a scale ceased, it was felt, to be human; they belonged to the elements.

This sense of terrible primordial grandeur, captured in flight and embodied in *The Twelve* by Blok (1918), was summed up in the final whimsical "chapter" of Pilnyak's *The Naked Year* in 1922:

> CHAPTER VII (the last, no title):
> Russia
>   revolution
>   blizzard

The snowstorm motif has a tradition in Russian literature as a back-ground for crucial, irrational acts.* In early postrevolutionary fiction, the motif was blended with the mysticism inherited from the Symbol-ists and with naturalistic pictures of bloody violence.

Short stories prevailed, the genre lending itself well to capturing dramatic moments snatched, as it were, out of the welter of events. The style was generally modernistic, refined and sophisticated in the works of educated writers, flamboyant and melodramatic in those of proletar-ian newcomers to literature. All pictured the plight of helpless villages and provincial towns, captured in turn by the Reds and the Whites, subjected to ruin and murder at each change of master. All suggested ancient Russia, the prey of Tartar invasions and of the peasant mutinies of Razin and Pugachev. A wasteland emerged, snowbound, lawless, doomed to destruction, a nightmare country where wolves roamed following in the wake of madmen as bloodthirsty as wolves, where

> through towns and villages and hamlets the blizzard of the Revolution whirled in a stormy dance, thundering, whistling, yelling, shooting . . .

and where there were

> whistling whips, animal-like yelling, people like stumps of flesh crawling in bloody mud, faces distorted in Mongolian smiles, spilled intestines, broken bones, . . . Scythians, Polovians, Tartars.[1]

In the mid-twenties the trend changed. Novels reappeared, with slower tempos of action, vaster scopes of events, and characters more complex and capable of development. The theme of the Revolution, popular as ever, assumed an ideological hue. Bloodshed lost its mystical garb and became a relentless struggle between two hostile political orders. Scythians gave way to the enemy ambushed in the neighboring village, and the blizzard, to actual fighting. The modern Pugachevs and Razins—trigger-free, sensuous, drunk with power—vanished, as did squeamish, bespectacled students in the Red Army ranks and that Bolshevik Nemesis, "the awesome man in a leather coat." They were replaced by tough, taciturn commissars fiercely dedicated to the Cause.

It took another decade before, meeting the demands of Socialist Realism, authors endowed the ideal Bolshevik in retrospect with prole-tarian origin, iron will, and strict Party discipline. Thus, in the works

---

* For example, a traveler's marrying a stranger in Pushkin's *The Snowstorm,* a flinty peasant's dying to save a servant's life in L. N. Tolstoy's *Master and Man,* and a soldier's shooting his unfaithful mistress in Blok's *The Twelve.*

of the Fellow Travelers the Revolution wandered in the snowstorm; in those of the *émigré* authors, dwelt in a Cheka cellar; and in those of the proletarian writers, lived with partisans in the woods. Whatever the author's ideology, the Civil War was painted with a bold brush and in vivid colors. Ever present were death, blood, and tears. Blood, as usual, was shed mostly by men, tears by women.

The Civil War in Soviet fiction is a man's world where women play only a secondary role. They are extras: haggard mothers with starving children in their arms, refugees fleeing before the advancing enemy, wives sobbing over their husbands' dead bodies. But as protagonists they are few, except in short stories, where they are often centers of a dramatic episode or of a psychological problem. In novels they drift among the panorama of events, adding a touch of color to the somber plot, introducing the element of personal emotions into an atmosphere of ideological and military contest. Women help to characterize the male protagonist by bringing out the good or the evil in him. But they are only participants in the march of events which are being shaped by men.

Nevertheless, the literature of the 1920's developed two types of Civil War heroines. One—a proletarian—is a woman comrade, a dedicated supporter of the Bolshevik cause; the other, invariably of middle-class background, is a romantic adventuress. Since reality provided actual living models for both types, the choice between them at that time was determined either by the artistic endeavors pursued by the Fellow Travelers and their imitators, or by the early proletarian writers' efforts to serve the young Soviet State. With the ascendance of the latter approach—codified eventually into Socialist Realism—and the parallel waning of the former, the romantic adventuress disappeared from the Soviet fictional world, leaving no issue. It was the woman comrade who was succeeded during World War II by the patriotic Soviet woman fighting for her Fatherland.

THE ROMANTIC ADVENTURESS

The romantic adventuress is much more prominent in the fiction of the 1920's than is her earnest counterpart, just as the blizzard revolution overshadows the ideological struggle in it. The adventuress is invariably young, lovely, and above all, pointedly and aggressively feminine. In fact, femininity is her outstanding characteristic, since her very role in a work of fiction consists in being a maverick woman among a great number of men.

Ostensibly, she serves as fighter, investigator, and typist; but she also assumes all feminine guises, and impulsive and seductive as she is, tends to take men away from the vital matters of politics and warfare. She thus becomes at best a distraction, often a disruptive influence, and seldom is of much value to the Cause, even when she honestly tries to be, which is not always the case, because the Revolution has its camp followers.

The camp followers, with the exception of Lyolka (in B. Lavrenyov's *The Wind*, 1924), a former prostitute who leads her own fighting band of desperadoes, are employed in the bureaucracy of the new regime and are known as the typing misses (*pišbaryšni*). The proletarian writers ignore them; the Fellow Travelers, making no attempt at ethical evaluation, use them as instruments of the heroes' destruction. They are wisps of evil produced by the war and constitute a separate group from the "Marusyas," the bourgeois amazons who actually serve in the ranks of the Red Army. Both nicknames were widely used in life as well as in fiction.

In contrast with the women comrades, who pursue a political goal, the romantic adventuress is mere flotsam on the stream of the revolutionary strife. This is not just because these women are moody and reckless; so are many commissars. Nor, it seems, is the fault with their noble or bourgeois background, since most of the period's dedicated "leather men" are also of nonproletarian origin. The reason is that the romantic adventuress still seeks in the midst of wartime chaos traditional feminine prizes: love, or on a less exalted level, pleasure and luxury.

Seductive Femininity: The Camp Followers

Any Soviet reader today could easily identify camp followers as the class enemy. These girls were alien to the proletariat by birth and upbringing, coming as they did from bourgeois homes or homes of the landed gentry. They obviously had gone over to the winning side for personal gain; finally, they infiltrated the Bolshevik ranks, and by their wiles managed to endanger the reputation of its trusted men. But in the

1920's the villains' patterns were not yet clearly recognizable. In the first place, the Party welcomed anyone from the intelligentsia who was willing to cooperate with the regime, and the nascent wartime bureaucracy needed the services of the typing misses. Secondly, since they were patently indifferent to any political creed, they seemed unlikely to turn traitors; it was even conceivable that they could be converted to Communism, and at least one dedicated commissar came to grief trying to educate such a siren politically (Nina in O. Brik's "Not a Fellow Traveler," 1923).

In any case, Soviet men found them irresistible, these pretty, kittenish creatures from an alien world, "etherial and delicate, sweeter than a confectioner's cookie," their laughter "tinkling like tiny silver bells" and their "luminous hair and . . . rustling, lissom, perfumed skirts" bewitching onlookers.[2] Predatory, parasitic, foolish, they flutter about Army and Cheka offices, file records, and type decrees and orders, often helping their illiterate bosses to sign them. Greedily, they seek the comforts of life and are experts at making men provide them. Any men: White officers with whom fictional typing misses invariably associated in the past, and these gone, Red commissars. The latter may sometimes prove their match in cynicism—like Comrade Laytsis, who is riding the crest of the wave of mass arrests with pretty, moronic Olenka Kuntz, in Pilnyak's *The Naked Year*. During the day Olenka types arrest warrants for Laytsis' signature in a Cheka office set up in a former convent; nights they meet behind the altar in the convent's chapel. In the end the wave engulfs them, too. Usually, however, the camp followers ensnare good men in whose lives women had meant, so far, but little: there are crude, fleeting romances with erstwhile sailors and with busy Party workers who have neglected family life. These men are helpless against the consummate, seductive femininity which is these girls' stock-in-trade. During a night search at a rich merchant's house, for example, Commissar Pushkov sees Taynka "sitting on her bed—white, slender, frightened. She presses her little hand to her full bosom, shoves her plump, rosy little foot into a black stocking, misses it, seizes a garter prettied with tiny red bows. It's too much for Pushkov,"[3] and he orders his men out of the charmer's house. So begins their romance.

The thoughts and feelings of the temptresses themselves are not presented, for psychological analysis is not practiced in Soviet literature; and the reader's knowledge of the characters is either to be deduced from their behavior or is imparted directly by the narrator. Still, while the commissars are revealed as ascetic, tormented souls or as primitive and temperamental "children of nature," the women, almost inanimate in their puppet-like, passive brightness, are mere tools of destruction. The tragic denouement is always provided by the Party, which metes out justice without delegating the task to a capricious and possibly politically illiterate Nemesis. No allowances are made for good intentions, and vice is punished—whether in knights, rebels, or cynical parasites and their mistresses—in a spirit of perfect impartiality. In *Chocolate* (1922) by A. Tarasov-Rodionov, the ideologically impeccable Cheka executive Zubin falls victim to Elena's greed and stupidity; for twenty pounds of chocolate she becomes a counter-revolutionary agent, and for the same amount of gold tricks Zubin into signing a prisoner's release. The affair is discovered, and the Party considers it expedient to shoot both for the sake of its prestige.

Occasionally, the victims try to break the spell and regain their freedom, but in vain. In A. Yakovlev's *Wanton Rebels* (1922) the ignorant, boisterous Commissar Bokov, who terrorizes the whole town at the instigation of his Ninochka, gets drunk at a boating picnic and attempts to throw her into the river in traditional Razin style. Sobered, he continues as before until a special committee of the Party (*trojka*) has them both shot.

The typing misses survived in Soviet literature until the advent of Socialist Realism, when they were replaced in the executives' offices by women secretaries, efficient, middle-aged, and crusty. But they had been gradually losing their demoniac sex-appeal. The "blizzard" mood of reckless lawlessness, and the atmosphere of mystical chaos paramount in 1922, abated as the decade advanced, and finally temptresses vanished with it like soap bubbles, without a trace. Indeed, the works in which they appeared have remained out of print since the 1920's, and the very fact of their onetime existence is largely ignored by Soviet historians of literature and is therefore unknown to the vast majority of young Soviet readers.

Thwarted Femininity: The Marusyas

The Civil War amazons nicknamed Marusyas are more complex characters than the typing misses. With a few exceptions (to be considered separately) they too stem from the bourgeois camp, but did not leave it for mercenary considerations. The driving force in their case was a desire to escape from an unhappy home, or to follow a man they love, or just an urge to join the great adventure, so as not to be left out of it. Politically they are uneducated and lukewarm. If they fight valiantly, and on occasion, ruthlessly interrogate White prisoners, it is not out of hatred for the enemies of the Revolution, but because they insist on emulating men in everything. The establishment of the dictatorship of the proletariat is of little concern to them. They sport men's clothes and haircuts, chain-smoke, swear, and affect a disdainful attitude towards love. And all the while they are starved for love, for its tenderness, its elation, its sense of owning and belonging. " 'I would like to call him "my man," as peasant women do,' " confesses an amazon wistfully, adding that, in spite of her Army costume, she yearns for her lover to caress her condescendingly, as one pets a cat.[4]

For the most part, bourgeois amazons fall in love with ideologically sophisticated heroes, and unlike the typing misses, have no use for the exuberant Soviet Razins. This, however, and their status as comrades-in-arms, only serves to widen the gap between their urge to be attractive to men and the way of life which deprives them of the feminine charm which the camp followers use to such advantage. Naturally enough, the Marusyas are shown as emotionally unstable; their thwarted femininity finds an outlet both in reckless courage and in ungovernable hysteria.

They are capable, like Nadya in Yakovlev's "Without Shores," of leading a group of hesitant fighters in a successful attack, and exasperated by a lover's coldness, of shooting a prisoner during interrogation. Like Katya in Nikitin's *Fort Vomit* (1922), they abhor sex because of a traumatic youthful experience, live a life "as stern as an axe," and become Cheka prosecutors. Then suddenly, prompted by spring, they not only frankly approach their male colleagues but also peruse the prisoners' files in search of a suitable candidate. Actually, they are sisters of the melodramatic, sensuous heroines of decadent prerevolutionary fiction. Helplessly floundering in the troubled elements of the Revolution, they are "victims who drifted away from the familiar shores of life but reached no new ones. And nobody knows when [they] will reach them—if ever."[5]

But guiding amazons to the safe shores of life was not the main concern of the authors (and perhaps in the early 1920's they were not yet quite sure what these shores might be). Thus the romantic adventuresses belong to the hour of strife, and their ultimate fate remained a matter of conjecture. Only two Marusyas continued living into peacetime, their fighting days shown in a flashback, but they are high-strung and impulsive rather than hysterical, and stem from Dostoevsky rather than from Artsybashev. One is A. N. Tolstoy's Olga, in *The Viper*, a dazed bourgeois waif who, having followed a partisan leader through the thick of the Civil War, survives his death, but fails to adjust to life under NEP, and meets with a tragic end. The other, Leonov's redhaired Suzanna, in *The Soviet River* (1930), once had walked out of her eccentric parents' home straight into the camp of a roving guerrilla band, but eventually settles down rather prosaically as a chemical engineer and a co-builder of the first Five-Year Plan. Both girls preserve a certain masculinity in attire and manners; and though Suzanna does marry, it is she who proposes.

Looks and clothes play an important part in the characterization of the bourgeois amazons. Understandably, these women are exotic, colorful, and even occasionally gaudy. Marina, mistress of the redoubtable Commissar Gmyrya in Gladkov's *The Fiery Horse* (1922), "smelled of blood and of milk. . . . fire was spilled like smoldering dust between the black rays of her eyelashes, leech-like her lips curled, and one could not tell whether with joy or hatred." Lyolka, whose beauty ensnared the brave Commissar Gulavin in Lavrenyov's *The Wind*, was "a big woman with thick, dark eyebrows, cherry-colored cheeks, lips red as tomatoes, full and juicy. . . . dressed in a brand-new, grey sheepskin coat, pink hussar breeches with silver stripes, patent leather boots with spurs; she had a silver-mounted saber hanging at one side, a sheathed automatic pistol at the other, and her black, shaggy Cossack cap sported a red bow."[6] The looks of Marina and Lyolka, of course, are exaggerations, almost caricatures; living and fictional amazons were ordinarily content to bob their hair and wear a soldier's uniform with a revolver in their belts. Male reactions to this garb range from respectful admiration for A. N. Tolstoy's lovely Olga, who "slim and tall, her hair in a dark, trim bob, her short sheepskin coat cinched with a belt, passed, spurs ringing, along the barracks through clouds of cheap tobacco smoke," to ribald jokes at the plump Fioza, a provincial merchant's runaway wife, donning quilted khaki Army pants and blouse (in V. Ivanov's *Blue Sands*, 1923).

These amazons never forget that they are women masquerading as men and insistently use their disguise to contrast with and enhance their femininity. Not all aspects of femininity, however, are acceptable. Maryutka, in Lavrenyov's *The Forty-First*, is explicitly warned by the enlisting commissar against childbearing (a detail deleted in later editions as immodest). But otherwise the question of maternity is not raised by the fiction of the 1920's, and neither are other possible biological and psychological problems. Doesn't a sensitive woman recoil before bloodshed, for instance? Would she not rather tend the wounded than kill? Bourgeois amazons show no such squeamishness, and with the exception of Varya, in Fadeev's *The Rout* (1926), who deserves a special discussion, fictional heroines of the period are not cast as nurses. Isn't camp life too hard for them? They invariably enjoy enviable health which, as well as their loveliness, is not affected by the hardships of warfare. In short, femininity, conspicuous as it is in the characterization of the romantic adventuress, assumes primarily the form of sex appeal. All of them—the passionate and virginal Olga, the aloof Suzanna, the hysterical Vera, the earthly Lyolka—exude it. And all other features are toned down or glossed over.

The bourgeois Marusya, in spite of her active service in the revolutionary ranks, shared the lot of the mercenary and predatory camp followers in that she did not survive the establishment of Socialist Realism. There are several reasons: her nonproletarian origin, the stigma of decadentism attached to it, and particularly her lack of revolutionary zeal. As was mentioned before, many a proletarian partisan leader is lawless and unpredictable, and many a model commissar is of bourgeois descent, but their dedication to the Cause is their main characteristic, and this eventually secures them the status of Soviet heroes. The female of the species, given to suicidal attempts, tinging her military performance with sadism and hysteria, proved less acceptable than the male.

Three heroines, however, outlasted the eclipse of the romantic adventuress: Maryutka, of Lavrenyov's *The Forty-First*, Varya, of Fadeev's *The Rout*, and Bakhmetev's Froska, of the short story bearing her name, later renamed "A Mistake" (1924). These are borderline cases. As working girls, they faithfully serve, as Maryutka phrases it, "the poor proletariat who is after its own rights." Yet they lack the singleness of purpose which distinguishes their opposite numbers, the pioneer women fighters of proletarian fiction, and seem to be motivated by class instinct rather than by class consciousness. Their chief and obtrusive characteristic is again femininity—romantic in Maryutka, earthy in Froska (both bona fide partisan fighters), and a combination of the two in Varya, who, too full of the milk of human kindness to take up arms, is a nurse. Moreover, each of the three becomes involved in an affair with a class enemy, an enormity of which Soviet fictional heroines are seldom guilty. Still, he remains to them a class enemy, a spiritual alien, and in the case of the two amazons he is unhesitatingly sacrificed to duty. Eventually, with adjustments ranging from minor editorial text cuts to the author's rewriting the story, these three romantic adventuresses achieved the permanent status of New Soviet Women.

Maryutka, in looks and temperament, could serve as a representative of romantic Amazon: she is "a slender little reed, [with] red braids tucked under a brown, shaggy Cossack cap, slanting eyes burning with a crazy, yellow, feline fire." What is more, though practically illiterate, she writes poetry. On the other hand, she also meets the qualifications of a woman comrade: she is of impeccable proletarian descent, chaste, stern, and an excellent shot. Her count of despatched White officers, whom she loathes, stands at forty when she misses her forty-first, and he proves her undoing. While conveying him by boat to headquarters, with orders not to let him fall alive into the hands of the Whites, Maryutka is shipwrecked and stranded on a deserted coast with her handsome prisoner. In spite of mutual class hostility a passionate romance follows. When Maryutka identifies a rescue boat which reaches them after several months as the enemy's, she unhesitatingly carries out her orders, shoots her lover—and falls in hysterical grief on his body: "'What is it I've done? Wake up, beloved one! Oh, my blue-eyed darling!'"

Contemporary critics, while acknowledging Maryutka's dedication to her stern duty, easily identified her as romantic Amazon and Lavrenyov himself as a Fellow Traveler.[7] But the story was a success, eventually became a Soviet classic, and was even adapted as a film. It was easy to excuse a girl of nineteen for forming a liaison with a dashing officer, particularly in such propitious circumstances. And the tragic denouement, inevitable in any case because of class hatred, endowed Maryutka with the halo of a classical heroine who resolved the conflict between love and duty in favor of the latter. If the shot fired by Maryutka was a reflex rather than a conscious decision, it is argued that her carrying out the order instinctively, as it were, was all the more to the credit of her military discipline.

Varya, in *The Rout*, probably owes her survival to the importance of the novel itself. She is not its protagonist, but even as a secondary character she was likely to cause some embarrassment by her loose morals. Since, however, no cuts could be made in later years without seriously impairing the fabric of the already famous novel, and since Varya was one of the few working class heroines in Civil War fiction, she stayed in Soviet literature much as she did in the partisan unit—part of it, but slightly a dissonance.

Besides, much in Varya could be (and was) explained and justified. Her dream of poetic love atones for the coarseness of her relationship with her husband and numerous other partisans. In addition, her romance with the cowardly intellectual Mechik had remained platonic, allegedly because "she could sense a class enemy in him."[8] She nurses the wounded in their forest hospital with infinite devotion. And she is kind: large and placid, with smoke-grey eyes and heavy, golden braids, she is overflowing with a desire to comfort everything that suffers. "Not only her voice, but her whole being seemed to rustle and coo with kindness," comments the author.

Froska is a primitive specimen of the Soviet Amazon, burly and sensuous, and her nonproletarian love affair is actually an accident. Lost after a skirmish, she spends the night in an empty railroad car with a chance lover whom she takes for a fellow Red fugitive. When dawn reveals his officer's epaulets, Froska indignantly upbraids him as an enemy of the People, and since he is trying to stop her from warning the Reds of the enemy's approach, manages to kill him with a piece of rock and joyfully rejoins her unit.

The short story, insignificant in itself, would hardly deserve notice, were it not for Froska's interesting transformation into an acceptable proletarian fighter. Written as early as 1920, when Froska's living models were readily available, it was first published in 1924, with her name as a title.[9] It was included in a selection of Bakhmetev's works with the title changed to "A Mistake," in 1935, and in the 1947 edition a few cruder details were deleted. The next step was more drastic. In the 1953 edition, as well as in the *Collected Works* (1957), no intimacy whatsoever takes place between Froska and the officer, and it is he who shoots and wounds her in a futile effort to prevent her warning the comrades. Thus the wayward amazon Froska of the 1920's thirty years later becomes the typical female combatant in the Civil War, portrayed in retrospect under the auspices of Socialist Realism.

THE COMRADE-IN-ARMS

In the fiction of the 1920's the woman comrade is barely outlined; she is but a harbinger of things to come. A simple working woman obeying the ringing call "the Revolution is in danger," she takes up weapons unfamiliar to her sex in order to reinforce the ranks of the fighting proletariat. Unglamorous and dedicated, she is granted by the author and her fictional comrades alike sober recognition, and at her death, a soldier's scant tear.

The proletarian amazon first made her appearance in 1923 in D. Furmanov's *Chapaev*, an account of an actual Civil War campaign loosely knit into a novel. It was not an impressive appearance: far from being cast as a heroine, the New Soviet Woman was an all but anonymous private in a regiment formed by worker volunteers from a provincial factory. " 'There are twenty-six of us women in the regiment, comrades,' " one of these factory girls tells the crowd who is seeing the volunteers off to the front. " 'We have realized that this is a decisive moment for the whole country, so it means that we, too, have to join. It is a must, that's all.' "[10]

Indeed, that was all, but it established a pattern which was subsequently developed. There is nothing exotic in the proletarian woman fighter, nothing of the enchantress Circe. Her decision to join the Red Army, seen by the Soviet critics as "natural and artistically convincing,"[11] is made spontaneously and is due not to infatuation with a Red Army man or ideological sophistication (she never has any), but to her inborn class-consciousness. The battle of the sexes, prominent in the works of Fellow Travelers, does not enter the picture; nor do these women fight for their own emancipation, except as part of the new order which is to be established after victory.

The contrast between their femininity and the grim brutality of wartime conditions, so coquettishly used in the characterization of the Marusyas, in proletarian fiction merely stresses the urgency of the revolutionary struggle. It is not that the contrast is disregarded by proletarian writers, nor is femininity spurned by them as means of characterization, but both are studiously kept free of sexual accents. Frivolity, impulsiveness, and seductiveness are ignored in favor of selflessness and dedication, basic feminine virtues. Men are cooperative.

Surely, in works by proletarian writers they could not show less political alertness than did their counterparts portrayed in works by Fellow Travelers: after all, equality of women belongs to the A B C's of Marxism. Hence men recognize and value the woman comrade's virtues, even though they are aware of the incongruity of her presence in their ranks. They joke at her unwarlike appearance and unimpressive military qualifications; they may (rather obviously prompted by the author) grow sentimental over a pretty girl who is being subjected to hardships and danger; but these reactions are secondary. What matters is the common understanding that fighting for the Revolution "is a must" for all. As a result, an attitude of comradeship is carefully sustained: if a woman does her proletarian duty like a man, she is his equal, and her contribution to the Cause should be appreciated.

Women themselves live up to their position of equality. They do not use their clothes (blouse, pants, top boots, a cap perched on short-clipped hair) either to enhance their femininity or to repudiate it. Female soldiers, they simply dress their part, just as, being soldiers, they carry a rifle. Unlike the romantic Marusyas, they never tantalizingly flaunt their masculine costume before their comrades-in-arms; whenever practical, they even wear skirts. And they neither smoke, swear, nor drink. Moreover, in contrast to the romantic adventuress, the woman comrade is not always young and not necessarily beautiful. Furmanov established this principle when he introduced Marfa the weaver and Marusya Ryabinina. The former, thirty-five years of age, broad-shouldered, with a wide, slightly pockmarked face, "had parcelled her kids out to orphanages" in order to join her factory's regiment; and the latter, nineteen, has "a small, red pug nose, lively hazel eyes boring through a hedge of dark eyelashes, and brown hair, unevenly bobbed and sticking out in coarse little bunches."[12]

Marfa's ultimate lot is not revealed, but Marusya's is a stern and pathetic story. She has no biography outside the Red Army; she joined, she served, she died fighting for the Cause:

It happened at the battle of Pilugino. Guns roared and howled. Bombshells imprinted kisses of fire on the blue oval of the sky. . . . Marusya walked in the line. The heavy rifle weighed down her tired, tense arms; her eyes burned with a passionate fire; but on her open, pure, girlish face there was a smile. . . . The very first bullet was for Marusya; it hit her right on the forehead . . . the waves [of the Volga River] caught her up, and . . . away they rushed the girl's warm corpse on their undulating green backs. . . . Many are the girls such as you, Marusya, who, faithful unto death, were taken away from us in those days of bloody strife.[13]

These two proletarian amazons—the sturdy, homely middle-aged housewife and the young, innocent, courageous girl—blazed the trail for the fictional heroines of the 1930's and those of World War II. The third—a loving woman, the Red soldier's perfect mate—came from a pen incomparably more skillful than that of Furmanov.

Sholokhov's Anna Pogudko of *The Quiet Don* as a woman comrade in Soviet literature is unique in many respects. In the first place, she is Jewish, which would have made her an isolated case even among the romantic adventuresses. Next, she is an educated girl and a member of the Party, though Red Army girls in proletarian literature are usually unschooled and politically unsophisticated. Finally, she alone among her kind is affected by the sight of blood, death, and executions of the White prisoners. Everything about her—her characterization, the relationship with Commissar Bunchuk, her death—is executed in vivid, naturalistic colors. She is plain (in 1928, sugary prettiness or rustic beauty in Red Army women was still a decade away) and wears a quilted military coat and heavy boots several sizes too large. She is seen dusty and sweaty, wading in the mud, fighting lice and typhoid fever; the reader is not spared any ugly detail of her mortal wound and agony. Yet, with A. N. Tolstoy's Agrippina (in *Bread*) for a possible rival, she is the one Civil War heroine who can stir the reader to sympathy and perhaps to admiration.

The setting of Anna's romance is so lurid that it precludes any possibility of a romantic glow. At times, she has to fight an emotional revulsion towards her Chekist lover, who himself is racked with nightmare memories of his own atrocities. Sholokhov neither justifies nor glamorizes Bunchuk; the man does his duty as he sees it, and hates the enemies of the Revolution the more for his exterminating them. But for Anna the artist draws the line at manning the machine gun. Romantic adventuresses could, with hysterical zeal, conduct Cheka investigations; at least one heroine of the Civil War, cast as a charming ingenue in the 1930's, was shot by the Whites for her efficient services in the Cheka (Tanya in V. Gerasimova's "Pity," 1934). But Anna Pogudko fought and died as a true proletarian amazon: a woman soldier.

IO

Between the Wars

✴

THE CIVIL WAR AMAZON
UNDER SOCIALIST REALISM

The popularity of the Soviet amazons did not match fictional interest in the Civil War theme, which continued into the 1930's. The two great Civil War novels, A. N. Tolstoy's *The Road to Calvary* and Sholokhov's *The Quiet Don*, introduce no women fighters during the period except for Tolstoy's Agrippina, who wanders from *Bread* (1937) into Part III of *The Road to Calvary* (1941). Anna Pogudko lived and died in Part I of *The Quiet Don* (1928). Otherwise, except for a few insignificant short stories featuring victims of the Whites' ferocity,[1] women comrades seemed as extinct in the 1930's as were the exotic Marusyas. Then in the last three years of the decade, when the threat of war was looming dark on the horizon, there began a mass revival of historical fiction. The emphasis was on times of stress, times when the Russian people fought the foreign invader or the class enemy in the Revolution. And the theme brought back the woman fighter participating in the common effort of the proletariat during the Civil War.

By that time, the Amazon's living model of a generation earlier, the actual woman in the Red Army ranks, could apparently be considered a historical personage. In the words of a Soviet critic, when "a master writer of historical fiction scans History in search of typical situations, he sees a historical personage as a typical character: this constitutes the basic feature of the genre as demanded by Marx and Engels."[2] Thus, another critic explains, "in Civil War combatants, writers seek and find the characteristic features of the people of the future, those people who are now our own contemporaries. This is what determines the historical novelist's selective choice of facts and events as well as the specific details of characterization."[3]

In this way, then, the Soviet Amazon of the Civil War was endowed in retrospect with the traits which, in the late 1930's, were assumed to be typical of all Soviet women. These traits included, besides such wartime essentials as "holy class-hatred" and military prowess, the peaceful virtues required of fictional heroines engaged in the building of socialism: modesty, a sunny disposition, and sweet naïveté for girls; marital faithfulness, domesticity, and prolific motherhood for women. Obviously, producing an artistically acceptable combination of these characteristics was no mean task; it proved but a moderate success in Agrippina, at the hands of A. N. Tolstoy, and an hilarious parody at those of A. Karavaeva in Lena, the heroine of *Lena of the Crane Grove* (1938).

The presence in Red Army ranks of women fighters of lesser moral stature was recognized, but they were firmly dismissed as nontypical: a black sheep cannot represent the whole flock. The following conversation between two patently representative heroines of the Civil War, 1938 vintage, may help to illustrate the point:

"Good for you!" laughed Masha [seeing Lena slap a soldier who was trying to kiss her]. "That's the right way to treat them. There are so few of us girls in the Army, we must be very careful; otherwise we'll lose our men's respect in no time at all."

"Do you remember that dissipate girl from the Ufa Regiment we saw the other day?" [Lena asked].

"Don't even mention her! I would simply throw her out of the Army! Everyone is pawing her, treating her without any respect; her voice is hoarse and deep like a man's; she reeks of tobacco, is dishevelled, slovenly; her boots are caked with mud—why, she doesn't seem to be a woman! Never be like her, dear, and give in to no man, remember!"[4]

The introduction of proper femininity into the characterization of the woman comrade may be responsible for her having never developed leadership, the distinguished quality of the Soviet hero. The absence of prominent women commissars in actual fact would not necessarily have precluded their existence in the fiction of the 1930's. A heroic girl leading enthusiastic partisans to victory could have caused no more raised eyebrows among readers, veterans of the Civil War, than in all probability did the starry-eyed ingenues. But leadership was definitely not a feature a Soviet writer wanted to observe in contemporary women, and therefore, not one he would try to discover in the women of the past. The male commissar, from his first appearance in Russian literature, had been constantly developing, undergoing changes in quality of military leadership, in degree of Party discipline, and in ideological interpretation of the Revolution. Women fighters, however, as types, were arrested in their further development. Like Marfa the weaver, Marusya Ryabinina, and Anna Pogudko, their descendants in Soviet fiction considered joining the Red Army a must for a proletarian girl, served, faithfully carrying out orders but never issuing them, and fell into three distinct age groups with resulting differences in characterization. The only novelty was the introduction of a particular brand of feminine respectability which a decade earlier had been denounced as bourgeois.

THE FAITHFUL MATE
AND THE INGENUE

The model of a Soviet proletarian woman fighter is Tolstoy's Agrippina; she has all the necessary prerequisites. An illiterate orphan, working as hired help at a rich kulak's house, she kills her master when he attacks her, joins the Red Army, and meets there Ivan Gora,* a neighbor from her native village. Stern, taciturn, and beautiful, she goes at his side through the hardships of the Civil War, as a soldier and wife. The boots she wears and the pants that replace her tattered skirt, she took off a Cossack whom she had killed in a skirmish. A good shot, a disciplined soldier, she nevertheless "has none of the 'emancipated' contempt towards proper womanly concern for her husband's comfort, makes no vulgar demands for equality in petty household chores."[5] She washes his shirts (in the night, so that comrades will not make fun of her), nurses him when he is wounded, and accepts his

* An almost symbolic figure, hailing from his legendary namesake, "Ivan the Mountain" of Russian folklore.

judgment in all things. When he is killed, though she is stunned with grief, she goes on living to bear his child and then returns to their regiment taking the baby with her. " 'One is so sorry for her,' " says another woman in the novel. " 'Hers is such a difficult disposition. She's a one-man woman.' "[6]

They all are in 1937 and 1938, the years of a bumper crop in amazons in Soviet fiction, and they seem to have been created on the same pattern. There is Natasha in A. Perventsev's *Kochubey*, a nurse, but whenever necessary also a fighter, a combination which meets the principles of both revolutionary service and gentle femininity. Here she is, marching with

> the two hundred thousand men retreating to the Kalmuk steppes . . .
> wrapped in an Army coat, carrying a rifle. Her head was bowed, and
> she could hardly be distinguished from her comrades-in-arms; she had
> fought side by side with them against the rich Cossacks. Under her
> heart, with growing insistence, a child was moving, conceived in so
> turbulent a time. . . . At her belt bobbed a bundle, the layette which
> Roy had managed to provide for his future son.[7]

The brave commissar Roy is killed, and his son, like Ivan Gora's, is born posthumously.

Beside the similarity in life stories, all these typical women share other resemblances: in looks—they have strong bodies and thick braids, which are no longer sacrificed to camp life conditions; in their love— they display the full, serene love of a mistress and a wife; and in their sober acceptance of proletarian and military duties.

Women of the older generation are not barred from active participation in the war effort, though their contribution is naturally smaller. They are rather grotesque in appearance (which Marfa the weaver, in Furmanov's *Chapaev*, was not, in spite of her plainness), but they serve as another proof that winning the Revolution is everybody's task. Sasha Trubka, in Tolstoy's *Bread*, has a sharp tongue, a reputed liking for vodka, small, pale eyes in a wrinkled face, and gray hair straggling from under a Red Army cap, a relic of her son, who was killed in action. She carries a gun and proves that she can use it in encounters with "White bandits," but her real contribution to the Cause is in raising a regiment of lumberjacks to defend besieged Tsaritsyn, a feat which Red Army agitators had been unable to achieve.

Marya the washerwoman (in V. Ilenkov's *Ivan and Marya*, 1937), a powerful woman with a topknot of mousy-colored hair and size twelve shoes, follows her husband into the Red Army when he volunteers. She becomes, the author asserts, "the most important fighter in the regiment" by protecting it, with her tub and suds, against the wartime scourge of typhus. She dies in the trenches, fighting to the last and felling the attacking enemy with her natural weapons—buckets of scalding lye.

The strangest amazon in the fiction of the 1930's to combine a woman's feelings with masculine valor is Klavdya Vavilova in V. Grossman's "In Berdichev." She is thirty-six, a Red Cavalry commissar, swarthy, ungainly, masculine. Her lover, fighting by her side, is killed in a battle over a provincial town, Berdichev. Their unit retreats, but Klavdya stays behind in the house of a Jewish tailor, Tuter, to have her baby.

> Behind the door, a hoarse, mannish voice went on screaming. The words were so strong that Tuter, after listening for a while, shook his head and spat on the ground. It was Vavilova, who, frantic with the pain of the last moments of labor, was fighting God and the cursed lot of women.
>
> "Now this is something," said Tuter, "this is something. You can tell it's a commissar who is having a baby. Now my Beyla, all she can think of yelling is 'Oy, mama, mama, mama!' "[8]

A week later, when Beyla comments on the Commissar's fussing over the baby " 'like any crazy Jewish mother would,' " Tuter shrugs philosophically: " 'What did you expect? Do you think a woman can become a man just because she wears leather breeches?' " Yet, in another fortnight her unit returns, and Vavilova joins it, leaving the baby in Beyla's care: " 'It's a must.' "

In addition to the women fighters, there are the ingenues, new versions of Marusya Ryabinina. These are young girls, light as blossoms, naïve and winsome. They are enveloped by an aura of maudlin sentimentality: they are *so* eager to serve the Cause, plead *so* charmingly to be allowed to fight the enemies of the People, awaken *so* tremblingly to the magic of their first love. Though they come as a matter of course from exploited working families, they are primarily *Russian* girls, not just members of the international proletariat. They are demure, blush at the mention of illicit love, giggle at being offered a cigarette, wear skirts with their uniforms, and have beribboned blond braids or funny flaxen pigtails. In short, they are a complete contrast to that shocking combatant from the Ufa regiment, and of course, to the brash fighters called Marusyas in the 1920's. They are, however, amazingly efficient.

Karavaeva's Lena, for example, does valuable intelligence work, catches enemy spies, kills traitors, and gallops under fire across enemy lines to deliver dispatches. When, at the end of the novel, she marries a worthy commissar, the reader feels that for a heroine of her stature even such reward as this is hardly adequate. There was some disagreement among the contemporary critics as to the book's artistic level,[9] but its ideological value was apparently unquestionable, and having survived all changes in political trends, the novel was included in Karavaeva's collected works in 1957.

It will be observed that beyond the 1920's woman's role in the Civil War becomes increasingly auxiliary. Women help men to do their hard and cruel job, but stay away from participation in actual bloodshed. Agrippina, for instance, as the heroine of *Bread* in 1937, stabs her master with an awl and later kills a Cossack in a face-to-face encounter. But in 1941, having reappeared in *The Road to Calvary*, she is simply shown "sending bullet after bullet" after the retreating enemy without seeing the results of her marksmanship. As to Lena, she breezes through scenes of violence as screen stars do through scenes of storms and earthquakes—without any harmful effect to her emotional makeup.

But even though the heroine keeps away from the more drastic forms of revolutionary struggle, tragedy stalks her steps. She knows heartache at the death of a lover; sometimes she is wounded or even killed. On the other hand, this erstwhile amazon, rehabilitated within purposeful historical fiction, is spared the sense of frustration and the inferiority complexes which tormented her a decade before. She accepts her biologically predetermined secondary status in the army, much as the Soviet woman of the 1930's accepted it in civil life, and is rewarded by peace of mind and a sense of duty well done. Whatever calamities she has to suffer come to her—to use a term which she herself would reject—as acts of God.

II

The Great War
for the Fatherland

❧

WORLD WAR II IN RUSSIAN FICTION

In 1933 a Soviet critic, Leytes, attacked the "hundreds and thousands" of female characters in bourgeois fiction who had served to "sugarcoat and ennoble the war theme. They were as stereotyped as those girls on gaudy picture postcards who, as symbols of military glory, tenderly bend over a hero lying dead on a field of battle with arms spread and a smile on his lips."[1]

Within a decade, however, the girl and the hero had reappeared in the works of Soviet fiction featuring World War II. All the usual patriotic components of war fiction were present: the contrast between a peaceful landscape and the destruction of war, the native soldiers' heroism and the atrocities of foreign invaders. Human suffering, the loss of life and property, and personal tragedies provided the plots. There were stories of valiant mothers, proud to see their sons die for the Fatherland and for Stalin, and stories of the adoption of war orphans. Love, of course, figured prominently: romance blossoms in trenches and hospitals, and amputees who had despaired of their wives' affection return home to find that they have underestimated its sterling quality. The naïveté of the plot and the primitivity of character drawing, common to popular wartime fiction everywhere, were enhanced in the case of Soviet literature by the practices of Socialist Realism, already established and reaching the peak of influence during the postwar period.

The scale of destruction inflicted on Russia by the war and the horrors endured by the population account for the unflagging popularity of the war theme after the war. In the following years there were fluctuations in the treatment of the theme, paralleling those in Party policies and perhaps reflecting a cooling of passions, which allowed some improvement in the artistic level. But there were no marked differences in writers' attitudes, such as there had been in Civil War fiction, for several reasons. First, all writers had followed the same literary method, that of Socialist Realism, since 1934; second, no exotic or proletarian approach to the debacle was possible: it was the story of the Russian people repelling the invader.

In addition, a motto appeared, increasing in force as victory became certain, and finally developing into a leitmotiv of Soviet war fiction. In dramatic stories of besieged Leningrad and Stalingrad, of fleeing refugees, and of the hardships of German occupation, fiction told of "how simple Soviet Russian folk achieved the stature of heroes." The accent during the war was on "Russian" and afterwards on "Soviet"; subsequently the two were assumed to be synonymous, a trend known in literary criticism as "Soviet patriotism."

THE COMBATANTS

The woman participant in World War II shares most of the characteristics of the Civil War Amazon, but there are several differences. In the first place, she could no longer be considered an unusual, peculiarly Russian phenomenon. Living and fictional women in uniform had become familiar figures in the West, and if their role was auxiliary, that of the Soviet women had become increasingly so, too. Next, Soviet women's active participation in the war, however heroic, is no more than what is expected of them. With the equality of sexes accepted as an established fact, it follows that if an average Soviet man becomes a hero in an emergency, so should a Soviet woman. Nevertheless, women are still given extra credit for heroism: after all, they are not drafted into military service; they volunteer. Therefore they not only equal men in dedicated performance, but by joining, obey the call of patriotic duty, as their mothers a generation before obeyed the ideological must.

Lastly, Socialist Realism's endeavor to create typical Soviet characters caused the World War II heroines to become completely two-dimensional in comparison to the Marusyas, the romantic adventuresses of the Civil War. Their psychological pattern is reduced to a mere outline, and they react in a standard manner to a set of circumstances construed into a standard plot. But since these plots are based on situations which did not exist during the Civil War, heroines developed certain new characteristics and specialties. In the Civil War women served as partisans or nurses; in World War II they also belong to all auxiliary services. Moreover, war effort on the home front, shown in the kolkhoz and industrial novels of the period, provides the plot theme in about half of postwar novels, and women are prominent in these.

The Amazon's main feature, femininity, reappears in the World War II heroine in modified form. The contrast between a woman's gentleness and the brutality of war continues to be stressed, as well as the incongruity of her effort when pitched against the enemy's power. But unlike the heroes of Civil War fiction, men of this period often disapprove in principle of female participation in the war. " 'Fighting is no job for a woman,' " they say. " 'Don't we have enough men to do it?' "[2] This attitude, however, is meant to affirm masculine strength rather than to disparage feminine weakness. War heroines are mostly robust, and Russian women have been quite used to hard physical effort—a fact deplored by prerevolutionary fiction as a sign of Russia's backwardness, and until recently, praised by Soviet fiction as proof of socialist progress. Still, a woman wounded or tortured by the Gestapo touches the reader more poignantly than does a man, especially if she is very young—or very old. This may be why the type of fighting woman such as Marfa the weaver (in Furmanov's *Chapaev*) is almost absent in the fiction of World War II. Middle-aged women perform bravely on the home front, while those fighting the Germans are young, as were Furmanov's Marusya Ryabinina and A. N. Tolstoy's Agrippina; or, without a precedent, they are very young—teenagers and even children; or they are gray-haired grandmothers.

While age naturally determines the heroine's appearance, it has no effect on her behavior: young or old, she is ready to serve her country and to die for it if need be. Old women help partisans, provide information on enemy forces, and occasionally kill Germans stationed in their homes and are hanged for it—like Zakharovna in L. Seyfullina's *On Her Own Land* (1946), who sets fire to her house in the night. Little girls carry messages, refuse to divulge the hiding places of their partisan relatives, and are subjected to bestial cruelties, as is Zina in P. Pavlenko's *Happiness* (1947), who had fingers chopped off both hands by the Germans "right there, in her own room." But incidents like this are few, even in wartime fiction, and scenes such as German soldiers' raping a child on the scaffold prior to public execution were toned down in later postwar editions.[3] In action female soldiers are as brave as men: "They fought for twenty-four hours, not a whit behind other soldiers," an eyewitness reports with pride in a wartime novel. Numerous and unobtrusive, they serve on the front line as machine gunners, as marines, as telephone and radio operators, and as partisans in forest dugouts. Occasionally the spotlight rests on their heroic performances and deaths, particularly if they have an actual prototype, posthumously decorated.[4] But generally they are extras, perhaps bringing a ray of happiness into the life of a brave officer who is the protagonist in the story.

Since the writers concentrate on showing how *average* Soviet people develop into heroes, women soldiers are studiously kept unglamorous. A few romantic beauties with golden braids are lost in the mass of sturdy, plain girls in ill-fitting uniforms. They wear blouses, top boots, and either skirts or breeches, depending not on coquettishness but on practicality. Their hands are frostbitten, their hair untidy, their voices hoarse because of rough weather, not, as with Marusyas, because of smoking and yelling. It is as if authors in their choice of heroines followed the directions given by that recruiting officer who answered the question whether women volunteers should be accepted with: " 'Yes, by all means. But choose sensibly and with discrimination. We have women [in Russia] who are going to fight better than many a man. All those who are young, healthy, childless, especially when they are good in athletics, know how to use a gun, and have a fighting spirit are acceptable.' "[5]

Their civilian occupations are as pedestrian as their heroism is lofty. The contrast, for example, between Shura's prewar career as a nursery aide and her death in capturing singlehandedly a machine gun is startling, as it is intended to be (in G. Berezko, "The Commander," 1944). The salesgirl Manya, caught by the enemy on a reconnaissance assignment, scribbles a proud epitaph for herself on the wall of her death cell: "I did not talk."[6] The reader feels that the full military honors with which she is buried are due to her and to many girls like her. Even their names are common: if a count were taken, it would be found that the majority of women characters in Soviet war fiction are called Manya, Tanya, or Anya, with Katya, Ola, and Lena as second choices.

Nurses in wartime fiction are even more numerous than women soldiers; hardly any novel is without them. They too are plain and average, but have soothing and compassionate feminine charm. "Little sister," the wounded call them, and "mother," and we are told that hearing a young woman answer a much older man with "Yes, son, I'm coming" does not seem strange.[7] Moreover, nurses are the most human among women characters. Even the standardly angelic ones, of the type deplored by Leytes, call for a smile rather than a shrug. And the freckled, snub-nosed young things, nicknamed "sparrow," or "button," or "bun," compare favorably with Karavaeva's saccharine Masha of 1938, even though they too are tagged with her "funny flaxen pigtails." Perhaps the reason lies in the difference between a writer's using models furnished by actuality and his creating imaginary, didactic characters in a historical novel—though Karavaeva claims to have known personally the living models of both Masha and Lena.

At any rate, most of the "little nurses" are not implausible and are even occasionally made touching through the use of a skillful detail. One could cite, for example, the well-worn boots of a dead girl found in a frozen forest, and a small mirror in her first-aid kit; the tears on the round face of an eighteen-year-old who, frightened to distraction, crawls nevertheless out of the trenches to fetch the wounded.[8] And there is the American gift parcel with pretty underwear and a berib-boned bottle of perfume which is awarded to Lena Gnatyuk in recognition of services above and beyond the call of duty in besieged Stalingrad:

> She stood, embarrassed and awkward in her bloodstained uniform blouse too narrow for her big bosom, loaded with medical kits, wearing wide, loose pants and big, square-toed boots. She was trying to hide her large hands with short, blackened nails. . . .
>
> "What use is all this to me now?" she asked. And the officers felt uncomfortable, realizing how clumsy and unattractive the girl felt at that moment—and how proud.[9]

None of them was to see the end of that day. The officers were killed in the trenches; Lena, with a group of her wounded, in a basement shelter; and the gift parcel was delightedly picked up by a marauding German soldier.

There are other women—middle-aged nurses and surgeons, tired and begrimed with the blood and dust of war. Some are gruff, like nurse Yulya Dmitrevna, the heroine of V. Panova's famous war novel, *The Train*. Some are kind, as are the physicians Levitan in Grossman's *For the Just Cause* (1952), Levkoeva in E. Kazakevich's *Spring on the Oder* (1949), and Müller in B. Polevoy's *The Home Front* (1958). But all are efficient, skilled, and indefatigable. Yulya Dmitrevna, moreover, has the distinction of really coming alive for the reader.

The gallery would have been incomplete without the glamorous young surgeons (who, artistically, range below their humbler sisters) like Dr. Koltsova, also in *Spring on the Oder*. Always lovely and elegant in her well-cut military coat, she looks like St. Clara of Assisi when at work, tireless and self-possessed in the operating room, "a small bleeding universe full of groans, where her large, lake-like eyes shone evenly and calmly above the white gauze mask and slim, rubber-gloved, skillfully moving hands."[10]

Looking for examples of continuity in characterization, we meet the Civil War amazon Maryutka of Lavrenyov's *The Forty-First*. Considerably changed under Socialist Realism, she now is Staff Sergeant Bondarchuk (her first name is not revealed) in Lavrenev's "The Tea Rose" (1943), drilling discipline into a darkly handsome recruit, Georgie (*Žora*). His eyes, "coal-black marbles," retain the spell of the "ultramarine blue marbles" of Maryutka's dashing lover, but the "yellow feline" eyes of Maryutka have faded to a standard blue; her red hair, to pale gold; and, in short, the rough, rusty-brown little reed has evolved into the sentimental tea rose of the title. She is still a sniper, but no longer writes poetry and would not fall in love with a White officer even if White officers were still around. Staff Sergeant Bondarchuk rescues Georgie from a dangerous spot where she herself had sent him in the line of duty, while normally the situation should have been reversed, the man protecting the courageous but weaker woman. The slip was duly detected and reproved by the critics. The objection was not to a "tea rose" in the role of a sniper (there was even a living prototype, on whom Lavrenyov also wrote a feature story),[11] but to the strained military relationship between these two, combined with a love affair. It was denounced as psychologically untrue and artistically trite, "just fiction, skillful and unemotional."[12]

Wartime love stories in the 1940's were indeed unimpressive, and the "this is no time for love" motif was as valid as it had been in the old days, in fact, even more so. It was not so much that romance in such stern times was unsuitable, perhaps unpatriotic, but that there was not enough time for it. This is why the criticism leveled against Simonov for having made Saburov and Anya's love story so joyless in his *Days and Nights* (1944) seems unfair.[13] The scene is besieged Stalingrad, an inferno, compared to which Civil War fighting seems a skirmish. An hour of sleep and a warm meal have become oases in an arid desert of blood and fire. Captain Saburov and Anya, though they tremble for each other's safety, literally have no time to give to their love, because he is responsible for the defense of his position and she, a nurse, for the care of her wounded. In the end she herself is mortally wounded.

Another Anya, in E. Kazakevich's *The Heart of a Friend* (1953), and her Captain Akimov are more fortunate, at least in the first stages of their romance. There are furloughs, and there is an opportunity, denied to Saburov and his Anya, to register their marriage in a dingy office which of late has been registering chiefly deaths. But fate's generosity does not extend beyond several days of a honeymoon. Akimov returns to the front, and Anya, who works at the headquarters as interpreter, soon has to return to civilian life to bear their baby. The days of Commissar Vavilova, who had her baby between participating in two cavalry attacks, are past, and as her commander assures Anya, grieved at such an end to her military usefulness, " 'bearing children nowadays is also important State business.' " Akimov is killed in action, and Anya is left to dedicate her life to the daughter whom he had never seen. Still, Vavilova as a type did not vanish without an echo. Faina, a middle-aged officer with streaks of gray in her black hair who has lost a leg in battle, gives birth to a premature baby on board a hospital train (in Panova's *The Train*). When she refuses to tell the sympathetic *politruk** anything about herself except that she needs no help, the swarthy face lighted by a cigarette and the hoarse voice seem familiar.

Whenever no marriage takes place, writers do their best to justify the fact. In *Spring on the Oder* nurse Glasha and her major, an understanding high officer explains, live like a model married couple, and theirs "is a real, not a camp love." There are several such cases in post-thaw fiction of the late 1950's. There is, for example, Rita in

* A party member assigned to a military unit and in charge of its political morale.

Baklanov's *An Inch of Ground* (1959) and Tonya in his *South of the Main Offensive* (1958) and Nina in Andreev's *I Want to Go on Living* (1958). When the monogamic principle is lacking—for example, in Yu. Bondarev's *Fire for the Batallions* (1957) Shurochka, in the words of a buddy, falls asleep at one end of the trenches and wakes up at another—the blame is put on the war. These girls, young and living in constant peril, want at least to secure a short moment of happiness with the man they really love: this is what Grossman's Lena Gnatyuk says, as Sholokhov's Anna Pogudko said before her. This does not quite explain the other men whom a girl does not really love, but Soviet writers cannot use the routine argument that morality is always loosened by war, because general rules are not necessarily supposed to apply to Soviet reality. Accordingly, illicit liaisons in the Army were simply absent in wartime fiction and rare in that of the postwar period, though they have been treated leniently in the era that followed.

THE CLOAK-AND-DAGGER SET

Generally, female spies can be grouped into two categories: the naïve teenagers who are caught and die as martyrs and the glamorous young women who emerge victorious from apparently hopeless difficulties. The subsequent fate of the latter is a matter of some concern to authors: adjustment to normal life may prove difficult. In one case, the heroine, Anyuta in *The Fiery Earth* (1945) by A. Perventsev, marries an understanding young partisan, but only after living a while among the apple orchards of her native kolkhoz, waiting for "fresh winds to purify her soul" of the slime of her wartime experiences.

There are many teenagers employed by the underground in occupied territories to gather information and carry messages across the front line. Several of these had living prototypes, like the heroines of A. Fadeev's famous novel *The Young Guard*, which was based on Gestapo documents captured during the German retreat from the Don Basin. Ula, Maya, and Klava became patron saints to a postwar generation of Soviet schoolgirls, who pledged, individually and collectively, to model their lives on them. Young heroines of the underground represent pure tragedy, and not just because they sacrifice their lives willingly and proudly, as priestesses deposit an offering on the altar in a temple. Selfless and intent, they feel no pity for themselves or for those they love, no regrets for the youth and happiness they are forfeiting. Their story is that of dedication alone. Passion has no place in it, though a ray of poetic romance, fast extinguished, may fall across their gloomy path. Chaste, lovely, and stern, they die as flowers broken by a storm—and the simile here is not a chance one. Ula is compared by the author to a white water lily, and her fate is symbolized by the lily plucked from her luxuriant hair and thrown underfoot; Valya's face (in Kataev's *For the Power of the Soviets,* 1949) was, we are told, like a delicate flower, and on her way to her execution she is holding a twig of acacia in her "parched lips, dark as a small dry wound."[14]

Another of the *Young Guard* girls, Lyuba Shevtsova, represents the junior group of that glamorous new wartime heroine in Soviet literature, a female spy. This *emploi,* requiring talent, daring, and resourcefulness, vies with that of the nurse in war fiction popularity. It seems, however, to have created some problems for the authorities in charge of regulating Soviet literary output. This is apparent from the drastic changes in later editions of wartime works featuring Soviet Mata Haris, and from the fact of their absence from new, postwar fiction. The strange case of Tatyana Polovtsova, whom Panfyorov lovingly led over fifteen years, through five separate novels, to an unexpected and ignominious end, will be discussed later as proof of the change. The case of Zhenya Müller in Polevoy's *The Home Front* may provide another.

The nature of the problem seems obvious. In order to obtain information, these young women had to associate with the German military, and during the war no effort was spared in showing these men as monsters of cruelty and debauchery. However useful these girls' task, however repugnant to them, it still involved immoral behavior of which a Soviet woman should never be guilty. Seducing willing dupes came easily to lovely, chic young women, invariably excellent dancers and singers; and the authors either implied or stated that the affair did not go beyond a mere flirtation. Before the situation became critical, the information was usually secured, or else discovery and death struck simultaneously. Still, the drunken orgies which for some reason Soviet fiction writers considered the best opportunities for spying did not fit the framework of literary morals obligatory since the 1930's: they just did not make good educational reading.

These temptresses have little in common with the camp followers of the Revolution who used to seduce commissars in the fiction of the

1920's. They are free from the vulgar sexiness of Lyolka in Lavrenyov's *The Wind* and from the insidious sex-appeal radiated by Tarasov-Rodionov's Elena in *Chocolate*. They use their good looks as they would a weapon and wear pretty clothes like costumes in amateur theatricals. In Fadeev's *The Young Guard*, blue-eyed, cherry-lipped Lyuba, setting out on a reconnaissance trip, packs lace-trimmed under-wear and her best silk dress in a small suitcase, curls her golden tresses, pulls "flesh-colored silk stockings over her plump, creamy legs."[15] Yet such scenes are not introduced for piquancy. And when Panfyorov's Tatyana in *In the Land of the Defeated* (1948) enters an elegant carriage wearing perfume, a stylish dress and hat, and long black gloves, she is not gratifying personal vanity. These are soldiers setting out on encounters which may prove a service to their country—or a death warrant to themselves. Naïvely seductive details of the heroine's beauty and elegance are meant to arouse in the reader a feeling of admiration and regret: such loveliness, such courage, such waste!

It goes without saying that in Soviet fiction no German temptress tries to obtain military information from a Russian officer. Whether this never happened in actuality or was inconceivable to writers is impossible to tell.

Soviet Mata Haris do not hesitate to take human life, but this does not, it is understood, detract from their femininity; for a delicate woman to turn murderess is part of the war's horror and a measure of the People's wrath. In postwar fiction, however, butchering German villains fell out of favor. A good example is provided by the scene in which Russian girls attend an orgy arranged by German officers and stab their partners on a signal from suddenly attacking partisans. In a later edition the task was left for the partisans to accomplish.[16] But as a rule, Soviet women fighters are on the receiving end in scenes of bloodshed and death, either as grieving witnesses of their comrades' misfortune, or as victims themselves.

THE THAW AND AFTER

In the late 1950's the number of works dealing with the war theme grew significantly. The case of Zhenya Müller, nineteen, a Soviet intelligence agent, may serve to gauge the change. Hers is still the part of an ingenue, a typical Soviet girl heroically serving her Fatherland, but it is played with less melodrama and in modified conditions.

Unlike Lyuba, Zhenya is no free-lance amateur; she is trained and directed by military intelligence men. Her native command of the German language and her Nordic prettiness (her father was a Russified German Communist) enable her to secure a position as an interpreter with the Germans. There are no orgies, no tortures, and her employers do not attempt to seduce her, particularly since she is engaged to Kurt.* Kurt, a personage who would have been quite impossible while the war lasted, is another Soviet agent: a German deserter, anti-Nazi, son of a Communist—in short, a living proof that there can be good Germans. Zhenya is mortally wounded when they escape after completing their assignment, which includes the shooting of a Russian traitor, performed by Kurt in Zhenya's presence.

In the light of Zhenya's story the fall of Panfyorov's Tatyana Polovtsova becomes less of a puzzle. Plainly, times have changed, and after the thaw certain details formerly considered proper are no longer so. Accordingly, not only does the role of Mata Hari disappear, but the woman who can play it well, the *femme fatale*, must also be shown as spiritually alien to the Soviet way of life.

The reader first meets Tatyana in 1947, in *The Struggle for Peace*. She is a painter, specializing in scenes from factory and kolkhoz life, happily married and mother of a small son. When the enemy occupies her town, she succeeds, after a short flirtation, in stabbing to death the sadistic German commander and escapes with her mother and son, who perish from German bullets. Tanya suffers a nervous breakdown. In 1948, in *The Land of the Defeated*, she recovers, and trained by the Army in using firearms and concealing her feelings, becomes an agent. She then miraculously secures much vital material from the Gestapo and murders a death camp director and his wife. Laden with fame, she is reunited with her husband (a war hero in his own right), has another son in 1949, in *The Great Art*, and settles down to live happily ever after as a secondary character in *Musing* (1959).

Panfyorov's series had several new editions with, on the whole, only minor changes, consisting mainly in the deletion of the gaudier details. Tatyana was hailed by the critics as a representative of heroic Soviet

---

* In Zhenya's case this is true, but a feigned engagement is a routine device for warding off importune admirers.

womanhood and a product of Soviet education, though it was recognized that Panfyorov had minimized the achievements of the Soviet
intelligence service by exaggerating both Tatyana's luck and the ob-
tuseness of the Germans.[17] Then in 1960 Panfyorov produced a novel, *In
the Name of Youth*, reintroducing all the principal characters who had
inhabited the thirty-odd years of his writing career. In this strange
curtain call, which proved prophetic because Panfyorov died in the same
year, Tatyana is demoted to a Soviet villainess. She sports a pony-tail
hairdo, a masculine gait and manner, paints abstracts, takes a lover (a
cynic and an admirer of Western art who leaves her), and is on the
verge of insanity. Her husband, in despair, becomes an alcoholic and
commits suicide. Too late, she realizes her criminal folly, and at her
husband's funeral everyone turns away from her.

It is difficult to explain such cruelty to a favorite heroine, unless the
author is sacrificing her on the altar of Stalinist morality. The literary
Old Guard, the conservative wing of Soviet writers to which Panfyorov
belonged, had opposed the thaw from the start. They deplored all its
innovations—the criticism, however cautious, of Soviet reality; the
apolitical themes; the emerging characters of juvenile delinquents, unfaithful wives, and modernist artists. Surely, Tatyana's downfall could
not but serve as a warning to the young women of the post-Stalinist
era. If yielding to the evil Western influences so destroyed a veteran
heroine of World War II, it certainly would destroy an average citizeness.

The theme of World War II in Soviet literature has proved surprisingly vital, and the thaw did not seem to affect its popularity. Besides
Polevoy's *On the Home Front*, starring Zhenya Müller, several monu-
mental novels could be mentioned—K. Simonov's *The Living and the
Dead* (1959) and *One Is Not Born a Soldier* (1963–64), and A. Kron's
The Home and the Ship (1964), for instance. But if the volume of the
output, compared to the earlier periods, was not materially affected,
the writers' approach did change. With the "cult of personality" held
responsible for all the human suffering of Stalin's era, it was natural that
the disastrous military blunders of 1941–43 were not forgotten. Arrests
of excellent officers and devoted Communists on trumped-up charges,
scenes of unfair trials and deportations, unnecessary carnage on the
front, the atmosphere of suspicion and frustration corroding the
Army—these became the prevailing themes.

The trend had an unexpected effect on the role of the amazons in

Soviet fiction. Since they had seldom held a rank higher than that of a major (and even then only in the capacity of surgeons), since there were no female politruks and no women at headquarters except typists and interpreters, and since no fictional heroine had ever been shown as inmate of a labor camp, the amazons receded into the stage wings of the war novels. There have been, occasionally, women who deviate from established patterns, as, for example, Eva in P. Nilin's *Across the Graveyard* (1962). She is as loyal and courageous in her intelligence work for Soviet partisans as is Fadeev's Lyuba, but, in the words of a critic, less resistant to the temptations facing a young, attractive woman in her dealings with the German officers.[18] Perhaps for this reason she is more human and plausible as a character.

On the whole, however, women in war fiction have become inconspicuous and standardized. The darling "little nurses" and snipers, the well-disciplined intelligence agents are still around, and the military still fall in love with them. But unless the trend changes again, the heroic amazon in Soviet fiction faces extinction.

IV

THE INTELLIGENTSIA

12

The Intelligentsia,
the Bourgeoisie, and
the Revolution

❧

Postrevolutionary fiction made no sharp differentiation between the intelligentsia and the bourgeoisie. Because in fact and in fiction the majority of the members of the Russian upper and middle classes were hostile to the Bolshevik revolution, authors relegated them all to the enemy camp together. In Sholokhov's *The Quiet Don*, for example, such divergent characters as General Listnitsky, merchant Mokhov, and even the kulak Korshunov all speak the same political language and come to the same disastrous end.

On the other hand, the question of class origin, particularly in works portraying the Civil War, was subordinated to the characters' ideological allegiances, and many a sincere Communist of nonproletarian background was cast as a revolutionary hero. Levinson, the courageous commissar of Fadeev's *The Rout*, is of Jewish bourgeois origin, as are several of the commissars in Yu. Libedinsky's *The Week* (1922) and the narrator in I. Babel's *The Red Cavalry* (1926).

Political feuds rifted families. In Gladkov's *Cement*, Communist Ivagin kills his brother, a White officer; in A. N. Tolstoy's *The Road to Calvary*, Bulgakov, a high official in the White Government, delivers his daughter Dasha to the police, and his two sons-in-law fight on

opposite sides; in Veresaev's *The Dead End* (1922), Professor Sartan-
ov's daughter Vera and his nephew Leonid are Communists, but not his
daughter Katya, who cannot become reconciled to the atrocities of
Revolutionary strife.

Even during the NEP period, however, the intelligentsia was beginning to be favorably distinguished from the bourgeoisie. The latter
continued to stand, as always, for a reactionary way of life, for hypo-
critical religiosity, and particularly, for petty love of property. But the
intelligentsia, as was widely known, had denounced this *Weltanschauung* even before the Revolution and certainly had been on no
friendly terms with the Tsarist regime. Moreover, except for sullen
criticism, the bourgeoisie had nothing to offer the young Soviet State,
while the intelligentsia possessed what was now desperately needed:
education and professional and technical skills.

Thus, engineer Kleist came to be forgiven for his former wartime
hostility and helped Gleb Chumalov to rebuild the factory in *Cement*.
And engineer Gabrukh, in spite of his unquestionably capitalistic habits
and morals, was granted an important position both in the factory and
in the novel in *Natalya Tarpova* by S. Semyonov. Plotting White
officers, like those in Sholokhov's *Virgin Soil Upturned*, Part I (1932),
survived in literature for the natural duration of most of their prototypes' lives, but became rare after World War II. Of course, they still
continued to appear in works set in earlier periods, such as *Father and
Son* (1963–64) by G. Markov and *Virgin Soil Upturned*, Part II
(1960).

During the Five-Year Plans the bourgeoisie as a social group disappeared almost completely from the world of fiction, but the intelligentsia assumed an even more prominent role. Non-Party specialists, usually
engineers, carefully avoid political issues and receive good salaries for
efficient performance of professional duties. For them this is a period of
participation and adjustment (*prisoposoblenie, perestrojka*). Some are
lukewarm and adjust but half-heartedly, like engineer Renne in L.
Leonov's *The Soviet River*. Others sincerely try to participate, as does
Captain Kutasov in Yu. Krymov's *The Tanker Derbent* (1938). But
none of them equals the social usefulness of proletarian characters
because of their congenital social vice: the objective, reasoned attitude
towards the Soviet industrialization which they are privileged to build.
The Stakhanovite workers' enthusiasm and their brilliance as innovators are favorably contrasted with such cold, asocial skill.

In the industrial novels of the 1930's and occasionally of the postwar period, members of the prerevolutionary intelligentsia are introduced as wreckers and saboteurs. They are cynical and brilliant, and cunningly pose as zealous builders of Socialism; but they are invariably unmasked by alert intelligence officers. Of these, Granatov, in V. Ketlinskaya's *Courage*, is a good example; Professor Kozelsky, an intellectual saboteur who underestimates the values of Soviet literature, is another (in Yu. Trifonov, *Students*, 1950).

Basically, however, members of the former intelligentsia are no longer necessarily considered outsiders in postwar fiction. The young people, born after the Revolution, are products of Soviet education; the middle-aged had belonged to the university Komsomol in the formative years of NEP and the early Five-Year Plans. And a few venerable old intellectuals, having faithfully served Soviet society for three decades, refuse to retire and want to serve to the end—like the chief construction engineer, Vladimir Ippolitych, in V. Panova's *The Factory Kruzhilikha* (1947).

The new, authentically Soviet intelligentsia is, of course, a separate element, integrated with and recognized as part of the toiling masses. The distinction, reserved after the Revolution only for proletarians, was extended to kolkhoz members in the 1930's; and by the end of World War II professors and engineers, surgeons and bureaucrats had also arrived as the *tiers état* of the monolithic Soviet society. Freed from the old stigma of bourgeois descent and education, they have since enjoyed the prestige not only of worldly learning but also of what might be termed theological education in Marxist dogma. Invariably possessing excellent professional skills and ideological competence, they live and work as Communists in the way pious, educated people profess and consciously practice their religious beliefs.

Accordingly, their position is comparable to that of learned monks in medieval society. They have greater responsibilities than do the uneducated members of the toiling masses, and the importance of their duties entitles them to certain privileges. Throughout the postwar decade in fiction, the accent was on these duties and their excellent performance; but after the thaw it was privileges that came into focus, and the executive section of the "third estate," the "privilegentsia," came under criticism. It was accused of a variety of shortcomings, the choice of which was rather obviously determined by changing political trends. Thus there were bureaucratic vices such as red tape, neglect of workers' welfare in favor of production norms, and padded statistics; there were the mortal sins of pride and gluttony, the old bourgeois sin of snobbery, and the new Soviet sin called the cult of personality. But these black sheep are exceptions to the rule. The bulk of the Soviet intelligentsia—the professionals and the huge hierarchies of the bureaucracy, the armed forces, and the Party—have all been portrayed as honest, hard-working people, the cream of Soviet society. And it is they, rather than workers or peasants, who occupy the center of the stage in contemporary Russian fiction, just as the former intelligentsia did before the Revolution.

LADIES IN PREREVOLUTIONARY RUSSIAN FICTION

It has been shown in previous chapters that peasant and proletarian women play an insignificant role in Russian literature before the Revolution. There are a few notable characters from the merchant milieu, to mention just two Katerinas: Ostrovsky's, in *Storm* (1860) and Leskov's, in *Lady Macbeth of the Mtsensk District* (1865). But the overwhelming majority of women characters belongs to the educated strata of Russian society: aristocracy, landed gentry, and the upper- and middle-class intelligentsia.

It would be difficult to discuss the collective, static character of a prerevolutionary Hero in Russian literature. Even if an established literary type were chosen—the superfluous man, for instance—progressive changes in his education, social role, world outlook, and way of life would preclude the success of such an attempt. Pechorin, Rudin, Oblomov, and Chekhov's Ivanov share little beyond their typical frustrations, and even these stem from divergent sources. But with women characters it is different, because they are shown not so much within a social group or a political era, as within an emotional atmosphere which basically remains unchanged.

To begin with, the education of girls had not improved much over the passing decades. From Griboedov's Sofya in 1823, to Pomyalovsky's Nadya in *Molotov* (1861), to Chekhov's *Three Sisters* in 1901, they had been brought up by French governesses at home or in "establishments for young gentlewomen," until, at seventeen, they were ready for marriage. Once married, they would begin to build their nest, oblivious of everything else.

> "Yes, apart from her interest in the house (she does have that), and dress, and the *broderie anglaise*, she has no interests [muses Levin on Kitty, his bride]—not in my work, the estate, the peasants, nor in music, even though she is quite good at it, nor in reading. She does nothing and feels perfectly satisfied."[1]

Needless to say, they may not stoop to work. Widowed Katerina Ivanovna, in *Crime and Punishment* (1866), in order to save her children from starvation marries Marmeladov, and because he drinks, her stepdaughter Sonya for the same purpose becomes a prostitute. But nobody, including Dostoevsky, had apparently thought of work as a possible solution for them. A gentlewoman was confined to idleness in her home as inexorably as the baba was to drudgery in hers. The outside world belonged to men.

Because of censorship, Russian fictional characters could not openly become involved in political activities, but at least for men there were discussions of needed social reforms and participation in progressive movements. Women characters, however, take no part in these, not even in the trend for their own emancipation, except for a few secondary mavericks and one protagonist, the eccentric Vera in Chernyshevsky's didactic novel *What Is to Be Done?* (1864). Authors themselves tend to treat harshly the women who meddle with problems rightly belonging to Man. In *Virgin Soil* (1877) Turgenev rescues pretty dilettante Maryanna from the Populist movement by finding her a husband but leaves plain Mashurina to its frustrations. And the would-be revolutionary, Sukhanchikova in *Smoke* (1867), is one of Turgenev's best female caricatures. Even Chekhov, in *The House with the Attic* (1895), seems to favor sweet, indolent Missy over the efficient, social-minded Lida. And of course Tolstoy emphatically discourages his female characters from any activities except childbearing, at which they are quite good.

The heroine's personal characteristics are subordinated to the purpose of her being attractive to men. To conquer hearts ingenues wield charm, *femmes fatales* exude sex appeal, and the effectiveness of domesticity and unselfishness rates high with any good woman. Authors seldom consider it worthwhile to endow heroines with intelligence: most, like Natasha Rostova, "do not condescend to being intelligent"[2] any more than to learning boxing. But while they have no use for masculine accomplishments, women respect them. Natasha, who neither is interested in nor understands Pierre's intellectual pursuits, considers them nevertheless very important because they are her husband's. For the same reason Turgenev's Elena, in *On the Eve* (1860), dedicates her life to the cause of Bulgaria's independence, and Chekhov's thrice-married "Darling" (1898) dedicates hers consecutively to vaudeville theater, the lumber business, and veterinary medicine.

Prerevolutionary fictional heroines do not lack courage, but they show it only in fighting for love. For the sake of love they defy social conventions, morality, and law; they forfeit reputation, temporal life, and eternal salvation. Tatyana's letter to Onegin, Anna's leaving Karenin's home, and the multiple murders committed by Leskov's Katerina are but different levels of a struggle for fulfillment in love. Defeated, they commit suicide, like Tolstoy's Anna and Ostrovsky's Katerina; or else they surrender and take the veil, like Liza in Turgenev's *A Nest of Gentlefolk* (1859).

THE IMAGE
OF A SOVIET HEROINE

It should be remembered that such a mode of living encompassed, as it were, within the precincts of love is not exclusively characteristic of Russian fictional womanhood. Romance has ever affected the heroine more than it has the hero, for practical and psychological reasons. To quote Byron (*Don Juan*, Canto I, CXCIV), "Man's love is of man's life a thing apart, / 'Tis woman's whole existence." What was Gretchen to Faust, Ophelia to Hamlet, Penelope to Ulysses compared to what their lovers were to these women? The fact is that a man, however deeply he is in love, still has other interests in life and other duties, whereas the woman has none. Charles Bovary has his patients and the necessity of earning a living, but what does Emma have to fill her life apart from her quest for love? Nor does the situation seem to be limited to a certain historical period. A hundred years after Mme. Bovary's death, Paule (in Simone de Beauvoir's *The Mandarins*, 1954) serenely assures Henri that her time is well spent in staying idly at home and being in love with him. " 'But being in love is not an occupation!' " he remonstrates. "She interrupted: 'Excuse me, it is for me' " (p. 118). And this is why a Soviet fictional heroine differs from her sisters elsewhere: she is allowed, even expected, to have other important problems than those created by love.

It is, indeed, unfortunate that the birthplace of this unusual character happened to be Soviet fiction. Her living prototype is not, as Soviet critics insist, the exclusive product of Communist society. After all, educated, economically independent women, actively contributing to social, political, and scholarly fields, have become a part of twentieth-century reality not only in the Western world but also, increasingly, in Asia. Yet she does not appeal as a model to writers of contemporary Western fiction, which emphasizes the problems of sex. Her psychological sensations, so important in the age of realism, seem to be of little interest to the average reader. In Soviet fiction, on the other hand, this cultured, self-supporting woman is subjected to shallow and inadequate portrayal because of the rigid behavioral patterns of Socialist Realism. If the average Soviet reader does not always enjoy her company, it still allegedly is beneficial to his spiritual development and so serves the didactic aims of Soviet art.

It would be fascinating to see an artistically convincing, three-dimensional fictional heroine capable of some interests besides romance. Not instead of—romance is the pivot of a work of fiction—but besides it. Could she experience the *Weltschmerz*, a Nietzschean super-woman complex, a religious crisis? How would she carry on a political struggle, persevere in the pursuit of a scientific discovery, solve an ethical problem within her profession? In short, once the ghastly adage "men must work and women must weep" is no longer true, can a female character be conceived within a framework other than emotional?

To repeat, Soviet authors have not achieved this goal, but they have tried, and were they to be freed from political interference, they might succeed. But in their efforts down to the present time, and it seems likely, for the future, they have concentrated on female characters of the intelligentsia rather than on factory and kolkhoz women. The latter have remained on a primitive level of psychological design, straightforward and righteous in solving their always practical problems. This is not to say that women from the Soviet upper and middle classes are complex, three-dimensional characters; within the framework of Socialist Realism they cannot be. But the typical educated woman has been allowed a wider range of plot situations and more opportunities to show her emotional reactions to them. During the post-Stalinist period, as will be shown, she was even occasionally left to make personal decisions without the customary help from the omniscient author. This New Woman of the Soviet intelligentsia made her entrance after World War II. Until then, educated women in Sovietland were aliens: those of the 1920's in fact, those of the transitional 1930's in spirit.

13

Transitional Characters of the Twenties and Thirties

❦

It is unfortunate that, unlike the great Russian realists, the Fellow Travelers did not create any important women characters. Leonov's Nastya (in *The Badgers*) and Liza (in *The Road to the Ocean*, 1936) hardly qualify; his Tanya (in *The Thief*, 1927) is a symbol of femininity rather than a living woman, and so is Olesha's Valya (in *Envy*, 1927). Esfir in Kaverin's *Artist Unknown* (1931), as well as women in the works of Babel and Pilnyak, is an episodic character. Even Katya and Dasha, in A. N. Tolstoy's *Road to Calvary*, are not really the trilogy's heroines, except in the first part, *The Sisters* (1921), which belongs to the prerevolutionary period.

In general, women from the upper- and middle-class milieu did not play an important role in the fiction of the 1920's. They were too insignificant to count as enemies of the Revolution, and they did not have the professional skills which made their men desirable collaborators. Also, because of its pedestrian and strictly utilitarian quality, the topic of their adjustment to the new order offered few interesting possibilities to the plot. Men accepted or rejected the Revolution on ideological grounds, but women either exploited the weaknesses of the new regime, as did the typing misses, or blamed it, with feeble, helpless hatred, for their economic privations and social downfall. Many whining, foolish, frightened women, usually wives of businessmen or of

White officers trying to escape abroad, serve as a Greek chorus lamenting the passing of the old order, but they seldom have any individual spoken lines. Nor, in contrast to the powerful conservative camp in village fiction, do they have any influence on the plot.

It will be remembered that the whole milieu was from the start considered doomed to destruction. It was, therefore, not a question of how its women would fit into the classless society, but at best, whether a few of the more valuable individuals among them could be rescued. In the 1930's, several such rescues were accomplished by means of rehabilitation through work, and these cases deserve separate discussion. But in the 1920's women characters, in most cases secondary, were used either as symbols representing the decadence of their class or as cases illustrative of a social problem.

THE DECADENT FEMALE

The representatives of the decadent group usually come from the pens of Fellow Travelers and are linked to prerevolutionary Russian literature. Proletarian writers seldom seem to notice their existence. L. Leonov's Manka the Blizzard, queen of the underworld at the time of the NEP (in *The Thief*), and K. Fedin's impetuous Varvara in *The Brothers* (1928) hail directly from the high-strung, unpredictable heroines of Dostoevsky. And the typing misses, already discussed as the camp followers of the Revolution, continue the tradition of the morbid heroine,[1] fashionable on the eve of World War I, with the added characteristic of being mercenary.

The group also includes the homewreckers, the "young ladies from the city," who made Party executives of peasant origin divorce their uneducated wives. Such is Katya in Zamoysky's *The Bast Shoes*, who took Praskovya's husband away from his family and later left him for a man of her own class; and Antonina, who seduced Darya's brave Sofron in Seyfullina's *Mulch* (1922); and Nina, the "little snake," who alienated the affections of Vasilisa's husband in Kollontay's *Vasilisa Malygina*. In this last case the couple were class-conscious proletarians, which made it the more shocking.

The star of NEP anti-heroines (though just an episodic character within the novel, *The Twelve Chairs*, 1927, by Ilf and Petrov) is Ellochka the Cannibal. With her vocabulary of thirty words and her efforts to out-dress an American heiress featured on a magazine cover, Ellochka is easily the most foolish female in Russian fiction, not excluding Chekhov's Darling. If, however, one were to look for literary antecedents for this paragon of mean vulgarity (the untranslatable Russian *pošlost'*), it is not the kind-hearted Darling who comes to mind, but Bely's plump "Angel Peri," Sofya Petrovna in *St. Petersburg* (1913). Dissolute and vicious, Sofya Petrovna "was distinguished for her extraordinary vegetative qualities." But Ellochka herself, explain the authors, "had no particular distinguishing features and did not need them. She was pretty."

There are other female drones in the fiction of the 1920's, less notorious than Ellochka, but just as representative of the species: Safo, the languid wife of engineer Gabrukh (in Semyonov's *Natalya Tarpova*), and Sonchyk, the morphinist stepmother of the self-appointed proletarian, Favsta (in Nikiforov's *The Woman*). There is the depraved Agnya (in D. Chetverikov's "Routine," 1925) with her sixteen-year-old daughter Lara, who boasts of using cocaine and plans on becoming a prostitute; this promising youngster robs her parents of money and jewels and becomes leader of an underworld gang. There is Nina (in L. Gumilevsky's *The Game of Love*, 1930), who, impersonating a factory girl, tries to seduce the Party investigator working on the case of her embezzler husband. And there are also the heroines of two best-sellers by P. Romanov—Tamara (in *Comrade Kislyakov*, 1930), who covets a career of a movie star, and cheated by a cynical foreign producer, commits suicide; and Margarita (in "Problems of Sex," 1926), who, with her doctor husband and architect lover, grapples in vain with the problems of free love in the new society: " 'Now supposing that her soul will still be mine,' " the good doctor ponders, " 'but the rest of her will belong to the architect. Who then should support her? Even though I will have the use of half her person—perhaps the most valuable half—still, my keeping her for the architect would seem odd.' "[2]

Finally, there are numerous older women who, rather than being portrayed as human beings, are openly used by the authors as symbols of the decaying past. Aristocrats like the degenerate Princesses Ordynin (in Pilnyak's *The Naked Year*) and bourgeoises such as Olesha's fat, dissolute Anichka Prokopovich (in *Envy*) and the dim-witted widow Gritsatsueva (in *The Twelve Chairs*) can serve to support this contention. Since no symbolic characters exist under Socialist Realism,

these repulsive women subsequently became extinct in Russian literature.

THE LOST GENERATION

The allegedly corrosive influence exerted by bourgeois mores on Soviet
society can be best observed in two notorious novels of the 1920's
dedicated to student life: Gumilevsky's *The Dog's Lane* and Malashkin's *The Moon from the Right.* The deplorable state of morals among
Soviet youth of the period has already been discussed: sexual licentiousness, drunkenness, and hooliganism were rampant in village and
city alike, and did not spare the ranks of the Komsomol. But the
deterioration of morals in the university milieu was considered especially dangerous because of its added taint of decadentism.

Vera, the heroine of *The Dog's Lane*, has a tragic life ending in her
being murdered by a rejected lover. Her husband, a student like
herself, has forced her to abort a baby whose birth would have made
further studies impossible for the parents, a recurrent plot situation of
the period. As a result, their marriage is wrecked. After the divorce
Vera becomes a neurotic, and while insisting that all she cares for in life
are her studies, she reportedly entertains four men in one night. Malashkin's despondent heroine Tanya, who confesses to six men to Vera's
four, has twenty-two shortlived marriages—some of them legal—and
attempts suicide. She owes her rehabilitation to dropping out of college
and settling down to hard work in her native village with a Communist
husband—her twenty-third, and hopefully permanent, mate.

Soviet critics noted that both girls were basically good and were
ruined by decadent influences alien to their class origin. Vera came of a
worker's family, and Tanya grew up in a quiet village, though her
father did keep a small grocery store, and this, presumably, could have
made her susceptible to vice.[3]

Worst of all, debauchery among the students (who are all members
of the Komsomol) is advertised as "freedom from bourgeois prejudices" by young sophisticates of bourgeois extraction, such as the
notorious, jug-eared Isayka Chuzhachok in *The Moon from the Right.*
His speech on the subject, delivered from a tabletop to a drunken
audience smoking drugged cigarettes, is a travesty of the teachings of
the Marxist pundits whom he extensively quotes. This naïvely terri-

fying orgy, called by participants an Athenian night and complete with
girls naked under transparent dresses, was blasted by literary critics as
the epitome of depravity, unworthy of Soviet fiction. The "in the
attic" orgies in V. Lidin's *The Renegade* are a carbon copy of those in
The Moon from the Right, as is the plot in which the heroine (also
named Tanya) commits suicide.

With the establishment of Socialist Realism, orgies and drug addicts
vanished permanently from Soviet fiction. Drinking and illicit love
affairs among students did not reappear until the 1960's, when, for the
first time in almost thirty years, it was admitted that the happy Soviet
youth had their problems. Even then, however, writers showed much
restraint in their portrayal of these chance cases of youthful immorality, and the reader is always assured that virtue is bound to triumph
eventually. In N. Morozov's *On the Bend* (1960), for instance, wicked
Dina is only a secondary character. The hero escapes her wiles and is
rescued and rehabilitated through the dual salubrious influences of work
and love for a good Soviet girl. This girl, Valya, plays approximately
the same role as Tanya's last husband in *The Moon from the Right*.
The case of Galya in V. Aksyonov's *A Ticket to the Stars* (1961) will be
discussed later.

Of course, the two Tanyas and Vera are also unusual characters in
the fiction of the 1920's. Not every girl who came to study in the city
was necessarily ruined, but she had every chance to be unless she
possessed great strength of character. P. Romanov, a Fellow Traveler
and a dedicated observer of contemporary mores, succinctly states the
problem in a short story, "Without Cherry Blossoms" (1926), and
offers a solution of sorts in its sequel, "The Big Family" (1927). The
stories, widely noticed and discussed at the time, deserve attention.

Sonya longs for love, but feeling lonely on a beautiful May evening,
settles for one brief encounter in the dingy dormitory where the boy, a
fellow student, lives. A spray of cherry blossoms which Sonya buys on
the way in spite of his cynical comments is, of course, symbolic. It
withers on a window sill, while, on returning home, Sonya pours out
her disgust and sadness in a letter to a friend. Rejection of bourgeois
prejudices proves to be not all evil, however, and the student Komsomol
proves kinder to Sonya than her own mother, who curtly orders her to
get rid of the baby she is expecting. What is more, while Panya, in
Platoshkin's *On the Way*, and Ketlinskaya's *Natka Michurina*, faced by
the same predicament, were jeered by members of their factory Kom-

somol, Sonya is surrounded with friendliness and even admiration, as a propounder of new morality and "a genuinely free woman." She is also granted the triumph of denying the baby's father any rights to it: like other female pioneers of progress she will raise it alone.

Avant-garde as this attitude may be, it was not the most extreme. Children, authorities such as Kollontay insist, should be raised by the State, not by parents: "A class-conscious mother should achieve the spiritual level at which she would no longer make a distinction between 'my child' and 'your child,' but would remember that all children are 'ours,' children of a Communist, toiling Russia."[4]

The doctrine is not without an echo in the fiction of the period, as was shown in *Cement*. But writers are less than enthusiastic in its support. Nikiforov's Vera Serdobova (in *The Woman*), who insists that "giving children over to the State should be compulsory, so that parents would be prevented from thwarting their development,"[5] is childless, and so hardly a spokesman for mothers. Gladkov, instead of making Nyurka profit by "collective education," allows her to die of neglect in the appalling conditions of a children's home.

B. Stepnoy (in *The Family*, 1922) offers Lyubochka, however, as another sacrificial lamb to Marxist ideas. It is Lyubochka's father who places her in the home where, he was told, 200 out of 350 infants have died so far. " 'In time of starvation,' " he says, " 'everyone must starve. Why should *our* baby necessarily be included among the survivors?' "[6] The mother, Nadya, feels different; it was during her stay in the hospital with typhoid fever that her husband was able to practice his egalitarian principles. At his suggestion, they get a divorce, because he feels they should not risk having another baby who would again make it impossible for him to study and for Nadya to keep her job in the office. "This novel," says its preface, "bares and inequivocally states the question: should the family continue [as an institution]? And the answer is definite and inexorable."

This obviously negative answer was unacceptable to women and the source of much conjugal distress. The time was near—only a decade away—when a woman's desire for a home would begin to be recognized as natural, and subsequently, as commendable. " 'There is nothing one can do about it,' " a husband will remark resignedly in 1937. " 'It's a biological phenomenon; they are building a nest!' "[7] And a combination of efficiency on a man's job with female accomplishments will be admired in 1941: " 'What I particularly like about her,' " a suitor of Zina the chauffeur will say, " 'is her being always so feminine. She can really speed up that car of hers till your heart stands still from fright; but yesterday I saw her as she was waiting at the wheel by her boss's office, knitting so fast, and adroitly, and smiling to herself.' "[8]

The climax of the trend is reached in the postwar decade when a woman's attachment to the home is taken for granted, as is her ability to combine professional duties with those of a housewife. In 1951, a male discussion on whether it is right that after work a man expects rest and comfort at home, while a woman has to attend to chores, is simply wound up with the appreciative statement: " 'Our wives somehow manage to have time for everything.' "[9]

In the 1920's, however, home and family are reefs on which many a marriage is wrecked in Soviet fiction. Not in the worker or peasant milieu, it should be noted, but in that of the intelligentsia, for reasons economical or ideological, or as in Stepnoy's *The Family*, for both. In Brazhnin's *The Leap*, a young Party executive leaves his bride, Yulochka, because of her bourgeois efforts to beautify their room in a communal apartment. (Young couples aspire to no other home in Soviet fiction.) In V. Veresaev's "Marina's Sickness" (1931), the heroine leaves her husband because of his hostile attitude towards their expected baby, whom she had insisted on having. They are both students and now face sleepless nights warming up formulas on an oil stove in their one room and taking turns in cutting classes to stay with the baby. For these considerations Marina had given in to her husband's arguments before and had one abortion, but then she became literally sick with longing for motherhood, and to satisfy it is now ready to suffer any hardships. In Veresaev's "Isanka," the heroine's mental anguish at her inability to solve the same problems made her the standard-bearer of Soviet students in 1928.

" 'How can a little rug obstruct the Revolution?' " wails Tanya, in G. Alekseev, *The Shadows of the Future* (1928). But her Komsomolets husband keeps protesting in the name of Revolutionary progress against a strip of rug, tulle window curtains, a pink lampshade, and other such "petty-bourgeois notions of cosiness." It is hard for poor Tanya to forgive this masculine insensitivity to her homemaking efforts: it had not been easy to save the needed money on their meager budget nor to buy the articles secondhand in the free market. For that matter, at times it was even dangerous: in *The Family,* before NEP, Lyubochka's father barely escaped arrest trying to buy a pacifier for her.

Generally, in the period preceding the establishment of Socialist Realism, the nobler the hero, the more he opposed a comfortable home, treating it as a vestige of the bourgeois past. In *The Birth of a Hero* (1930) by Yu. Libedinsky, Shorokhov, an old Bolshevik and a ranking Party official, harasses his pregnant young wife Lyuba until she escapes with an understanding Komsomolets. Shorokhov is no monster; on the contrary, he loves Lyuba and suffers, but—a critic explains—in Lyuba's placid embroidering, her pretty bedroom slippers, and a treasured meat-grinder in the kitchen ". . . he recognized the old enemy, the primordial, eternally recurring, hated forms of life. . . . [This is why] he overcame in his soul this immoral love . . . he strove to free his [future] child from the influence of the reactionary family atmosphere of which Lyuba was the embodiment and which was hostile to the socialist future."[10]

Thus, love and marriage have as many vicissitudes in store for young women from the middle class as for their proletarian and peasant sisters. True, they are never brutalized (as peasant brides still were in the fiction of the 1920's) and seldom seduced or abandoned. But their difficulties, created by environment in both the physical and psychological sense, are no less acute for being less obvious.

FEMALE DRONES AND THEIR EMANCIPATION

There is no question that many of the works featuring the middle-class milieu in the 1930's came from the pens of mediocre writers and deserved the accusation of "appalling, cheap vulgarity" (*potrjasajuščaja pošlost'*) leveled against them by contemporary critics. The late 1930's in particular brought a crop of petty adventures of provincial wives. Some are unfaithful to their busy husbands out of sheer boredom, like Lyuba in L. Rubinstein's *Another's Love* (1936) and Vera in A. Pismenny's *In a Small Town* (1938). Others, like Marya, also in Pismenny's novel, fill their days with gossip, or at best, with organizing amateur theatricals. Still others just dream and endlessly talk of true love, like Varya in V. Kurochkin's "A Complicated Affair" (1938).

All these women share one characteristic: none of them is working outside home, or for that matter, in it. They have servants, euphemistically called homeworkers (*domrabotnicy*), and are little interested in housekeeping, children, reading, or anything except love, romantic or sexual, as the case may be. In short, they are drones leading a vegetative existence in the midst of the allegedly exhilarating atmosphere of constructive labor. Too indolent to assume the part of villainesses, they are nevertheless negative characters, though not always necessarily meant to be that. What their authors had strived—and failed—to achieve was psychological complexity.

Female drones did not become extinct in Soviet fiction with the development of Socialist Realism. They have been useful as foils to hard-working, authentically Soviet women; as occasional warnings that remnants of bourgeois vices are still lingering in the Soviet society; and finally as reminders that deficiencies caused by environment can be remedied by work. The first two devices of plot and characterization are standard and have been scattered throughout the works of contemporary Russian fiction; the third, just as common, has never been so forcibly represented as in *The People We Meet* by Yu. German. This novel, whose separate chapters appeared in magazines beginning in 1932, was published in its final and considerably changed form in 1936, when it became a subject of animated discussion.

German's heroine, Tonya, belongs to the generation of Natka Michurina and Isanka, that is, to the Komsomol youth of the NEP period. She is, however, their complete opposite. While they bubble with an excited desire of achievement, Tonya is indolent and simply drifts toward whatever life may have in store for her. Orphaned at sixteen, she first lives by selling her parents' belongings, then without love marries a seaman—a smuggler and a drunkard. After his opportune death in an accident, she accepts the proposal of a prerevolutionary maître d'hôtel, an elderly man whom she does not love and whom she betrays in a chance and futile liaison with a NEPman. She sinks deeper and deeper into sloth. Even her child and the two-room apartment are cared for by a servant.

Yet, Tonya is not a worthless person; she is intelligent, sensitive, honest. But she suffers from a paralysis of will, a total inability to pursue a goal in life, and worst of all, to find a goal. Rescue comes in the form of the model couple, Ivan and Zhenya, the latter, one of the first young women doctors in Soviet fiction. They persuade Tonya to leave her husband (who, in despair, beats her savagely) and shelter her and the child until she recovers. In the healthy atmosphere of this Communist household Tonya at last finds her place in life. She proves a success in kindergarten work and marries a dedicated officer of the Secret Police.

In spite of this happy ending, critics gave but qualified praise to the novel. Tonya, it was said, has the mentality of "a slave, a kept woman, a harem female, a parasite," though the fault, admittedly, is not hers but that of the men in her life. Critics also pointed out that she owed her rescue from the morass of bourgeois existence to luck and not to her own efforts, a non-Soviet way of solving psychological problems, making Tonya into "a Sovietized version of a Turgenev type of young girl." One critic, in charitable, though somewhat backhanded recognition, allows Tonya a useful role in Soviet fiction: "Antonina represents the arrière-garde of the army of socialism," she says. "If people like her have started marching forward, then it shows that our victory is indeed near."[11]

A. N. Tolstoy uses subtler skills than German in transforming Katya and Dasha—pretty, pampered, and frustrated in their quest for a great love—into the contented and useful schoolteacher and nurse. The sisters are not changed solely by deriving noble satisfaction from work well done. To them that work is primarily a haven they reach after having been tossed for years by the waves of the Revolution. They have endured loss of home and property, physical danger, loneliness, and heartache; they have been separated from each other and from their husbands, who were fighting on different sides and whom for a time they thought dead. Since the sisters' dedication to their jobs coincides with the family's reunion at the end of the Civil War (both husbands, moreover, are now officers in the Red Army), the reader, if he chooses, may discount the role played in Katya's and Dasha's bliss by their sense of social usefulness.

Within this period two more works should be mentioned as typical examples of bourgeois mentality cured by the panacea of work. In L. Vaysenberg's story, *The Housewife* (1937), Lyusya wrecks her marriage through her petty attachment to furniture and china knicknacks. Then, forced to sell some of these, she gets a job at a china factory, does very well at decorating dishes, and blossoms into a happy citizeness, wife (she wins back her estranged husband), and potentially, mother. In 1937, a good woman inevitably yearned for motherhood, and the story ends with Lyusya tenderly dandling her infant niece, whose crying used to irritate her in the past.

In A. Malyshkin's novel, *People from the Far Provinces* (1938), Olga, a small-town *femme fatale* deserted by a lover, contemplates suicide. Instead, like her contemporary Steshka in *The Village Bruski*, she enrolls in a course for tractor drivers, and again like Steshka, becomes a different woman. Happy and proud of her efficient performance ("though nowadays her manicured little fingers are all black and blue with bruises!" comments the author gleefully), she is reunited with her husband, a good Soviet man who is engaged on the construction of a gigantic plant in Siberia. There, it is understood, they will live happily ever after.

In the character of Olga there are echoes of her namesake in Chekhov's "The Grasshopper" (1893), who did not realize her husband's moral stature until she lost him. Of course, in Malyshkin's novel Chekhov's point is destroyed by the inevitable happy ending. So it is in Yu. Krymov's *The Tanker Derbent* (1938), where the notorious Soviet "grasshopper," Musya Basova, is slow to realize that she is married to the foremost Stakhanovite hero in Russian fiction. For the two subsequent decades of Socialist Realism fictional heroines would be duly appreciative of their mates. But it is interesting to note the revival of the grasshopper motif in one of those short stories of the 1960's which have been so strongly indebted to Chekhov. For Olga, in E. Kazakevich's "By Daylight" (1961), the shock of discovering her late husband's worth in a conversation with his wartime comrade is softened by the fact that she had already remarried and borne another child. While this can hardly be considered a happy ending, the poignancy of her tragedy is largely lost.

14

Women of the New
Soviet Intelligentsia

Women of the Soviet intelligentsia are purely a product of Socialist Realism. Peasant and proletarian characters in Russian fiction originated in the 1920's from the pens of writers representing their respective milieux, and during the 1930's, developed into the typical heroines of the kolkhoz and industrial novels. Over these years the Fellow Travelers portrayed the decline of the prerevolutionary bourgeoisie and intelligentsia, whose lot they subsequently shared by disappearing from the literary scene. But the women of the Soviet intelligentsia first made their entrance on the eve of World War II, introduced by Soviet writers (no other literary groups had existed since 1932) within the streamlined framework of conformities—ideological, emotional, and those of the craft of fiction.

As a result, they lack a pattern of continuity, and except for a few shortcomings such as the vanity and sloth inherited by negative characters, they have no ties with the past. They were born into the world of Soviet fiction like Athena from the head of Zeus, adult and fully armed ideologically. In the postwar decade, Stakhanovite women truck drivers and milkmaids are spiritual and blood descendants of Katya Dolga and Dasha Chumalova. But dedicated teachers, doctors, and engineers are only occasionally related to their social predecessors. They are daughters of kolkhoz and factory families, or as times goes on, of schoolteachers and Party workers, thus becoming the second generation of Soviet-educated intelligentsia. If orphans of old Bolshevik revolutionaries, particularly of the Chekists, they are proud of their blue blood and usually have inherited a courageous spirit.

That these young women owe their professional and personal excellence to the salubrious Soviet environment is endlessly emphasized. The lover of Nastya, the heroine of Nikolaeva's *A Story about a Director of the MTS and Its Chief Agronomist* (1954) and the agronomist of the title, muses on her thus:

> She grew up in an excellent family. Her father is a well-known steelworker; her brother was posthumously awarded the Red Star for heroism. She attended one of the best Siberian schools, received her practical training in one of the best kolkhozes. She never saw human meanness, lived among excellent people, faced lots of difficulties . . . naturally the result was a character like hers.[1]

And Zhenya Maslova, a graduate student and protagonist of V. Dobrovolsky's representative novel on Soviet university life bearing her name (1950), says: " 'I know that I must live my life doing what is right. How else can I live? I was born under the Soviet regime; I was educated in a Soviet school; my mind matured in a Soviet university.' "[2]

As another result of their late emergence in literature, the protagonists of the intelligentsia are young. Soviet born and educated, they would have to be nineteen years old at most when first introduced as typical contemporary characters in the late 1930's. And of course, youthful enthusiasts—by that time also in their twenties—were the fashion in the postwar era of Soviet Patriotism. It can be surmised that, while their enthusiasm abated somewhat in the following decade, the simultaneous increase of romantic elements in the plot served to keep the age of the heroines under thirty.

In postwar kolkhoz fiction, it may be recalled, the Heroine is preferably middle-aged and a representative of the final stage of woman's emancipation. From the downtrodden baba, through Marya the Bolshevik and Praskovya of *The Bast Shoes*, she had developed into the innovator Avdotya of *The Harvest* and Marya, the kolkhoz chairman in the novel bearing her name. But in the milieu of the intelligentsia of the period, middle-aged women are secondary characters, as they also are in the industrial novels, apparently for the same reason: their daughters are allegedly more representative of Soviet reality and are therefore more entitled to the position of a heroine.

Naturally, not every young woman of the intelligentsia is cast as protagonist, but many are, both before the thaw and after. They either share the leading role in the plot with the Hero, as does Tina with Bakhirev in Nikolaeva's *The Battle on the Way*, or like Ksenya in Sheremeteva's *On a Distant River* (1952) and her namesake in N. Adamyan's *Zero-Three* (1961), they have the stage all to themselves. Some heroines even lend their names to the novel; Dobrovolsky's *Zhenya Maslova*, Koptyaeva's *Comrade Anna* (1946), Lvova's *Elena* (1955), and Rybakov's *Ekaterina Voronina* could be cited. And numerous short stories are dedicated wholly to young professionals intent on doing their duties to the best of their abilities.

We have already noted that the subject matter of Soviet fiction, and it is assumed, the fabric of Soviet life is work. The kind of work for which a fictional character is qualified determines his social status; the efficiency of his performance, his standard of living; its quality, his personal value. Apart from being an economic necessity, work is the one available outlet for personal ambition and the only possible medium for romantic dreams of achievement. It is also a form of equality, since everybody must—and must desire to—work. There is no such thing as a life of complete leisure, at least not a life of respectable leisure. Hence, as in kolkhoz and industrial fiction, the heroines from the intelligentsia are the women who work.

Work, as a rule, takes them away from home. A girl having completed her studies in the city may return to her native kolkhoz as an agronomist or a veterinarian, but generally Soviet authors like to send their heroines to far-off places to prove themselves in new surroundings. Holders of university degrees have no voice in the matter: after graduation a physician or an engineer is assigned to a job by her respective ministry. If all the graduates in a certain year were needed in the provinces, none, it seems, would remain in Moscow, except those few with influential contacts. Whenever possible and for sufficient reasons—a reunion with a fiancé, for instance—a young person may be granted the choice of a particular locality. But more often job assignments depend on luck, and scenes of excited waiting for their announcement are routine in student novels, a genre identical with the industrial novel in everything except the setting, which is a university instead of a factory.

The purely physical effort demanded from a professional girl is tremendous, and writers take great pains to describe it in detail. The

dramatic effect is enhanced by her youth, slenderness, lack of experience, by her courage in challenging the various obstacles on her
path. Some of these obstacles are normal in her profession, such as
complicated cases of illness if she is a physician, or construction troubles if she is an architect. Some are peculiar to Soviet conditions:
traveling long miles by reindeer, horseback, and sometimes on foot
over frozen roads, stormy rivers, and open country.

As a doctor, she is rushed from modern hospitals to snow-bound
villages to deliver babies in filthy Yakut huts and to fight smallpox
(Valentina, in A. Koptyaeva's *Comrade Anna*); as an engineer she
spends days and nights in tense, exhausting work improving ship-
building techniques (Zina, in Kochetov's *The Zhurbins*). As a
meteorologist, she spends stormy nights alone on island weather stations
(Arinka, in Yu. Pomozov's "On the Tsimlan Sea," 1953). As a manager
of a Siberian gold mine, she handles accidents and hunger strikes
(Natalya, in V. Ganibesov's *The Prospectors*, 1948). As a geologist, she
leads expeditions through the wild tundra (Galya, in K. Kloss's *The
Avant-garde*, 1940), flies over the taiga drawing maps from an airplane,
and is injured in an air crash (Marina, in A. Livnev's *Explorers*, 1950).
Yet physical hardships are only part of the story.

These women are not overly emphatic in the manifestations of their
working enthusiasm, perhaps because of the nature of their work,
which does not lend itself to Stakhanovite competition. And there is no
publicity about their excellent performance, no press interviews, pictures in the papers, or trips to the Kremlin to be congratulated by its
current occupant. All a professional woman may expect in recognition
of performance above and beyond the call of duty is a citation from
the government, such as that awarded Ksenya, a pediatrician in a small
Siberian town, for controlling the outbreak of scarlet fever in a neighboring village (in Sheremeteva's *On a Distant River*). But even such
cases are rare. Schoolteachers living in tundra and taiga among native
Siberian tribes—such as Tanya in T. Semushkin's *Chukotka* (1938),
Tanya in B. Gorbatov's "Veretgyrgyn" (1937), and Yula in I. Kratt's
"Yulalanna" (1938)—neither expect nor ever get recognition. Compared to them, the famed milkmaids are spoiled prima donnas.

Except for the joy of duty well done, these young women derive no
tangible benefits from their professional toil. Their salaries are modest,
and since they are in government service, may not be supplemented by
fees from grateful patients and students. Even a promotion to a higher

position usually means little more than increased effort and greater responsibilities, and these are quite high to begin with. A factory or kolkhoz woman, even if she is an innovator, is part of a team effort; in fact, had she insisted on isolating herself from her collective, she would have lost her status as positive character. But a professional woman, as part of the larger and wider spread collective of the working intelligentsia, lives wherever her job takes her, often alone in far-off and lonely places. Moreover, though any heroine in the Brave New World of Soviet fiction can count on advice and encouragement from experienced elders, an Alfa girl is expected to be able to accept responsibilities and make decisions—in short, to be completely on her own.

THE KOMSOMOL
SINCE THE STALINIST ERA

One of the main factors responsible for the ideological upbringing of the Soviet intelligentsia is, as ever, the Komsomol. But the years following the turbulent days of the NEP brought significant changes in its membership and psychological climate. Needless to say, the various distinctive groups such as outsiders and proletarians disappeared; since the beginning of the Stalinist era, the Komsomol in Soviet fiction has been a homogeneous body. Its members are clean-living, happy youths and girls, aged roughly sixteen to twenty-five, engrossed in their studies, or after graduation, in their professional work.

Problems such as those which used to plague their parents in the 1920's have all been solved. The "glass of water" theory had long been discredited, abortions outlawed, family life rehabilitated (indeed, encouraged), the question of whether "a little rug could obstruct the Revolution" answered in the negative, and "Athenian nights" vanished without a trace. Twenty years after "Without Cherry Blossoms," a coed certainly would not be branded as a reactionary for refusing to contract an illicit liaison with a Komsomolets: she would more likely be expelled from the Komsomol if she accepted. Members seldom get married before finishing their studies, even more seldom start families if they do, but somehow this does not lead to tragedies such as Isanka's or Marina's (in Veresaev's "Isanka" and "Marina's Sickness," respectively). In part perhaps, this is due to the improved economic conditions of student life, but the credit, as usual, goes to the Soviet environment, the family, and the Komsomol.

The Komsomol from the start has been the ideological nursery from which the best saplings were eventually chosen for transplantation into the Communist Party. Hence, the attitudes of the young members of the intelligentsia towards their Komsomol and the Party, which they expect to join in their middle twenties, differ from those of the populace in that the element of awe and mystery is absent. They are the initiated: every student acquires, as part of his college curriculum, a solid education in Marxism-Leninism (and/or Stalinism, depending on the period). Moreover, men may expect to achieve a prominent position in the Party hierarchy, though, as will be discussed later, women cannot count on that.

Therefore, the relationship of Komsomol members to Party advisers is on a friendly business level, rather than that of a confessional. But Communist spirit and discipline are high. The first thing a heroine does on arriving at a new job is to report to the local Komsomol and assume some responsibilities, usually connected with her profession—for instance, lectures on hygiene by physicians or on literature by teachers. As before, the Komsomol membership has the collective duty of watching over and passing judgment on each other's ethical standards and the quality of professional or scholarly performance. The same, incidentally, is true of the Party membership, though during the post-Stalinist decade voices were raised arguing that, in both institutions, personal life should be exempt.[3] And, as always, they answer the Party's call to duty. It could be the building of the Moscow Underground, as shown by A. Nozdrin's coeds in *Line One* (1938); or the building of a trans-Siberian oil pipeline during world War II, as in the case of Tanya, under whose leadership feats of endurance were performed by youthful technicians of both sexes in V. Azhaev's *Far from Moscow* (1948); or the cultivation of the virgin lands in Siberia as it was for the heroes of D. Granin's *After the Wedding* (1958).

Religion, unsurprisingly, plays no role in the psychological makeup of these Komsomol members. The anti-religious demonstrations which were an important part of Komsomol activities in the 1920's have long become obsolete. Conversions and sectarianism, which still furnish occasional plot material for kolkhoz fiction, are unknown among the intelligentsia as are, of course, superstitions. The latter are treated in Soviet fiction as part of the Christian faith, and the younger generation of readers in the Soviet Union would probably be surprised if told that the Church has always considered superstitions pagan and fought them as such. A few unsophisticated and very recent members of the young intelligentsia, such as Lyuba, a miner's daughter teaching kindergarten in Ketlinskaya's *No Sense in Living Otherwise,* may in moments of distress utter a short prayer. But, as the author hastens to explain, this is proof not of faith but of insufficient vocabulary: "She did not believe in God, but could not find other words to express her passionate request for happiness." Better educated heroines who could, would no more invoke God's help than that of Santa Claus. But neither, it must be added, do they turn to look at the portrait of Stalin for moral support as do women from the masses, who have simple Communist faith. Nor do they exclaim, "So, it was Marx's will that we should meet again!" as did the young sophisticates of the 1920's.[4]

They do, however, believe in progress and in science, and that through these humanity will eventually achieve happiness on earth, and in its continuity, an immortality of sorts. Since they do not doubt that this goal will first be achieved by the Soviet Union, led and guided by the Communist Party, the Party, the Fatherland, and Progress became to them almost synonymous concepts for which they have genuine loyalty and unstinted devotion.

It is necessary to make a distinction between the wage earners and the career women. The former—grade school teachers, laboratory technicians, nurses, librarians—in psychological makeup are only a notch above the sisters they have left behind in kolkhozes or mining district communities. The latter—physicians, engineers, scientific workers—are the sophisticated women of Soviet fiction. Both groups are capable of selfless dedication befitting a Joan of Arc, a Florence Nightingale, or a Saint Clara of Assisi. But girls with degrees acquired in special schools for peasants and factory workers (rabfaki) and through correspondence courses excel in the physical brand of heroism, while college-educated young women are superior in the ideological. The ensuing disparities in their characterization are of importance.

WAGE EARNERS

While readily accepting physical hardships, young professional women, unlike Stakhanovite working girls, do not undertake them for the sake of emulating men. They simply consider themselves fit for any profession, and should it involve hard conditions and strenuous effort, they accept these as a matter of course.

Since the mid-1930's, women in traditionally masculine vocations have been much in vogue in Soviet fiction. There are sailors, such as Lena, the ship-pilot, and Katya, the ship-cook; fliers, like Vera and Natasha; radio-operators on island weather stations in the Arctic, like Oksana;[5] and any number of technicians shown braving the elements on scientific expeditions, such as Nastya, in A. Karalina's *The Seekers* (1940) and Zoya in V. Starikov's "The Wind" (1954). Such exploits in no way impair their feminine image, either in the eyes of critics, who hail in them a "combined charm of a Turgenev's Russian girl and the willpower, self-discipline, and endurance of a conqueror of the grim Arctic land,"[6] or in the eyes of men. Katya, the ship-cook, and radio-operator Oksana even became centers of rivalry among their colleagues; and a girl flier's lover exclaims:

> "When she leaves the airplane and begins the fall—small like a pebble, my little darling! . . . there I am, standing and trembling at the thought that the parachute may not open . . . and suddenly it does, dazzling like a silver flower. . . . Sometimes I wonder, what is it I love in her? Well, of course her lips, her legs, her smile . . . but most of all I love her courage, her lightness, the victories she wins over her own self!"[7]

In the postwar decade the popularity of unorthodox skills diminished, though not by any means the readiness to work in routine jobs under difficult conditions. There exists in this period a whole crop of dedicated small-town librarians (like Lera in S. Georgievskaya's *The Silver Word*, 1955), school teachers (like Valya in Rytkheu's "Five Letters of Valya Komarenko," 1955), and nurses (like Shurochka in Sheremeteva's *On a Distant River*), all working hard and uncomplainingly, usually in Siberia.

It is interesting to observe how thin is the line separating these professional specialists from the skilled factory workers, particularly the Stakhanovites. Aspiring to higher degrees of education than the one possessed is inherent in any positive character in Soviet fiction. Nurses' aides, for instance, find time to study and to win the Soviet equivalent of a nurse's cap; graduate nurses strive to become doctors—and some do, like Varya whose progress from an illiterate Yakut girl to an outstanding surgeon is traced over a period of nine years in three novels;[8]

and busy surgeons dream of continuing research, and in time, of doctoral dissertations.

This trend is particularly noticeable among the less educated heroines, and the boundary between the toiling masses and the intelligentsia is constantly crossed by ambitious girls. The brightest among them may get a fellowship and acquire an academic degree. Student novels occasionally use them as foils to that inevitable negative character, the spoiled coquette, a professor's daughter. But one seldom meets them later as career women, because these usually belong to the second generation of the Soviet intelligentsia unlike, one might note, heroes who are self-made men. Mostly, the kolkhoz girls attend some professional courses in the nearest town, the factory workers combine their jobs with study in a rabfak, or both may take correspondence courses, as many housewives prefer to do. Sometimes they choose to apply their newly acquired skills at home, introducing new methods. In the period of varnished reality following World War II they are rewarded by being cast as protagonists, or by marrying one, or both.

One thinks, for example, of Dasha instructing miners in new techniques at the bottom of the coal shaft, of Klavdya growing new and sophisticated vegetables in her kolkhoz, of Grunya working near-miracles in a fish hatchery, of Katya fighting old-fashioned methods of raising calves—the list is practically endless.[9] If the agronomists Tonya (in *It Happened at Penkovo*) and Nastya (in M. Zhestev's *The Golden Ring*, 1958) are frustrated in their efforts at improving kolkhoz conditions, and if Akulina (in A. Yashin's "The Levers," 1956), resignedly continues teaching in an unheated classroom, this is because they are already living in a period when Cinderellas no longer ride in golden coaches.

Daughters of the masses, born under Socialist Realism, the wage earners follow in their characterization the general pattern of the typical Soviet girl of the period. Consequently, they can conveniently be summed up, as was Varya in Erenburg's *The Second Day of Creation*, as "snub-nosed Russian girl[s] with stout calves and . . . kind heart[s]."[10] They show less interest in pink dresses and cheap earrings than do their less educated peasant sisters; they are not so coyly sweet as the little pig-tailed nurses in the novels about the Civil War and World War II. But they too had been taught at school, simultaneously with the multiplication tables, that the earth belongs to the solar system and that the certain coming of Communism will save the world; and they are equally disinclined to doubt either of these axioms. If their feelings are not strongly expressed, they still are warm and proper; their principles are sound, and their morals impeccable. In the rare cases when they are not—like Katya's, in Kochetov's *The Zhurbins*, or Rita's, in A. Bek's *The Young People* (1954)—the girl is always the victim of a crafty seducer. Naïvely, she trusts him as she knows she can trust a Soviet man, and he fails her because he is not one in spirit: he likes all things Western, and he might even have traveled abroad.

Otherwise, since the introduction of Socialist Realism and the recognition of the Soviet family and morality in the Constitution, young love has invariably culminated in a visit to the marriage registration bureau (ZAGS) and a Komsomol wedding, as merry as those in the kolkhozes, if less exotic. Champagne, flowers, and group photographs are *de rigueur*. Wedding rings are exchanged—"a handsome ancient custom," according to a contemporary source,[11] and they are indeed so popular that sometimes shortages occur. The bride wears white and even occasionally a veil, and in 1961 a divorcee may expect to be denied the privilege of a Komsomol wedding, just as she would a church ceremony in the nineteenth century.[12] All of this is a far cry from the mores of the 1920's, when "free love unions" were customarily announced, when couples "signed up" in dingy ZAGS offices while the clerk was shouting, "Next!" or when a bride would count out her half of the license fee in small change.[13]

Married, wage earners make excellent wives, mothers, and companions of the hard-working builders of Socialism. They are usually builders in their own right, but are also allowed to be just housewives and mothers, provided they stay active in the affairs of their communities. Their chief characteristic, however, is that they are faithful followers. In that capacity they range from wives (occasionally uneducated) of workers with special skills to wives of influential government executives. A carefully observed convention is that both groups belong on equal terms to the Soviet spiritual aristocracy.

In extreme cases, they lead a nomadic existence, traveling over the entire expanse of the Soviet Union from whatever building project their husbands are engaged in to the next, often changing their own jobs to suit his. They raise their families in temporary huts, never own a piece of furniture, and are forever leaving behind a vegetable garden or a friendship. In E. Uspenskaya's *The Wife of Him Who Strides Forward* (1958), Anya, the teacher wife of a building engineer in charge of an impressive excavator, sums up the situation thus: " 'Sisters mine! we all are wives of those who stride forward. Brides of fliers and miners. Mothers of soldiers and geologists. Daughters of sailors and foresters. We are all wives of those striding forward.' "[14]

It is interesting, however, to note that in 1962 (in B. Polevoy's *On the Wild Shore*) Ganna, wife of a famous excavator but herself just a golden-hearted homebody, rebelled. After fifteen uncomplaining years of gypsy life, she sobs out an ultimatum to her astonished husband: unless this latest move to a project in the Siberian wilderness be the last, she will take the children and leave. And, she asks, what is the use of their wanderings and his fame? Who will remember it, anyway? Their boy, who is fifteen, has never even heard of Aleksey Stakhanov![15]

Nevertheless, Ganna does not carry out her threat, and the end of the novel finds her settling down in another temporary home. This time it is a pretty cottage for the project's elite, which will make it even harder to leave. Her next-door neighbor is the partorg's wife, Lamara, who also is following "him who strides forward," and has just left a deluxe apartment in Vladivostok.

Ganna's outburst is a recent, and so far, a lonely phenomenon. Since the first industrial novels, men in Soviet fiction "have loved their workshops as one can only love a human being,"[16] and wives have soon learned to let that triumphant rival take precedence of them. Zina, in D. Kasimov's "The Green Light" (1935), cheerfully concedes that her husband cannot spare the time to take her to the hospital, or to bring her and their baby home; a taxi will have to do on both trips. Valya (in T. Leonova's "A Wife," 1953), waiting with two small children for her doctor husband to summon them to his new job location, bears him no grudge for forgetting to send them money for groceries, rent, and tickets. After all, she loves this homeless, overworked man and is proud of him, too.

And there are any number of wives like the schoolteacher Maryanna (in Panova's *Seryozha*, 1955), who leaves a sickly child behind to follow her husband, suddenly transferred to the directorship of a remote State farm; or like the nameless wife of architect Loshakov (in Sheremeteva's *On a Distant River*), who demands to join her husband in a new town which he is building in Siberia. This readiness to follow her mate anywhere, succinctly worded long since in the Roman marriage vows—*Ubi tu, Caius, ibi ego, Caia*—is nevertheless acclaimed as a peculiarly Soviet virtue.

Generally, marriages in what may be termed the Soviet lower middle-class milieu are happy. Wives, whether wage earners or homemakers, are good cooks, and both spouses are faithful and fond of family life. Their relationship is rather like that in the workers' households; in fact, these couples often are workers until the husband acquires higher professional qualifications and moves to a higher position. When the wife achieves this status first, she is the one who is anxious to reestablish marital equality. For instance, Masha, in S. Sartakov's *Don't Surrender the Queen* (1960), having earned a degree in engineering through correspondence courses, immediately insists on her husband's doing the same. So, ten years earlier, does the agronomist Shura (in Kapusto's *The Bread Growers*) in a similar situation, and the author comments: "This [still] was the voice of ambition, yet it was no longer the determined agronomist speaking, but the woman, whose ambition consists not in being superior to the man she loves, but in seeing him superior to everyone else, including herself."[17] This being the correct attitude expected of a wife, misalliances have been a popular topic in Soviet fiction. Such marriages, between educated girls and simple proletarians, are frequent and will be discussed later in this chapter.

CAREER WOMEN

The first women to engage in liberal professions appeared in Soviet fiction in the early 1930's. Some of them, while completely integrated with and serving the toiling masses, had also inherited the sensual temperament and the less than credible brilliance of the New Women of the 1920's. It is not clear, for instance, how and when Fenya and Tanya in Gladkov's *Energy*, Part I (1932) received their diplomas: during the Civil War, the reader is told, they were homeless orphans living in the streets (besprizornye). But they miraculously become beautiful *femmes fatales* (Fenya, a petite blonde; Tanya, a sultry brunette) whose skill as engineers put to shame male colleagues from the prerevolutionary intelligentsia. And Masha, a physician in Panfyorov's *The Village Bruski*, Part II (1930), though a Party member and of impeccable proletarian descent, is more interested in sex than in medicine. Other characters remind one of the collaborating outsiders of the NEP period; Vera, a dedicated and able engineer in I. Erenburg's novel *Breathless* (1935) is an example. For one thing, her father was a lawyer;

for another, she prefers to prove her devotion to the Soviet Union by helping to build the town of Kuznetsk in Siberia, rather than by joining the Komsomol. Her mother dies believing that Vera has "outsmarted them," but this is not true; for Vera, in spite of the fact that she is loyal and Soviet-educated, does not qualify as a member of the typical Soviet intelligentsia.

Perhaps it is Zhenya, the young physician who rescued Tonya from the quagmire of a bourgeois life in German's *The People We Meet,* who can be considered the harbinger of the type which became established under the Socialist Realism. She is an educated, young Soviet woman who knows how to combine a happy personal life with a fascinated interest in her profession.

In the postwar decade this goal is achieved by career girls in much the same way as by other women in kolkhoz and industrial novels. In the case of the career girls, however, the accent is on showing characters within their profession rather than on displaying efficient production by means of characters. And the reader is allowed some insight into the heroines' thoughts and emotions, approximately to the degree possible in Western fiction of the eighteenth or early nineteenth centuries.

Romance for a career girl consists in reciprocating the respectful affection of an eligible young man whom she marries at the end of the book. But work to her is a challenge and a way of life. The reader is informed of the dosage of medicines she prescribes for her patients and of minute details in the operations she performs; he watches, step by step, her scientific experiments in laboratories; he thrills at the sight of a perfect piece of machinery which she turns out, after scrupulously reported efforts, as a triumphant engineer. Medicine, scientific research, and engineering, incidentally, are the three professions in which career girls most frequently appear in Soviet fiction. There are practically no scholars, professors, writers, or actresses,* and very few journalists. Arts are represented by several painters and sculptresses (mostly negative characters), but there are no women musicians and no poetesses. Artists of either sex, however, play but a small role in a literature whose avowed goal is to portray the average members of toiling masses. Therefore, this is scarcely a case of antifeminist discrimination.

---

* Anka in K. Fedin's *Bonfire* (1961, 1965) is an exception, but then she had dreamed of becoming an actress since childhood (in the two preceding novels: *First Joys,* 1945, and *An Unusual Summer,* 1948).

The career girl is one of the most popular types in postwar Soviet literature. Young, attractive, though never a dazzling beauty, she is introduced by a favorite plot pattern as having just received her degree and been assigned to her first job. She has taken leave of her friends and fellow students, of her family, perhaps of a young man. The story begins with her reporting to the authorities at the place of her employment and being assigned living quarters, usually a room in somebody's house. Should she find it necessary to improve something on the job—and she will—she will appeal to the administrative authorities of the district and will be helped by a dependable, wise Party secretary without whom no Soviet work of fiction is complete. She will find him chaste, selfless, and dedicated to the constant quest for the future under Communism. In fact, Sir Galahad, properly instructed in Marxism, would make a very acceptable Party secretary.

From this point on, her life will be determined by the technical problems of her work and by her own performance. A few examples may help to establish the pattern. Ksenya, a pediatrician in Shereme-teva's *On a Distant River*, gives up graduate work in Moscow to join her fiancé, Boris, a geologist in a small Siberian town. They plan on marrying at once, but he has to leave for field work in the taiga. She begins work in the hospital, discovers some unsatisfactory conditions there, fights them, and wins the community's sympathy. An opportunity occurs for Boris and her to transfer to jobs where they need not be separated, but Ksenya decides that she has no right to desert a district with four thousand children and no other pediatrician. The reader, however, can have no doubts that they will marry and be happy on their separate jobs: in the midst of tense work, Ksenya feels, " 'there is no time to think about personal matters.' "

Nastya (in Nikolaeva's *A Story about a Director of MTS and Its Chief Agronomist*) is fresh from school and naïvely enthusiastic. Finding that in the MTS not enough attention is being paid to poorer kolkhozes, while more successful ones get preferential treatment, Nastya protests, thus antagonizing the local authorities. She fights against them stubbornly, and in the end not only makes her opponents realize that she represents the Party's concern for the people's welfare, but wins the love of the opponent who is the first to appreciate her moral superiority.

Nina, a safety engineer in S. Antonov's "Her First Job" (1952), begins her career on a big construction project. While wrestling with

some unsatisfactory conditions, she antagonizes her director and workers, particularly one reckless and stubborn young man with whom, she
soon realizes, she has fallen in love. Unfortunately, he is engaged to a
pretty bricklayer, and Nina, refusing a chance to transfer to a less
harassing job, seeks to cure her heartache through the challenge of
further constructive work.

As these examples show, these are courageous girls. Secure in their
freedom from doubts, they are prepared to fight for what they are
certain is right at any cost to their career or personal happiness. Because
they are fighting human failings, or even iniquities, rather than nature,
the anguish they may suffer in the process is spiritual rather than
physical. This is not to say that a geologist lives in comfort in a forest
camp, or that a physician is not exposed to inclement weather on her
way to the patients; and everyone's working load is heavy, and hours
are long. But unlike women with less education, the career girls face
the challenge on a more exalted psychological level.

A career girl must know how to make decisions and accept responsibility for them. The scope of these responsibilities is not wide, because
the jobs as directors of factories, of hospitals, and of research institutes
are held, as a rule, by men. Still, if an accident is traced to her
negligence or even to a plain mistake, she faces court action and
possibly a few years in a labor camp (like Nina, in A. Smirnov's
"Engineer Nestorova," 1947). She has competitors in her special field
and is bound to make friends and enemies on her job. But in all her
professional relationships she uses her sense and not her sensibilities, her
brains and not her emotions. She is guided solely by the dictates of
duty. She is correct and reserved with directors, friendly with colleagues, helpful to and polite with subordinates; but the moment she
decides that any of them is deficient in his working performance, she is
up in arms and spares no one, herself least of all.

With that, career girls do not look pugnacious. On the contrary,
they rather resemble the delicate and prim heroines of Victorian novels. Usually small in stature (Ksenya, for example, is often taken for a
schoolgirl), fair, and blue-eyed, they are without a trace of coquetry in
their manner or dress. Nastya still wears her hair in two braids held
over the temples with black ribbon bows. This hairdo was her grandmother's choice on little Nastya's first day of school, and she has never
seen any reason to change it. " 'These simply are not the things this girl
is living by,' " the hero comments appreciatively.[18]

Not all career women are so indifferent to their appearance, though no positive character ever visits a beauty salon. They do use perfume and lipstick, but discreetly, since in Soviet fiction heavy makeup, and for some reason, manicures are the badges of villainesses, especially aging drones overly concerned with preserving their waning beauty. Nadezhda Bartoshevich (in V. Panova's *The Seasons*, 1953) and Alevtina Stepanova (in Yu. German's *The Cause You Serve*, 1958), for example, never smile as a precaution against wrinkles. But no respectable woman of their age (or, for that matter, of any age) is on record as using face cream for this purpose. And the mother of the seventeen-year-old Galya in Aksyonov's *Ticket to the Stars*, concerned about her daughter's reputation, angrily wipes lipstick off the girl's lips in public.

In any case, a heroine does not necessarily have to be pretty to be popular. The combination of old-fashioned femininity with professional skill is irresistible to men. The able engineer Iskra in Kochetov's *The Brothers Ershov* is described through an admirer's eyes as "about five feet tall; eyes small, black, snapping [she also wears glasses]; a snub nose; solid little legs, not too shapely . . . a little monkey in belted overalls, rather plump though small-waisted."[19] But a Soviet man is understood to be most susceptible to those details in the appearance of his beloved which prove her professional efficiency. Nina's husband inhales with relish the faint smell of antiseptics clinging to the clothes of his physician wife. Engineer Tina's lover cannot wait to "fiercely embrace the slight, tired girl, with a smoke-blackened neck and the smell of fumes lingering in her rough short hair."[20]

They are not slatterns, to be sure, and will wear a pretty dress as naturally as they wear quilted pants and clumsy boots on an arctic expedition. It is just that costume serves primarily as means of characterization, and positive characters do not consider clothes a matter of importance. To illustrate, Dina (in Polevoy's *On the Wild Shore*), as the frustrated wife of an executive who forbids her to practice medicine, is carefully described as wearing a scarlet sweater, tight slacks, and an elegant fur coat in a Siberian construction camp. After she leaves her husband in order to take up strenuous, utterly satisfying work in the camp's hospital, much is made of her white doctor's uniform and sheepskin coat which set off her new, subtler beauty. In V. Dudintsev's much discussed novel, *Not by Bread Alone* (1956), a mink coat figures so prominently that it could almost be considered a dramatis persona. A status symbol as elsewhere, it is sacrificed by the heroine to enable the hero to complete work on his invention, and is acquired by a lazy socialite who makes it a graduation gift to her pampered daughter, the hero's fiancée. Because the girl has no faith in the invention, she keeps the mink but loses the hero to the heroine.

The young professional woman, then, is unassuming and modest. It goes without saying that she is also innocent and chaste, at least until the thaw, when she may meet an unworthy man and prove too trusting. She is not, however, always cast as an ingenue. Beautiful, ambitious young women are also popular contestants to the title of the Heroine.

These are elegant young women—no childish ribbon bows for them—brilliant and proud, occasionally even haughty. Love for them is not a naïve boy-meets-girl story; it comes as a storm, a revelation, when they are in their late twenties, and sometimes after a traumatic earlier disappointment. And while love, as always, ends in happy marriage, its path is not uniformly smooth.

Nor are their lovers like the youthful colleagues whom the ingenues meet at a university dance or in classrooms. They are mature, strong men engaged in important work. Nonna's is Listopad, a widower, a former Army general and now the director of the gigantic plant where she herself is employed as an engineer (in Panova's *The Factory Kruzhilikha*). Marina's Ozerov is a partorg, also in a gigantic plant where she is employed as an engineer and married to an unworthy woman, who, fortunately, divorces him (in O. Ziv's *The Ardent Hour*, 1951). The romance of the Army surgeon, Major Alexandra Goreva (in P. Pavlenko's *Happiness*), and the much-decorated war hero, Colonel Voropaev, started after she had amputated his leg in the field hospital. And though Andrey, whom Marina (in D. Granin's *The Seekers*, 1954) has chosen among her many suitors, is an engineer like herself, he is an inventor of genius absorbed in his work, which is vitally important for the nation's economy.

That these brilliant women are ready to pursue their careers a step behind their mates is a curious feature in their characterizations—a form of patriotism as well as of sweet femininity. This is not just because of their love, but because theirs are outstanding Soviet men. Nonna, the reader is told, loves Listopad "because his perspectives and the scope of his interests are on the same scale as those of the whole plant, indeed, are identical, since he and the plant have become as one."[21] She is an able engineer, a first-class citizen in her own right, but has no illusions as to the place she is going to occupy in her future marriage. Although she is ill with pneumonia, he leaves her in order to attend an important business meeting in Moscow; and she thinks, during a hasty good-bye: "It is going to be this way, always. He will never give up anything in the name of love, will make no concessions. Giving things up, making concessions, conciliating, waiting, will be for her alone. . . . She took his big hand resting on her hair and kissed it."[22] And Marina, the self-willed, proud beauty, does not resent her fiancé's being hours late for a rendezvous. She realizes that after they are married

> she is going to sit and wait for him, exactly as she is doing at this moment. And he will forget about her, engrossed in his work. He is tractable and gentle so long as things go well with his project, ready to comply with her wishes in everything. But should she stand in his way, he will pass over her like a tank.
> "Will I be happy? [she asks herself] Yes. Why? Because I want it to be like this. This is the most difficult and the most precious thing in life. Is it so difficult though, when you are in love?"[23]

This relationship is illustrative of the position a woman occupies in Soviet fiction. Economically, she is completely independent; her education, career, civic duties, professional responsibilities, and rewards are similar in all respects to those of men. In short, an *average* woman is absolutely equal to an *average* man. But she is seldom allowed to be anything more than average, whether in good or evil.

Thousands of fictional works which have been produced in the three decades following the establishment of Socialist Realism, have used basically the same plot. Somewhere in the Soviet Union in a plant, a kolkhoz, or a hospital, good Soviet citizens work to bring Communism a step nearer reality. Their efforts, until the inevitable final triumph, are frustrated by the inertia of negative characters and actively obstructed by villains. There are a considerable number of women cast in both positive and negative roles, but there are no female villains. Women are never wreckers, or saboteurs, or murderers; they are not expelled from the Party, or sent to labor camps, or even found guilty of ideological deviations. A woman's wrongdoings are possible only within the domain of morals and manners, within the specifically Soviet way of life.

Conversely, however intelligent, educated, or dedicated a Soviet heroine may be, she does not rise above the invisible ceiling assigned to a woman's career. She may invent a laborsaving device, and overcoming the opposition of some negative character, gain general recognition; but this is no more than that which any secondary male character can aspire to in Soviet fiction. Heroes know greater vicissitudes, headier triumphs, and of course, are eligible to higher offices in bureaucracy and particularly in Party hierarchy.

A Party executive, perusing the list of candidates for the job of the Party representative in a research institute, crosses out two women's names: "It was not that he had a low opinion of women [as Party leaders] in general. In textile mills, schools, hospitals, cafeterias, a woman, he granted, could do all right. But for a research institute or a plant—surely, there was no shortage of men in the Party?"[24] This reluctance to put women into positions of responsibility in Party bureaucracy is shared by authors; they seldom do so. If they do, they seldom let the experiment end in success. The patent stolidity of women partorgs in the kolkhozes has already been mentioned, but elsewhere partorgs are exclusively men. On the rare occasions when a woman does occupy a position on the district level in the Party bureaucracy, she proves unsatisfactory. One district secretary, Anna in N. Virta's *Steep Hills* (1956), is intelligent but conceited; another, Agniya in V. Tendryakov's *A Tight Knot* (1956–57), is garrulous and lacks initiative. In two of Tendryakov's stories, Nina, the district secretary of the Komsomol, decorates her office with lace doilies to insure a cozy atmosphere, but stays insensitive to young people's problems (in *The Outsider*); and Raisa, the school superintendent, is a hysterical spinster and a bureaucrat (in *Chasing Fleeting Time*, 1959). It may be assumed that Tendryakov obviously had living models to choose from, but did not do so until the thaw.

Another point of interest is the attitude of educated women toward the West. The question does not arise for proletarian and kolkhoz women; as far as they are concerned, civilized life ends at the frontiers of the Soviet Union. Beyond lies a frightening world of exploitation and misery from which they are protected by the vigilance of the Party. This seems to suffice, for while men in Soviet fiction may occasionally vent their indignation at the warmongering capitalists, these women do not pay even this small token of interest to the outside world.

Women from the intelligentsia are naturally more cosmopolitan in their interests, though they never travel and their authors very seldom permit personal contacts with foreign tourists or diplomats at home. They learn foreign languages for practical purposes, scientific or technical, but if they ever read Western fiction they do it unbeknown to the reader. Still, especially since the thaw, they are exposed to foreign influences: fashions, records, movies, dances, even a few imported luxuries such as perfume. Somehow, they are even familiar with modern art, though—again, as far as the reader knows—they never visit any Western exhibitions.

Needless to say, positive characters are immune to Western influence; the average wage earner, the least sophisticated of the group, has little opportunity to be exposed to it; career women, as standardbearers of Soviet culture, spurn the decadent culture of the West. One talented girl, for instance, cannot master her role in a play staged by the drama section of the local Komsomol: she is simply unable to live the part of a heartless American girl.[25]

Conversely, negative characters, fascinated by deceptive glitter, seek Western contacts and become tainted by capitalist manners and morals. Because Western tastes are not only reprehensible but also expensive in the Soviet Union, such negative characters, as a rule, are members of the privilegentsia. Therefore they play a more significant role during the thaw than during the postwar period of varnished reality, when they were assumed to be few and unimportant exceptions in a near-perfect society. These women are to be met in artistic and intellectual circles. (Soviet engineers are no more exposed to ideological and moral contamination than are factory workers.) The acid test is their attitude towards Western trends in art. The corrosive influence of modernism was dramatized, it will be remembered, in the case of Tatyana, the Soviet Mata Hari in Panfyorov's *In the Name of Youth* (1960). A model of Soviet womanhood until she turned from painting kolkhoz scenes to modernistic portraits, she then went from frustration to immorality to ruin, her own and her family's. On the other hand, Yulya in Kochetov's *The Secretary of the Obkom* (1961) is a coquette who cynically boasts of her scandalous past—a lost soul actually—but she has the redeeming quality of being a good painter who dislikes modernism in art. True love and a happy marriage restore her to virtue. In both cases the message is made painstakingly clear by the two authors, staunch supporters of Socialist Realism.

In contrast, Nekrasov's novel *Kira Georgievna* (1961)—a rare example of unjudicious handling by a defiant writer—is a perceptive portrayal of a coldly egotistic, amoral personality. The heroine is an avant-garde sculptress, still slim and attractive at forty-one, who betrays her invalid husband with a brawny young model, while trying to win back her former husband, already remarried and a father. She not only goes unpunished, but is not even considered a negative character by her environment. This, however, a critic insists, is because she is so untypical of Soviet reality that the normal Soviet citizen is unable to discover her real identity.[26]

Marriage, whether to an executive or to a rank-and-file professional, does not interfere with a career woman's work. In this respect the Soviet middle-class ménage resembles that of peasants and proletarians. In the postwar decade, and until the thaw, it is free from the plot themes, such as jealousy, unfaithfulness, and divorce, traditionally associated with the milieu. But marriage, for women, does have its own set of problems, just as it would have had for men were they responsible for both their professional performance and the family life, as are women.

The "absentee wife" (*zaočnaja žena*) Annushka Lipatova, in Ketlinskaya's *No Sense in Living Otherwise*, is typical of all the professional women whose work involves long absences from home. Annushka, a geologist, is forever participating in expeditions to "places mostly unmarked on the maps," leaving at home her husband—an excellent engineer, who, out of loneliness, is drinking more than is good for him—and a daughter, who, raised by an aunt in another town, is growing up a regular tomboy. Nina, in Panova's *The Seasons*, also a geologist, spends ten months of the year away from her family, which consists of her husband, mother, and a little girl. Koptyaeva's *Comrade Anna*, manager of a gold mine, relies completely on a housekeeper for the care of her husband, child, and home; Kaverin's *Doctor Vlasenkova* (1952) relies on her mother-in-law. Irina, an engineer in A. Chakovsky's *The Peaceful Days* (1947), wife of a Party worker, leaves him to his job and follows hers to Siberia. Agronomist Valentina, in *Harvest*, and her husband, also a Party worker, have been married for ten years, and have never yet had a home together. In the last two cases, the couples are childless, and this makes a difference.

Doctor Vlasenkova, returning from a scientific expedition, finds that

> the apartment had been specially cleaned, the curtains freshly laundered and starched, the table set with wine, apples, and a cake baked in honor of [her] arrival. Little Paul, dressed in his best suit with a white bow,

small and roly-poly, was sitting on the sofa . . . he put his arms around [his mother's] neck and kissed her several times, repeating, "Tanya, you are here! You'll stay, won't you?"[27]

She will not, and this is precisely where the difficulty lies. Career women—who, incidentally, are not prolific mothers and seldom have more than one child—consider their professional responsibilities first, much as they would like to dedicate more time to their children. The latter, it may be noted, are brighter than their proletarian counterparts and often show as much individuality as any adult is allowed in Soviet fiction. There even exists a type of junior heroine, a pretty little girl, spoiled or neglected by her busy parents, like Comrade Anna's Marinka, or Annushka's Irishka. And it was only for these children's sakes that the basic premise of Soviet fiction, the priority of work over personal life, has been ever questioned.

The idea that a child needs a home and a mother was strongly stated by Gladkov as early as in 1932 in *Energy*. Miron, the partorg of a huge dam construction, and his wife Olga, a factory director, live and work apart, as they have since the Revolution. Eight years earlier, their son, Kiryushik, ran away from their desolate home and disappeared, leaving his parents to lifelong mutual reproaches. Gladkov's question—isn't a mother's place at home rather than on a man's job?—was not raised as poignantly again in Soviet fiction for the next thirty years, when the results of maternal absenteeism became apparent in their children's behavior.

It may be of some significance that the two most notorious young heroines of the post-Stalinist era, Galya in Aksyonov's *A Ticket to the Stars* and Kena in Chubakova's *I Want Happiness* (1961) have had no normal family life. Galya dreams of a movie actress's career and follows an affair with an aging film star by one with a former high school sweetheart. "This girl, at seventeen, has already lived with two men!" exclaimed horrified critics.[28] She has no father, and her mother is working as an inspector of schools. Kena, also seventeen, is a school dropout drifting on a stream of meaningless flirtations toward the final tragedy. She lives with her grandmother, who had brought her up, her parents, both engineers, having always been away on geological expeditions. As a final negative touch to their characterization, both girls are fond of jazz and dancing and indifferent to Komsomol activities.

As to the feelings of husbands and fathers in this matter, they may have been voiced by a Captain Trokhov, who wants his wife to stay home and take care of their son while he is at sea. " 'She wants to work, if you please,' " he says; " 'she wants to help build universal welfare with her own lily-white hands! Now, I can do that better myself for both of us!' " His own mother, he reminisces, had worked, and as a result, by the age of ten he was "a first-class hooligan." He does not want his son to have a similar childhood.[29] The reaction of the Captain's wife is predictable: she leaves him and has to be coaxed back. This is not, of course, because she is a poor wife and mother, but because she—a Soviet fictional Heroine—knows how to rate marital and professional problems in the order of their importance.

Marital problems depend on husbands. It is true that even the most understanding Party workers occasionally break down and insist on their right to have a homemaker for a wife. Andrey, in *The Harvest*, during a bout with influenza, implores Valentina to stay with him for a while. Lipatov, in *No Sense in Living Otherwise*, demands that Annushka return home if she does not want him to become an alcoholic. But these are only passing moments of weakness. A really worthy husband should be willing to say, as does Zinaida's: " 'I do not want our family to hang on you like a dead weight. . . . I want you to live and work to your fullest abilities always, notwithstanding the family, or even perhaps because of it!' "[30] She does, leaving the housekeeping and the babysitting to the grandmother. And in V. Ketlinskaya's *The Days of Our Lives* (1952) a factory director, Nemirov, proudly says to an elderly general he had met on the train:

> "My wife and I are almost comrades-in-arms!"
> "You are a very lucky man [replies the general, who himself is married to a pretty, fun-loving little woman]. And you should not mind her being too busy, her having too little time for you, her less-than-perfect housekeeping. A comrade wife! You do not realize, my friend, how much it means to have one!"[31]

And Nemirov agrees, forgetting how often he worries about his Klavdya's health, too delicate for her demanding job in a huge foundry, how often, in the evening, he would have preferred to find Klavdya waiting for him at home, rather than her mother, who keeps house for them.

Not all husbands are so understanding. That time-hallowed, universal favorite, the marital triangle plot, has been replaced in Soviet fiction by conflicts involving working attitudes. And in the milieu of the intelligentsia the ideologically guilty party is usually the husband. In the late 1930's, the popular plot was based on professional competition. Spouses responsible for rival construction projects steal workers from each other's crews, as in A. Pismenny's "A Husband, A Wife, and a Stovemaker" (1938); or they both submit a new machine model, and the wife's is chosen, as in N. Virta's "Marina" (1936); or, as in B. Vadestky's *The Test* (1941), a wife is in charge of several teams fighting a forest fire, and her husband, an engineer like herself, performs poorly on one of them. In the last two cases, the husband's resentment of his wife's superiority leads to a divorce.

Since World War II, most estrangements have been caused by a husband's insensitivity toward his wife's work. He may prove an egoist, like Valya's husband (in Yu. Bondarev's "Engineers," 1953): they are colleagues working in the same laboratory; he is unsympathetic with her professional problems and irritated by her neglecting household duties. Or perhaps he is like the husband of the schoolteacher Lyuba, who would "never speak to her of anything outside their home life; admired her figure, her eyes, but never showed any interest in her work, her thoughts. Once he said to her: 'Give up that school; you are a married woman now.' " Or, like Zhenya's husband, he will go even further, and dismiss her desire to resume her work as chemical engineer after the birth of their son with the cynical comment that " 'a woman wants a job for three reasons only: when she needs money, or tries to catch a husband, or seeks to impress someone.' "[32]

Moreover, such attitudes, unworthy of a Soviet man, are not limited to villains. It is possible for heroes, engrossed in their own important professional duties, to forget their wives' need for self-expression. In A. Koptyaeva's *Ivan Ivanovich* (1949), Olga's husband, an excellent doctor completely absorbed by his practice, fails to recognize her legitimate longing to become a journalist. And Listopad, in *The Factory Kruzhilikha*, decides that his first wife, Klavdya, should give up her college studies after they are married, and then allows her to lead a frustrating, lonely existence. Nonna, a critic darkly predicts, with her readiness to recognize Listopad's superiority, may well become the next victim.[33]

Disappointed in her husband, the heroine will renounce him and suffer, though not excessively, because she no longer can be in love with him. On this point literary critics are unanimous. "A Soviet woman demands mutual respect and equality in marriage. . . . When she stops respecting her husband, love, too, is gone," says one, and another asserts:

> For a Soviet woman—the human being, the fighter, the builder, the citizen of the great Soviet land—love, in the old sense of psychological and physical attraction, however warm and tender, is not enough. The Soviet woman herself can—and wants to—be an active participant in the magnificent construction [of Socialism], to fall in step with the man she loves, as they march together in the column of the builders of the new world.[34]

Although this psychological pattern may seem unplausible to the Western reader, it does not necessarily seem this way to the Soviet reading public. Could a medieval woman love an atheist, a Victorian lady a man of loose morals, or any heroine at any time a traitor? A good woman in Soviet fiction cannot love a man who takes her work, a basic Soviet virtue, lightly. He is alien to her moral and psychological climate.

Unfaithfulness being restricted to villains (in the postwar decade, at least), the best solution, authors and characters alike seem to think, is for the heroine to get a divorce and marry another, better man. To young Soviet readers this is so obvious that a teenage girl can comment on *Anna Karenina* as being "rather boring and somehow difficult to understand. If you feel you must take a different husband, do so. What is all the commotion about?"[35]

This is not to say that divorce is taken lightly in the middle-class milieu of the period: far from it. But everything in the life of the Soviet fictional heroine depends on her work. Her standing in the community, economic independence, self-respect, and happiness in her personal life ("sometimes erroneously referred to as *private* life," remarks a critic)[36] are possible only within the context of work. She is—and is meant to be—a living illustration of Engel's maxim that the emancipation of women presupposes as its first condition the return of the entire female sex to work.

Still, however large work looms in Soviet life, fiction also offers glimpses of entertainment. Entertainment in the milieu of the intelligentsia—as indeed elsewhere—depends on locality. The inhabitants of Moscow and Leningrad attend concerts and plays, frequent museums (visitors also pay their respects to Lenin's mausoleum), mingle with crowds at parades on national holidays. Restaurants are seldom mentioned, but stopping at a delicatessen to buy a bottle of champagne and hors d'oeuvres for a home party is habitual. Social life, consisting of exchanging visits with friends and colleagues, is quite lively. Food at such receptions is described in some detail, but even during the postwar period of varnished reality the stress is on the hostess's culinary talents rather than, as in kolkhoz fiction, on Soviet plenty. The company, whether young or middle-aged, is congenial, the conversation (mostly on professional matters) animated. No one gets drunk, but everybody smokes excessively—except women.

Such receptions are the rule everywhere: in student dormitories; in wage earners' homes, consisting of one room in a communal apartment where bath, kitchen, hall, and telephone are shared with other tenants; in the homes of the professional intelligentsia, who may rate two such rooms; or in a separate apartment occupied by some members of the privileged elite. But social and family life at all levels centers upon a dining room table, over which an orange lampshade spreads the mellow atmosphere of a happy home.

The farther from the capital, the greater the role played by the orange lampshade. The provinces have no restaurants; the local movie theater is slow in changing its programs; the organizing of dances, amateur theatricals, and national holiday celebrations is the responsibility of the local Komsomol. Long walks and possibly a movie are all a young man can offer his date, but fortunately, at all social levels young girls are fond of walking. And truck drivers seem to be on hand to offer a tired couple a lift; taking a taxi, even in Moscow, is rare, except among the privileged elite. Private cars are practically nonexistent in Soviet fiction, and executives are reluctant to let their families use their chauffeured cars. But dancing and romantic walks are for coeds. Although a career woman, if unmarried, may go to concerts, wives, and particularly mothers, limit their cultural pleasures to visiting with friends and attending official celebrations of national anniversaries, which, in any case, unite all ages and classes in elaborate mass scenes of loyal enthusiasm.

THE SOVIET ELITE

During the first decade of Soviet literature, Party workers without formal education but well-versed in Marxist principles often achieved prominence as self-made men. Yet writers at all times have reminded their readers that even the privileged Soviet elite—Army generals, learned academicians, directors of gigantic Siberian plants—were born in peasants' and workers' homes and owed their prominence primarily to the education which the regime had made possible. For their own part, these men have always been conscious of their debt to Soviet society, but this has not necessarily been the case with their mothers, who, naturally, belong to a different political era, or with their wives and daughters, who all too often have been spoiled by opulent conditions.

These men are seldom happy in family life, perhaps because they are too completely engrossed in the performance of their demanding duties: statistics on fictional executives suffering heart attacks from overwork and tension could make an interesting study. In any case they have little time for their womenfolk, particularly for the illiterate mothers, who, like Zhdarkin's (in *The Village Bruski*), bring to their children's elegant homes "the peculiar sour smell of a peasant hut." Some of these crabby oldsters (like Mother Drozdova in Dudintsev's *Not by Bread Alone*) stay with their prosperous sons; others only come to visit and mourn the men's former good looks which intense work has ruined (like Listopad's mother in *The Factory Kruzhilikha*). And some, like old Mother Varygina in N. Zhdanov's "A Trip Home" (1956), die neglected in their shabby kolkhoz huts—though not before the thaw.

Wives of busy executives are the only members of the Soviet intelligentsia who do not invariably work. They are secondary characters, sometimes serving as foils to protagonists, but it is nevertheless possible to discern two types within this group: the dignified helpmate of a distinguished Soviet man, and the woman representing the Soviet *nouveaux riches*.

The first character was established as a type during the thaw. In the preceding decade, the existence of a privileged elite within Soviet society was not acknowledged, even by implication, and the good wives of executives worked. Teachers Polina in Azhaev's *Far from Moscow*, Katya in Ketlinskaya's *The Days of Our Lives*, Varya in Katerli's *The Far Journey* (1954), Anna in Tendryakov's *A Tight Knot*—all were wives of ranking Party workers. In the post-Stalinist era, it has become acceptable for them to be simply homemakers and to enjoy the one-family apartment, the chauffeured car, and the suburban villa bestowed on their husbands in recognition of services to the State. But in order to keep her status as a positive character, this woman has to be a busy mother, like Galitskaya in *The Battle on the Way*, and an attentive wife, like Anna in Kochetov's *The Brothers Ershov*. If she has had a professional education, once her children are grown she will hold a job, even if her husband, like Sofya's in Kochetov's novel of that name, is a secretary of the District Party Committee (*Obkom*); and civic activities are as obligatory for proper wives in the privileged elite as philanthropy was for Victorian ladies. At the start of the thaw, it was hinted that a middle-aged housewife may feel frustrated if she has sacrificed her career and youth to her husband and to children who now no longer need her—as do L. Volynsky's Klavdya Petrovna and A. Musatov's Nadezhda Egorovna in the short stories bearing their names (both, 1954)—but such cases are hardly typical.

The lazy, snobbish wives of Soviet executives are the direct descendants of their predecessors, the bored, often decadent wives of the prerevolutionary Russian intelligentsia and of the busy builders of Socialism in the 1930's. They are negative characters, usually middle-aged, ranging from foolish, gossiping coquettes like Pava Romanovna in Koptyaeva's *Ivan Ivanovich*, to the catty Mme. Ganicheva who cheated Nadya on the sale of the famous mink coat in *Not by Bread Alone*, to wicked, rapacious Nadezhda Bartoshevich, who involves her husband in illegal profiteering which leads to his suicide in Panova's *The Seasons*. They are poor wives, though unfaithfulness with them is rare and limited to the second generation of the privileged class. The latter, young women spoiled by overindulgence and luxury, are living proofs that the drones—foolish, permissive, and insensitive—are poor mothers as well.

While the importance of a good home is exalted by Soviet fiction, children, being products of Soviet society, may grow up ideologically and morally perfect in any conditions. Anya (in *The Wife of Him Who Strides Forward*) was brought up in an orphanage; Olya (in Kochetov's *Youth Is With Us*, 1954) and Kapa (in his *The Brothers Ershov*) in model Soviet families; and Katya (in *The Seasons*) as daughter of Nadezhda Bartoshevich. Yet all can be considered flowers of young Soviet womanhood. When, however, a young boy or girl fails to measure up to the fine qualities implicit in the name of Soviet-educated youth—and in the fiction of the 1960's juvenile delinquency has increased alarmingly—the fault is usually assumed to be the mother's. This seems strange, because mothers, whether good or bad, have hardly any speaking lines; their influence could only be exercised through their personal example, which seldom is really shocking.

No rapport exists between them and their children. No girl, for instance, ever turns to her mother for advice or has a heart-to-heart talk with her about a first romance. It is easier to find examples of filial love and confidence bestowed on the father. Unfortunately, though he is a fine person, he is usually a henpecked husband and too completely absorbed by the problems of his job to spare time for those of his daughter.

The young women from the elite fall short of the standard requirements of perfection often enough to become a separate fictional type known as the "little doll" (*kukolka*). This devious female, balanced within the plot by an ingenue, has appeared in every student novel since the emergence of that genre, and the romantic plot—parallel to the main plot, which features the victory of Soviet scholarship over Western influences—has presented the hero's infatuation with this beautiful, heartless coquette. As a rule, she is defeated by her rival, the familiar, modest, snub-nosed girl who is pursuing her studies with a fierce intensity of purpose and loyalty.*

This plot situation is not limited to student novels or to the post-Stalinist period, and it has several variations. The little doll may be reformed by hard work in the factory. Aching with fatigue, her once manicured fingers bleeding, her face smudged, she will endure, and emerge from her ordeal a new person. Such a transformation is possible at all levels of the privileged class ladder. For example, Tanya (in Katerli's *The Bronze Spinning Wheel*), whose "famed worker" parents rate the lowest rung, is as spoiled as Lyusya, who is a general's daughter (in Andreev's *The Wide Stream*, 1953); and "stylish Inga," as her gang calls her (in Dementev's *I Am Entering Life*, 1958), belongs somewhere in the middle. Inga distinctly resembles sophisticated Favsta in Nikiforov's *The Woman*, who, forty years earlier, had also escaped from her opulent home to build Socialism with bleeding hands and

* The latter type may be illustrated by the example of Katya, in Svirsky's *Hail, University!* (1952), a linguistics student who denounces the Marrist deviations of several colleagues at a meeting, and reveals her intention also to send a memo on them to the Central Committee of the Party and to Comrade Stalin. (The linguistic theories of Nikolay Marr [1865–1934] had been denounced by Stalin in 1950.) She is rewarded for her zeal by the unanimous support of the students and an immediate proposal of marriage.

marry a proletarian. And this resemblance seems to confirm again the proposition that, while typical heroines of the intelligentsia are wholly Soviet, less-than-perfect characters can be traced back to their prerevolutionary forebears.

Restored to the simple joys of the truly Soviet way of life, the girl may also win the hero's love. Tanya and Inga do so, but not Lyusya: by the time she emerges from the factory, Sergey is already in love with a kindred soul and spiritual equal, Tatyana.

Not all little dolls are reformed; in fact, most remain to the last negative characters, whose example serves the didactic purpose of Soviet literature as efficiently as any heroine's. Allochka (in Dobrovolsky's *Zhenya Maslova*) or Lilya (in Svirsky's *Hail, University!*) or Zina (in Bek's *The Young People*)—all capricious and vain, with pretty clothes and golden curls—serve to prove that beauty and wealth handicap rather than promote true happiness. These girls may be intelligent, but treat their studies lightly; they may inspire love, but are incapable of deep feelings. Married, they develop into cold, sensuous, selfish women, such as Irina in Ziv's *The Ardent Hour* and Ludmila and Tatyana in Ketlinskaya's *No Sense in Living Otherwise*—undeserving wives of outstanding Soviet men, whom they make thoroughly unhappy.

In short, though the little doll is not an Ellochka the Cannibal—this she could not be, having been born and raised within Soviet society—she is not integrated with Soviet life spiritually. Among other drawbacks, this often ruins romance between her and the Soviet Young Man. A conversation between Lena and Vadim in Trifonov's *The Students* (1950) may prove the point:

> "I am studying music but this is not because I have chosen it to be my profession" [said Lena].
> "Then why do you?"
> "Because . . . a woman needs to know all kinds of things: how to dress, to sing, to look lovely. Don't you understand?"
> "I think I do. So, you are preparing for the profession of being a woman?"

And, ignoring her accusation of cynicism, he asks Soviet fiction's crucial question: " 'What is your goal in life?' " Lena bursts out laughing: " 'Good Lord, what a lofty expression, "the goal of your life!" You are being naïve! How can I sum up my plans for the future in one sentence? Moreover, I am not worrying about them at this point; my life is just beginning.' "[37] And Vadim, realizing that he and Lena are not speaking the same ideological language, turns for consolation to Olya, who is. Sometimes, however, heedless of the voice of reason, the lovers court trouble by getting married.

SOVIET MISALLIANCE

Misalliance, in the usual sense of a union between people belonging to different class levels, is impossible in integrated Soviet society. But a spiritual misalliance created by differences in ideology, education, and habits has always been a favorite topic in Soviet literature.

In the fiction of the 1920's, love knew no social barriers. There was the unfortunate (and rather sordid) romance of Nina, the village teacher, with the Civil War veteran and Komsomolets Sergey in Karpov's *The Fifth Love* (1925); and the love of Natalya Tarpova, a pedigree proletarian in Semyonov's novel bearing her name, for the cynical engineer Gabrukh; and of course, the numerous deplorable affairs of good Communists—proletarians and peasants—with the typing misses and the homewreckers from the intelligentsia. But these romances, though in some cases involving marriage, were not really misalliances; rather, their theme was love for a class enemy, and since the protagonists' relationships were devoid of any tenderness, respect, or understanding, the right word for their ambivalent feelings seems to be infatuation. A mixture of sexual attraction, too powerful to resist, and of instinctive class hatred, too deep-rooted to ignore, the relationship is invariably a source of anguish to at least one participant, and ends in tragedy.

This plot pattern did not survive the establishment of the postwar trend of Soviet Patriotism, which, among other things, assumed both class enemies and sensual infatuation equally nonexistent in the Soviet Union. Misalliance, however, involving a little doll's marrying an uneducated worker, has been in vogue ever since World War II, but the reversed plot situation—the Prince's marrying Cinderella—has at no time been popular in Russian fiction. As early as the folklore tales, Tsars' daughters readily wed adventurous Ivan-the-Fools and presumably made them good, submissive wives. This optimistic assumption, reflecting, it seems, a faith in simplicity's superiority over sophistication, is shared by Soviet authors. Their version, naturally, opposes the lover's clean, Soviet-bred mentality to that of a girl spoiled by vanity and wealth, but the principle is the same, and is also applicable when the girl is as positive a character as the youth, but better educated. The bedrock of wisdom and virtue are, as ever, the masses.

So long as both lovers have the same Soviet *Weltanschauung*, disparities in their manners and tastes can be eliminated. A teacher fondly plans to make her fiancé, a Stakhanovite tractor driver, "change his socks regularly, shave, cut his hair, and clip his fingernails"—and she will. As to the disparity in education, any Soviet character, whatever his educational status, is working to achieve a higher one, and any Stakhanovite can be trusted to acquire a degree. So, should any girl feel the feminine urge to consider her mate a superior—for example, Rita, an engineer in S. Antonov's "The Grand Piano" (1955), hesitates to marry Lyosha, a stonemason, because she is not sure she can—she need only check the quality of his working performance. Rita does so, then confides in Lyosha's foreman, who sternly reproves her for snobbishly rating a Soviet worker beneath an engineer; and the happy union takes place.

Throughout the postwar decade such unions were automatically assumed to be successes. On the rare occasions when they were not completely so, the intervention of a wise partorg acting as a marriage counselor would set things to right, as happens in M. Zhestev's *Family Affairs* (1955). But in the 1960's a few disturbing cases began to indicate that possibly the pattern was changing.

In A. Andreev's *You Be the Judge* (1962), Zhenya, a general's daughter, elopes with Alyosha. Her snobbish mother has opposed their marriage because the youth, having failed at the university, is now earning a living as a mason. Instead of living happily ever after, the young couple constantly quarrel over their poor living conditions, and Zhenya, unable to stand it any longer, returns home. When, reproved by her sensible father, she goes back to Alyosha, she finds that he has already left with a party of Komsomol volunteers to work in the Siberian virgin lands.

Another story, that of a professor's daughter who follows a tractor driver to his kolkhoz in Siberia (in Antonov's *Alyonka*), hints that even in Sovietland sexual attraction may bridge the gulf of intellectual incompatibility. The wife (nameless) does walk out into a snowstorm when her temperamental mate turns his gun on a Rubens nude she has hung up in their hut: he "had no use for indecency." But he finds her, half frozen, and brings her home, where they make up; and—the husband insists—they have been very happy ever since.

The greatest shock to the readers must have been the case of Valentina, in V. Semin's *120 Kilometers to the Railroad Station* (1964). A schoolteacher married to a truckdriver, she leads a miserable existence because he resents her superiority in education, but refuses to improve his own. She finally dies in childbirth, victim of his maltreatment.

Parents have little to say in the matter of their daughter's marriage, whether or not it is a misalliance. Their approval is desirable, but not essential, and in any case, it is seldom refused. Mothers may object to a son-in-law whose social status is lower than theirs, but fathers, remembering their own humble beginnings, take the daughter's side. Financial considerations do not enter the picture, because both young people will get jobs, a room in a communal apartment, and will start their married life on a shoestring like any other Soviet couple, even if their families are well-to-do. And should the girl prove as sensible and unspoiled as, for instance, Kapa, daughter of an important Party official in *The Brothers Ershov,* and the youth prove as worthy as her Andrey, the marriage has every chance of turning out well. Thus, misalliances in Soviet fiction are possible only in cases of spiritual and ideological incompatibility.

15

The Thaw and After

🌿

THE CHANGE

Beginning with the thaw, the emphasis in fiction shifted from the portrayal of peasant and worker environments to those of the intelligentsia and particularly its recently developed upper crust, the priviligentsia. Consequently, it is in these two social groups that one can best observe the period's changes in plot and character drawing, and therefore, also in the patterns of the typical women.

Actually, as is evident from the previous discussion, patterns have undergone no basic changes since their establishment under the auspices of Socialist Realism, nor are such changes likely for its duration. Writers indeed had been invited to portray typical Soviet people as "whole persons," both with flaws and virtues, but at the same time they were cautioned to give priority to the latter.[1] There was, of course, a minority of atypical aliens whose hallmark, as usual, was their completely non-didactic quality, characters created and existing solely for their own sake. They did not follow patterns other than those of common human behavior. Enwrapped in their emotional experiences, always intense, and usually painful, they disregarded at will conventional moral standards without ostentation or remorse. In short, they could have walked unrecognized into the world of Western fiction.

Were they more numerous, protagonists of larger works, so to say, more aggressive, they might indeed have influenced the ways of Sovietland. But except for Nekrasov's Kira Georgievna, they appear in a limited number of short stories (still the favorite genre of contemporary Fellow Travelers), in which, moreover, they play a passive role. For example, Yu. Kazakov's Vika in "Adam and Eve" (1962) is not so much the heroine as a girl hurt by the hero's frustrations, while his Gusta (in "On the Island," 1963) is the girl whom the protagonist loves and leaves behind. Their feelings reach the reader indirectly, through the atmosphere of an impressionistic setting and through the recorded feelings of their lover. Needless to say, they do not serve as models for the continuing production of works designed for the education of the masses.

The proliferation of these didactic works goes on as usual. Though the conservative writers (still responsible for the bulk of fiction output in the Soviet Union) have obediently desisted from varnishing Soviet reality, they nevertheless denounce its failings discreetly and with moderation. Hence, as with kolkhoz heroines, giving characters a few modified accessories did little to affect their status as either positive or negative types.

The progressive writers did take advantage of liberalized conditions. They have not only exposed the flaws of Soviet life and mores, but they have also shifted the emphasis onto personal life, especially in drawing characters of educated women, showing them as also psychological, instead of exclusively social, phenomena. Nastya, in Nikolaeva's *A Story About a Director of the MTS and Its Chief Agronomist*, is a paragon demanding recognition and emulation; but Tonya, in Antonov's *It Happened at Penkovo*, is just a girl in love with a married man, and trying to find an honorable solution to the situation. Lena, Nastya's colleague and foil, is a coquette who has no real interest in her job; but the protagonist in Yu. Nagibin's "Get Off, We've Arrived" (1954) does not even condescend to take a job offering poor conditions. All four girls are professional agronomists, but in the case of Nikolaeva's Nastya and Lena this circumstance is the crux of their characterization: they exist *as* agronomists who succeed (or fail) in doing their duty for the kolkhozes and so for the Soviet economy. In contrast, Antonov's lovelorn Tonya and Nagibin's selfish little opportunist are just that, and their respective kolkhozes serve only as background.

Yet, the anguished cries raised by conservative critics at this rampant "de-heroization" of Soviet literature[2] have little justification: such young women are still legitimate inhabitants of Sovietland. They have kept their civic virtues and did not repudiate Soviet values, nor for that matter lose their inherent didactic properties. Noble human qualities which in model positive heroines are so often overshadowed by rigid dedication to the overfulfillment of production norms, in them become salient and therefore more effective features. And even their shortcomings are more likely to impress the reader because they are being used as an artistic rather than a didactic device. From the esthetic point of view they are, of course, superior to their uncompromisingly impeccable sisters. Besides, irrespective of authors' attitudes the thaw affected women characters in a different way than it did men. Military setbacks at the beginning of World War II; living conditions in labor camps; red tape, intrigues, and opportunism at all levels in bureaucracy; padded statistics in industry and in kolkhozes—all these newly popular topics, hitherto nonexistent in Soviet fictional plots, have concerned only men. The responsibility for the shortcomings concealed in Stalin's lifetime and revealed after his death was now squarely on the shoulders of male characters, as were also the difficulties of adjustment to the changed political situation. Women, through the very insignificance of their roles, were exempt from both. Whenever the burden of the plot is on political or social questions, they play accessory roles and remain true to the type patterns established in the preceding period.

This situation is best illustrated by the example of the two novels most discussed and best known outside of the Soviet Union: *Not by Bread Alone* by Dudintsev, and I. Erenburg's *The Thaw* which, it will be remembered, gave the post-Stalinist period its name. The third representative work, A. Solzhenitsyn's *One Day in the Life of Ivan Denisovich* (1962), has a prison camp for its background, and therefore, no female characters.

The change evinced in male characters is striking. Zhuravlyov (in *The Thaw*) and Drozdov (in *Not by Bread Alone*), both important government executives, are denounced by their authors for their impersonal, unswerving efficiency in following Party directives to the letter—qualities which up to that time belonged to the makeup of heroes. But Lena and Nadya, the men's respective wives, remain true to form. Led evidently by a woman's intuition (in this case political), they unhesitatingly recognize their spouses as villains, and accordingly, leave to marry worthier men. Both women are dedicated schoolteachers, each has one child whom she takes away from its tolerably affectionate father, neither is unfaithful while still married; and they probably will make excellent wives to their second husbands.

Nadya, in particular, is a typical follower sacrificing everything from a mink coat to good reputation to her lover's romantic vision of a machine which will produce perfect steel pipes. A dreamer, too engrossed in fighting for his invention even to appreciate Nadya's devotion properly, he finally asks her to marry him, but warns that his fight is not yet over:

> "Aren't you tired? [he asked.] What if I tell you: let us continue our journey?"
> Nadya did not answer. She only came nearer—and disappeared—because she did not actually exist; she was only a small, clear stream which he could use for drinking and refreshing his face on his hard journey.[3]

The impact of changes wrought by the thaw in women characters has been concentrated on morals, mores, and emotional values. The image of the Soviet Woman has remained untarnished: under any circumstances she has continued to be unselfish, honorable, and dedicated to her work. But quite a few taboos were lifted. It has been acknowledged that premarital and extramarital relations do exist in Soviet society and—even more shockingly—are not necessarily limited to villains. Novels like K. Lvova's *Elena* (1955), Nikolaeva's *The Battle on the Way*, and N. Davydova's *The Love of Engineer Izotov* (1960) introduced respectable career women having love affairs with married colleagues—featured, to be sure, against their workshops' background and paralleled by plots based on production conflicts. Other works, like Chubakova's *I Want Happiness* and M. Demidenko's *And They Will Call You Yurka* (1962), allowed that a young Soviet girl may enter an illicit liaison of her own will, and not as a victim of seduction. And Nekrasov's Kira Georgievna had a *succès du scandale* abroad and at home where, at forty-one, fictional heroines are plump, graying, and assumed to be immune to extramarital temptations.

It was not a question of Soviet literature's suddenly becoming immodest. Sensual descriptions are as severely banned as ever, no suggestive details are given—a pair of bedroom slippers, a robe, and a lampshade, provided by a thoughtful lover in Nikolaeva's *Battle on the Way*, touched off a blaze of protest[4]—and crucial love scenes end in blackouts. Nor are fiction's moral standards deteriorating: love, especially on the part of women, is always a genuine, deep feeling. In addition, all wayward girls repent in the end and either return to their forgiving fiancés, or disillusioned and chastened, try to build a new life on the ruins of romance. Aksyonov's Galya and Davydova's Tasya illustrate the first kind; Chubakova's Kena, Demidenko's Kira, and L. Obukhova's Tamara (in *The Splinter*), the second. But the problems of sex which had been assumed solved for twenty years were back, and unfortunately they were not always handled with good taste. At the hands of a number of talented writers they helped materially to enliven stale plots and humanize stereotyped characters. But numerous lesser pens simply proceeded (strictly within allowed limits) to spice with sex and romance the bland literary fare of the preceding decade.

Once the floodgates opened, the tide of what was scathingly termed "corny literary fodder"[5]—unsophisticated variations on the eternal theme of unhappy love—steadily mounted. The reading public, who, it was conceded, "was starved for books on love,"[6] queued in bookstores to buy these books out as soon as they appeared, and in libraries, to add their names to the long waiting lists. But the body of literary critics were considerably less enthusiastic. Disturbed primarily by the possible detrimental effect of these works on the masses, they expressed their concern in variants of Gogol's famous comedy line: "Why should our young people be exposed to the evil influence of free-thinking?"[7]

The main target of the critics was the most popular plot situation during the thaw: the heroine's love for a married man. Until then, the topic had been all but unknown in Soviet fiction. In the rare cases when such a forbidden passion was visited on a Soviet girl (married women were safe, by definition), she fought it firmly and successfully, as did Zhenya in Azhaev's *Far from Moscow* and Natasha in K. Kositsinsky's *The Front Line* (1951). The only significant exception is Valentina in Koptyaeva's *Comrade Anna*, but even so, her affair had no disastrous results: the flighty husband returned to his wife and was forgiven, and Valentina blithely married a worthy suitor.

This denouement, incidentally, is very popular in Soviet fiction, where everyone is entitled to a happy ending, the unsuccessful rival as much as anyone else; Kaverin's Mashenka, in *Doctor Vlasenkova*, Koptyaeva's Varya, in *Daring* (1958), and the heroine of Arbuzov's play *Tanya* (1938) are cases in point. But these happy endings, atoning for the young woman's disappointment in love, or sometimes the loss of a husband, occurred because all parties involved could be expected to act nobly. In the post-Stalinist period, however, such nobility was not necessarily the case, and the critics' concern therefore was not ungrounded.

The illicit love plot pattern has several variations, the favorite one assuming the hero to be a good man, married (which creates a guilt complex in the heroine), but unhappy in married life (which reduces her responsibility). In his youth, having mistaken infatuation for love, he had married a woman of bourgeois mentality who now has become a shrew, or at best, spiritually alien to him. One could cite many such wives: Larisa in Obukhova's *The Splinter*, Ksenya in N. Pogodin's play, *Petrarch's Sonnet* (1956), Liza in Chubakova's *I Want Happiness*, and Olga in Z. Rudskaya's *Next to Us* (1956), to name a few. Katya in Nikolaeva's *Battle on the Way*, however, found champions who argued that her only fault seemed to be her standing in the way of her husband's romance.[8]

Sometimes, however, the heroine's lover may prove to be a philanderer whose good wife either is unaware of his being one—for instance, Reshetov's wife in Lvova's *Elena*, or Terekhov's in Davydova's *The Love of Engineer Izotov*—or, having found out, has left him, as did Karelin's wife in *Zero-Three* by N. Adamyan and Valerik's in *A Farewell to White Nights* (1961), a play by V. Panova. Valerik even uses his wife's refusal of formal divorce as pretext for not marrying Nina, who is expecting his baby. These are, in actuality, cases of mistaken identity on the part of the heroine, and her tragedy consists in losing not her lover, but rather the man she had imagined him to be. Once she realizes his unworthiness, her love is gone.

The young women who misplace their affections in the fiction of the post-Stalinist era are not the vicious homewreckers of the peasant novels. Those never loved the men whose lives they were ruining, and the readers' and the author's sympathies were wholly on the side of the wronged wives. The modern homewrecker, on the other hand, is basically a positive character, a woman of charm, intelligence, and integrity. She is an understanding friend and a loyal colleague to her lover, completely unselfish, and it is she who suffers in the false situation, rather than the injured wife, who seldom is a sensitive person. At any rate, she is hardly a homewrecker in the literal sense, because as a rule illicit romances in Sovietland end in the lovers' parting, for a variety of reasons. The children's happiness, pitched against their father's infatuation, may win;* the Party may intervene, as in *The Splinter* and in *Petrarch's Sonnet;* or men may simply prove unwilling to divorce their wives, as in Davydova's *The Love of Engineer Izotov,* Tendryakov's *A Tight Knot,* Demidenko's *And They Will Call You Yurka.*

The heroine herself may also be married to an excellent or at least a tolerably good husband; a villain she would have long ago divorced. But affairs involving a double adultery are rare in Soviet fiction, and it is partly for this reason that the tragic loves of Tina in *The Battle on the Way,* of Elena in the novel bearing her name, and of Varya in S. Alyoshin's *Alone* (1956) became *causes célèbres,* unique and shocking.

The star-crossed lovers of *The Battle on the Way,* Tina and Bakhirev, both engineers employed in the same plant, are no Tristan and Isolde. Bakhirev is past his prime; Tina carries the scar of a former tragedy: her first husband was one of Beria's victims. Both are now married to good but dull spouses: Tina's second husband, moreover, is an invalid; Bakhirev's Katya, a conventional bourgeois homebody who cannot share his troubles in the plant as Tina does. Yet, what unites these two is not profession or ideology (Tina is not even a Party member); it is love, which looms unusually large against the background of a noisy argument over tractors. After Katya discovers their liaison and attempts suicide, Bakhirev decides to stay with his family, and Tina accepts his decision. She leaves for another job thousands of miles away, hoping that her husband will be comforted by a woman who has long loved him. Bakhirev stays to live down the scandal and earn back his children's confidence. Hard work is the only solace either can look forward to.

The book has flashes of genuine realism: Katya, handsome, bovine, and placid; her lively children; the lovers' final parting; their trysts in the sordid little room Bakhirev had managed to hire in the suburbs; the scene in which a cockroach scuttles over the oriental rug (a pathetic effort to conceal the ugliness of the room) and makes Bakhirev remark bitterly: " 'The era of Socialism is ill-equipped for adultery.' "[9] And the author succeeds in showing that the affair is neither adultery nor a glamorous passion, but a bond of deep feeling between two honest and sensitive people. And in this success lies whatever artistic value the book possesses.

* As in the case of the three Bakhirev children in *The Battle on the Way,* Boris' two babies in *I Want Happiness,* and Vadim's boy in *Kira Georgievna.*

Elena has no artistic value and can be compared only to the cheap, sensational novels which women from the lower middle class read so avidly at the turn of the last century. It is a melodramatic story of beautiful, talented Elena, a chemical engineer, who suddenly incurs a fatal passion for a handsome, cynical colleague, Reshetov, a married man. Torn between this infatuation and the remorse at having betrayed her beloved husband, Elena miscarries a child by Reshetov, nearly dies, but finally recovers, accepts a job in Siberia, and departs, leaving both husband and lover behind. It is not known whether the readers appreciated the descriptions of chemical laboratory experiments which occupy one-third of the novel, or whether they resented the critics' near-unanimous condemnation of its vulgarity. But the love story was a tremendous success, and the author was deluged with letters requesting that Elena be reunited with her husband.[10]

Alone differs from the bulk of the romantic fiction of the period in that it has two heroines equally deserving of the hero's love. Both are proud, sincere, honest women. Masha, Platonov's wife, is a teacher; Varya is an engineer working in the same institution as both Platonov and her own husband. After much anguish for both couples, their old parents, and the Platonovs' young daughter Nina, there is a double divorce, and Platonov marries Varya. The cost of his new, married happiness is the loss of Nina's affection and respect, and apparently some remorse for the fate of Masha, who is left to find what solace she can in her socially useful work.

Most often, however, the protagonists of an unhappy romance are a single woman and a married man. The reverse combination, so popular in nineteenth-century fiction, is limited in Soviet literature to a few cases of chance affairs where no true love is involved—as in the case of Kira Georgievna and of Tatyana Rusakovskaya, the red-headed sorceress in Ketlinskaya's *No Sense in Living Otherwise*. When both protagonists are free and in love, no affair is involved; they simply get married. Generally, the young Soviet girl still continues to follow Mefisto's advice to Gretchen to "grant no favors until the wedding ring is on her finger." And in all fairness, it should be said that no positive male character would have it otherwise when he is single. But in the popular plot pattern of the post-Stalinist period, he is married.

This pattern, to quote an exasperated critic, "promotes a single moral: 'Don't fall in love with middle-aged married men, girls; that's bad. They will just trifle with your feelings and then desert you.'"[11]

The heroines who disregard this sensible maxim are best represented by Tasya, in Davydova's notorious novel, *The Love of Engineer Izotov*. Engaged to Izotov, a worthy young man and an engineer like herself, the twenty-two-year-old Tasya is as naïve and innocent as a teenager. While Izotov is away on a business trip, she falls desperately in love with the handsome, flirtatious Terekhov, director of the plant where she and Izotov are employed. This is a real grand passion, and blonde Tasya is helpless before its impact. When Terekhov moves on to another flirtation, Tasya regains her senses and her love for her returned fiancé. Fortunately, she regains him too.

Because a happy ending is no longer obligatory in post-Stalinist fiction (though apparently readers still prefer it),[12] other heroines are less lucky. There is, for instance, Tamara, in *The Splinter*, whose lover accepts a job in Siberia after they both have been lectured by the Party district secretary on the immorality of their liaison. There is Kena in *I Want Happiness*, who loses her Boris twice: as a fiancé, when he realizes she is a coquette, and as a lover, several years later, when he chooses to stay with his family. There is Kira, in *And They Will Call You Yurka*, a freshman student who does not even want her cowardly lover to get a divorce and marry her. Instead, encouraged by the Komsomol, she decides to raise her baby alone, very much as did Sonya in Romanov's "The Big Family," thirty-five years earlier. And there is, of course, Galya, the controversial heroine of *A Ticket to the Stars*, who sacrificed her young love to the mirage of a glamorous career. While it has been occasionally suggested since the thaw that divorce may be preferable to a patched-up family life, the family's position as "the bedrock of Soviet society," stays unchanged. Illicit liaisons, when prompted by genuine love, are not judged harshly, and even infatuation may meet with understanding, but neither are considered typical of Soviet reality. On this, critics and readers are in perfect agreement, at least those readers whose letters are chosen by editors for publication in Soviet literary magazines.

THE PSYCHOLOGICAL CLIMATE

As has been demonstrated in this study, Soviet fictional women seem to be incapable of complex feelings. Perhaps, like Hardy's Bathsheba, peasant and proletarian women find it "difficult for a woman to define her feelings in language which is chiefly made by men to express theirs." But one would expect an educated woman to be reasonably articulate in revealing her intricate sentiments—if she has them. That this is not the case stems from the peculiarities of Socialist Realism, particularly from its lasting ban on anything irrational, subconscious, or abnormal in human behavior.

Hence, the most striking feature in the women of the intelligentsia is the sane and matter-of-fact quality of their emotions. Whatever spiritual anguish they may suffer, their reactions are rational, and they can control them. They never faint, or become hysterical, or suffer a nervous breakdown.* It is not quite clear what would happen to them if they did, because fictional Sovietland has no psychiatrists and no mental institutions. There are hospitals, where characters are taken in case of an accident, a heart attack, or pneumonia; a maternity ward figures in practically every novel; but a snake pit, or just an ordinary psychiatric ward, is simply nonexistent.

These women never seek oblivion in drugs or alcohol or attempt suicide. The only escape from heartbreak and the only hope for redemption is in work. Tina, Elena, and Kena will immerse themselves in work, and like a potent drug, it will dull the pain, and eventually achieve a cure. Their sleep, as a rule, is dreamless, but when they do have a dream, it is sensible and connected with waking reality. On these rare occasions one is reminded of Goncharov's Grandma Tatyana Markovna, who, after listening to her family's accounts of their "poetic" and "mysterious" dreams, declares that hers was about a stick lying on the snow, a fine dream "from which one need not wake up screaming."[13]

As in adversity, so in love, the heroine's sentiments are ingenuous and elemental. Both sophisticated career women and starry-eyed little nurses seem to accept the universally true love formula succinctly presented at a Komsomol meeting by a girl secretary: " 'Love is physical attraction combined with a community of social and cultural interests.' "[14] Physical attraction in Soviet fiction exists exclusively between two members of the opposite sex unrelated by blood, of legal age, and

---

* Works on World War II, where wartime tragedies and Nazi atrocities may cause a nervous breakdown, are exceptions. Tatyana, in Panfyorov's *The Struggle for Peace*, suffers one after losing her mother and child, but recovers in the next volume because, the reader is told, of good medical treatment; and she becomes the Soviet Mata Hari.

usually expecting to have issue from their union. In standard plots, no other possibilities are taken into consideration. As to the overwhelming importance of spiritual affinity, its role in love has been already discussed.

Chastity in a woman is assumed to be her natural state, and any departure from it an exception. True love also presupposes a certain freshness of feelings. For instance, in the magazine version of *The Battle on the Way*, Tina had been married twice before meeting Bakhirev, and the critics insisted that this made her passion for him less credible: "Were she freed from her excessive former [erotic] experience, it would be easier to believe that the young woman's emotions still remained largely unawakened and virginal."[15] Author Nikolaeva complied, and when the novel was published in book form in 1958, the first husband had disappeared.

Modesty, too, is taken for granted in women, and for that matter, in men, with the exception of villains; but even these are a tame lot. No character in Soviet fiction would openly admit to being overly concerned with sex. A kiss is the ultimate in physical contact, a robe in dishabille; no piece of underwear is ever on display. The absence of any suggestive details or love scenes has been already mentioned, and while of late, the use of unprintable words by negative male characters has been made apparent, they are never spelled out in Soviet publications.

Another reason for the simplicity of the heroine's psychological makeup is the rigid orderliness of the world she lives in. She is faced exclusively with predictable situations in which she knows she should act according to an established ethical code. She never questions the code or refuses to obey it. Nobody around her ever does. There are no Anna Kareninas; and even Virineya, or Aksinya of *The Quiet Don*—the sultry rebels of the 1920's—are inconceivable in contemporary fiction. The prejudices of a reactionary society which they had challenged have been replaced by Socialist norms of moral behavior, which are not supposed to be challenged, at least not by positive characters. A rebel cannot count on anyone's sympathy and understanding, not even on that of her lover. A conformist, on the other hand, may claim a few compensations, such as freedom from doubts, from the necessity of choice and decisions, from a feeling of insecurity.

Like the kolkhoz Heroines, typical Alfa women may be pleasant company for the reader. Of course, the twelve-in-a-box, mass-produced creations of professional Soviet mediocrities hardly qualify; but quite a few original characters by the more gifted authors deserve to be noticed. Nikolaeva's Tina, Panova's Nonna, Dudintsev's Nadya—to cite a few—are appealing in their integrity, in the sterling quality of their unselfish love and even in that of their thoughts, which are innocent of artifice and as tidy as their hair. Even so, because they breathe the unexciting atmosphere of the Soviet fictional world, they suffer from the ailments common to its inhabitants: they are predictable and transparent. Nothing they can do will ever surprise, shock, or disappoint the reader. They harbor no secret resentments or desires, have no deep-seated thoughts and emotions they would like to conceal. And, unfortunately, as Voltaire pointed out, "Le secret d'être ennuyeux c'est de tout dire."

Conclusion

In tracing the evolution of women types over almost half a century of Soviet literature, this study inevitably also reflects the actual changes which have been taking place in the Soviet Union. Yet, under the conditions peculiar to Soviet life (and to the detriment of Soviet art) the mirror held by fiction to reality reflects it at an angle determined not by the artist alone, but also by the current policies of the Communist Party. Hence, characters and their evolution have been presented here as products of Sovietland, the world of Soviet fiction, which is governed by its own laws and where the tide of change is synchronized with political fluctuations.

For the typological purposes of this study, the salient feature of Sovietland has been the uncompromising segregation of its inhabitants into positive and negative characters, both of whom serve to educate the reader ideologically. Heroines, a vast majority and assumed to be typical of their living prototypes, invite emulation of virtue, while the infrequent villainesses, allegedly leftovers of the prerevolutionary past, sound a warning against imitation of vice. The numerical ratio of these two groups varies, though not drastically, with the change of trends, as does the ratio of black and white in their characterization. At the height of the postwar period of varnished reality, negative characters all but disappeared, and the remaining few were so tame they seemed mere shadows of the resplendent heroines. In the post-Stalinist era, on the other hand, human weaknesses became acceptable in the heroine's psychological makeup and sterling qualities appeared in that of the occasional wayward women, mild Soviet versions of Western anti-heroines. Such concessions allowed for higher artistic levels of characterization, but the patterns, once established, have remained.

Alien characters, created independently of any patterns and without didactic purpose, do exist on the margin of Soviet fiction, but are not present—or at least discernible—all the time. They are a small minority whose presence has been tolerated during the periods of liberalization, such as the 1920's and the mid-1950's, but who seem to go underground when the line is tightened. They have little, if any, influence on the permanent dwellers of Sovietland.

The evolution of female type patterns has been considered within three stages: the period preceding the imposition of the literary controls regulated by Socialist Realism, that of its absolute domination, and that of increased creative possibilities within its pale.

Between the Revolution and the early 1930's, Sovietland hosted a number of women characters who, albeit conspicuous at that time, did not continue into the next period. For the most part, they shared the fate of their living models: within a decade, the meek, illiterate girls who were victims of the village byt; the predatory typing misses, those camp followers of the Revolution; its enthusiastic but misguided standardbearers, the romantic Amazons; and the Komsomol's proponents of the "glass of water" theory disappeared in fiction as they did in real life. Other characters, such as women inmates of labor camps or prostitutes, were simply excluded from the world of Soviet fiction, and this ban continued even after many other "un-persons" had been readmitted under the thaw.

None of these women, psychologically still creatures of the past, contributed to the emerging positive image of the New Soviet Woman. But they did pass on to future negative characters some essential attributes of the old order, particularly those of "bourgeois mentality." For instance, the period's middle-class women, grasping and useless, and their spoiled, selfish daughters can be recognized in the social drones among the early Soviet intelligentsia and among the privileged elite of the postwar decades.

Simultaneously, the first type patterns were taking shape in works dealing with the emancipation of women. The theme, firmly rooted in Marxist teachings, was popular from the start: Neverov's "Marya the Bolshevik" (1921) was one of the first short stories to appear in Soviet literature; Gladkov's *Cement* (1925), starring Dasha, was one of its first novels. The woman comrade fought for the cause of the Revolution in the Red Army's ranks; the downtrodden baba and the proletarian housewife demanded free exercise of their newly acquired political and civil rights, marital equality, and sexual freedom; and bourgeois girls left their homes in order to build their lives independently within the changed world.

These were the pioneers of progress, aggressive, intrepid, ready to take on any adversary—domestic tyrants, public opinion, the whole enormous hulk of the prerevolutionary way of life. The keynote of their characterization was rebellion. Eager to destroy the old order, they were doing little to establish a new one, nor did they know exactly what it should be like. They denounced religion, neglected their homes, and dedicated all their time and energy to work in new Soviet institutions such as village and factory councils, the Zhenotdel, or the Komsomol. They were often hurt in this constant strife, but bravely endured heartache, the censure of their conservative milieu, and physical hardships. The weaker ones among them fell by the road, but the stronger (or the least sensitive) ones came out self-reliant and victorious. As the title of a famous novel by a proletarian writer (N. Ostrovsky, in 1935) phrased it, this was "how the steel was tempered," and how the patterns of the typical Soviet women were first adumbrated.

With the installation of the code of Socialist Realism in literature and the actual formulation of the principles of Soviet ethics by the Constitution of 1936, the fictional patterns crystallized and the New Woman mellowed and became domesticated.

From then on, the keynote of her characterization was moderation. If the real life of the Stalinist era was indeed built on the "cult of [his] personality," life in Sovietland was based on the cult of the average, paradoxically equated with excellence, as part of the postwar trend of Soviet Patriotism. The Heroine (and this was endlessly stressed), like her living prototype, was an *average* Soviet woman. There was civic heroism in her intensive everyday work contributing to the building of the Communist future, and as wartime fiction amply proved, a latent military heroism readily sprang up to answer the call of the Fatherland in danger. Yet, it was no more than what would be expected of her as a positive Soviet character, living (except for the World War II disaster) in a land of hard-earned peace and increasing plenty and guided at all times by the wise and benevolent Party and its representatives.

She is no longer fighting for her rights—they have long been recognized—and instead has settled down to enjoy them. Her good husband, himself a changed man, appreciates her value as wife and mother, her excellence as social and professional worker, and her magic gift of succeeding in all these capacities simultaneously. An unworthy husband she still could divorce, but not a good Soviet man, and not for such reasons as sexual incompatibility or falling in love with another man. Her moral standards are very high and compare favorably with those of the pioneers. Young and married love, and usually also motherhood, sum up her personal life; work in her chosen profession guarantees her spiritual happiness. She covets no high positions in her job or in Party bureaucracy—which is fortunate, because none are granted. She is modestly happy in her sense of duties well done and is proud of tokens of recognition by the government such as citations and decorations or interviews in the local newspapers.

It is apparent that the basic pattern of the Heroine did not change with the thaw, except for her becoming more susceptible to human weaknesses. These, however, have penetrated only the domain of her personal life and do not affect the quality of her working performance. Unlike male characters, whose ideological and bureaucratic sins (resulting, to be sure, from the cult of personality) were now revealed, women in their inconspicuous jobs remained their meticulous, unquestioning, and efficient selves.

They do betray more interest in their appearance, adopt some new fashions, and are considerably less adamant than they used to be in following the paths of virtue. But the reader still has no difficulty in telling a positive character of somewhat less exalted standards from a negative one with some redeeming qualities. Of course, it has always been possible for a mildly negative character to be rehabilitated through work.

The reappearance during the thaw of some atypical characters similar to those of postrevolutionary fiction has already been noted. Absorbed in their personal affairs, they stay aloof from the current ideological and economic developments and do not conform to the usual patterns of behavior. In the post-Stalinist decade, the presence of these visitors from the outside world of fiction has been tolerated but tenuous, as well as that of the works in which they have been featured.

The development of the women type patterns in Soviet fiction has been synchronous with but varying within the four environmental groups into which this study is divided.

Prerevolutionary Russian fiction traditionally portrayed the peasant woman as the long enduring victim of the coarse village byt—a domestic drudge, ignorant and destitute. Early in the 1920's in the works of peasant writers she emerged as a rebel, a pioneer of progress, and a fighter for women's emancipation. She was endowed with an indomitable spirit: she could not have lasted through her ordeals without it. She was poor: the rich were evil almost by definition in early Soviet literature, as indeed they continued to be under Socialist Realism. She joined and supported Soviet institutions, took pleasure in exaggerated flouting of village customs and morals, and was indefatigable in promoting the establishment of kolkhozes and in fighting the kulaks.

The transition from the mutinous baba type to that of a devoted *kolkhoznitsa* took the form of a gradual spiritual awakening rather than, as before, that of a spontaneous rebellion. The process can best be observed in the characters of Panfyorov's Steshka (in *The Village Bruski*) and Zamoysky's Praskovya (in *The Bast Shoes*), especially because in both cases it was demonstrated in multivolume novels published over a period of ten years.

From then on, the kolkhoz woman becomes a Heroine, the truly positive character of Soviet fiction, outshining the Hero. Kolkhoz chairman, partorg, resourceful innovator, or just a rank-and-file conscientious worker in barns and fields, she is the pillar of the Soviet state. Stout matrons, timid ingenues, or spirited oldsters, they all share in the civic and personal excellence which had become an integral part of the pattern. A few flaws carefully doled out to positive characters by the authors as a concession to the spirit of the thaw did little to affect the image of the kolkhoz woman. Nor was it impaired by the comeback of negative characters, who had been practically unknown during the postwar decade. Descendants of the operatic hags and the women bootleggers of the 1920's were now simply innocuous old gossipmongers and vulgar village sirens. Nevertheless, when the emphasis in fiction shifted to city life and the intelligentsia, the kolkhoz and its inhabitants, suddenly revealed as drab, faded into the wings of the literary stage.

The proletarian woman, seldom featured in Russian literature before the Revolution, achieved no prominence even under the dictatorship of her own class. Gladkov's Dasha, in *Cement*, was, of course, the first and most famous New Woman, yet she has remained a lonely example of a proletarian pioneer of women's emancipation. Fanatically devoted to the Communist cause, ready to sacrifice everything in its service—including her marriage and the life of her child—Dasha was too formidable a character to invite emulation. Neither her colorless contemporaries of the 1920's nor their heirs, the comfortable matrons of the industrial novels under Socialist Realism, could equal her fighting spirit. Besides, they were not expected to do so. They were good housewives, efficient factory workers, virtuous, sensible—and insipid.

After the decline of industrial fiction caused by the thaw, the patterns of typical proletarian women failed to undergo even token modifications, such as occurred in the peasant heroines. The younger generation, however, proved more versatile in its development. In the 1920's zealous members of the Komsomol dedicated to its activities all the time they could spare from their factory work. Defying parental authority, they tried to build their lives on what they understood to be Marxist ethics, often with tragic results. The advent of Socialist Realism relieved them from the necessity of groping for solutions to their personal problems. New Girls vowed to Stalin overfulfillment of production norms, kept their promise, and were rewarded by seeing their photographs in the local paper, and after a period of decorous courtship, by marriage to a worthy young worker.

They, too, did not change after the vogue for industrial fiction was over, and the ingenue of the post-Stalinist period could have appeared in any work of the preceding decade. As to negative characters among the proletarians, they were even less conspicuous than in village fiction. A few non–class-conscious, lazy women in the 1920's, a few flighty ones in the post-Stalinist era, bring up the insignificant total.

Generally then, strange as it may seem, the patterns of typical proletarian women are the least original in Soviet fiction.

Fictional women participating in the revolutionary struggle were not wholly figments of the writers' imagination: in the 1920's, reality provided art with many unusual models. Accordingly, both the romantic adventuress and the woman comrade-in-arms could be considered actual, if often stylized, portraits. But in the 1930's, on the eve of World War II, fiction conceived of these modern Amazons as propaganda posters: they were contemporary Soviet characters costumed for the parts of youthful revolutionaries and reenacting the glorious, strenuous past. Works dedicated to World War II—contemporary and postwar alike—used a combination of both methods. The heroines in uniform, whether cast as soldiers, nurses, or in the new role of intelligence agents, were average Soviet girls and at the same time intrepid fighters ready to die for the Fatherland.

Understandably, with the exception of the early bourgeois Amazons, who were short-lived and actually belonged to the world of prerevolutionary fiction, they practically all are positive characters. If the personal morals of these young women sometimes do not match their courage and patriotism, wartime conditions are considered sufficient justification, even in post-Stalinist works rewriting World War II fiction from a new angle. What does affect the patterns of women comrades-in-arms in recent Soviet literature is that while war fiction after twenty years of peace continues to hold a position of importance, the role women play in it is progressively on the wane.

The women of the authentically Soviet intelligentsia have no forebears in postrevolutionary fiction. A few middle-class followers of the new order, like Kollontay's notorious Zhenya, hardly qualify. They were born as full-blown positive characters into the world of Socialist Realist fiction towards the end of World War II. In their case, therefore, no struggle for women's rights was necessary, and their positive status has always been conditioned by their proper use of these rights and by good working performance.

They were expected to—and did—behave as befitted the fledglings of the Soviet system, the products of its psychological and social structure. These women, prevalently young, raised in Soviet homes, educated in Soviet schools, and members of, consecutively, the Young Pioneers, the Komsomol, and in time, the Communist Party, are perhaps the purest representatives of Soviet fiction. At the height of Socialist Realism they are poised, secure in the sense of their own ideological and professional proficiency and in the availability of the Party's counsel in case of doubts. They are not simply trusting followers as are their uneducated sisters of the peasant and workers' milieux. They are members of the ruling class and have a highly developed sense of responsibility, although, subject to the invisible ceiling limiting a woman's career, they do not participate in any policymaking.

Though their tastes and interests are naturally more sophisticated than those of kolkhoz and factory workers, their moral standards, home life, and world outlook in general are the same. The fact that they usually had been born into one of these milieux or had married into it is a contributing factor. Besides, as this study shows, women of the Soviet intelligentsia are not a homogeneous group, but one which comprises the career women—mostly engineers and physicians—and the wage earners—teachers, nurses, kolkhoz agronomists, and the like. A degree of sophistication (a very modest one) can be observed only among the professionals with higher education and among the privileged elite, which, still bearing the stigma of spiritual affinity with the prerevolutionary middle class, is a hotbed of negative characters.

Career women and wage earners—earnest, sweet girls; brilliant young women; wives patiently following husbands wherever their jobs take them; and wives sacrificing family life to the demands of their own professions—are great favorites with Soviet writers. Older women either continue as model workers in their old age or take over their working daughters' duties at home.

Unhappy love affairs, which suddenly blossomed under the thaw, did not impair the heroines' professional performance. On the contrary, work provided the only escape from despondency and eventually a cure for heartache. Thus, even though women of the intelligentsia evinced few qualms in discarding most of the taboos of the Stalinist era, and though their emotional experiences were given considerable attention, they kept their status as positive characters and remained true to the pattern of fine, upright, truly Soviet women.

At the time of this writing, Soviet literature is half a century old. Its flat, two-dimensional quality is recognized by various literary critics; in the West the blame is put on the restrictions imposed by Socialist Realism; in the Soviet Union on the insufficient exploitation of its possibilities. Meanwhile, a whole class of mediocre writers is making a comfortable living by turning out an endless stream of fiction which follows safe, established patterns and introduces slight adjustments as necessary.

Still, some talented writers have time and again succeeded in creating living characters even without resorting to forbidden "formalist" devices. Nor did these cases occur exclusively under liberalized post-Stalinist conditions. In Paustovsky's "The Wind Rose" (1947) all is routine: the plot of seduction, the seaside resort setting, the stock characters, including a blasé poet, his foolish women admirers, and the kind janitress Auntie Pasha. Yet, the heroine is a living, proud, suffering soul. And so (in 1946, 1953, and 1959, respectively) are Panova's Lena in *The Train*, Dorofeya in *The Seasons*, and Valya in a short story bearing her name. Moreover, the latter three characters are revealed through personalized narratives conducted in the third person but from the character's own point of view—an ingenious way of circumventing the Marxist ban on the irrational in fiction.

On the other hand, the necessity of conforming to the current demands of Socialist Realism causes authors famed even abroad for their daring originality to produce perfect specimens of typical characters—perhaps as a price paid for works which otherwise could not have appeared. Thus, Nekrasov, the author of the notorious *Kira Georgievna*, also produced Valya (in *The Home Town*), as faithful in love and dauntless in war as Lord Lochinvar could ever have been. And the wayward heroine of Aksyonov's *A Ticket to the Stars* is balanced in *Colleagues* by two proper maidens, both in love with a heroic Soviet physician. Panova contributed such stereotypes as the prizewinning, naïve milkmaid and the stern cowbarn manager in *The Bright Shore*. Nikolaeva, in *The Battle on the Way*, besides creating the effervescent Tina, featured as heroine the model ingenue Dasha. The list of such concessions is long. And, of course, at the two opposite ends of the literary spectrum, there are writers like Kochetov, who apparently can create only within the pale of Socialist Realism, and a few known mavericks like Kazakov, who can create only outside it.

Changes in Soviet fiction are limited to details and never affect essentials. Fashions in working attitudes come and go, as Stakhanovism did, but work effort is forever given tremendous respect and recognition. Marriage and divorce, motherhood and abortions, illicit love affairs and chaste love—all at different times achieved prominence or were played down, but once defined, conventional morals have remained the bedrock of Soviet society. And certain basic attitudes and principles—Party infallibility (though its members may err), patriotism, social duty—are not subject to any changes.

Similarly, and closely connected with the above, the main premises of Soviet literature are unaffected by fluctuations on its surface: it remains a literature meant for the edification of the readers and to that purpose follows the guidelines of Socialist Realism. And the basic conditions of publishing in the Soviet Union—State ownership of the press, the Party's control of it, and the organization and role of the lone Union of Soviet Writers—constitute an integral part of the system.

Thus it is that the world of Soviet fiction has been, and largely continues to be, Sovietland, the world of the average, the everyday, the possible, where questions are seldom asked and never stay unanswered, and where sterling men and women stoutly work their way towards an unclouded future guaranteed by an immutable doctrine.

REFERENCE MATTER

Notes

CHAPTER I

1 A. Selivanovskij, "Na styke s krest'janskoj literaturoj," *Oktjabr'* (December 1929), pp. 176–90; D. Tal'nikov, "Literaturnye zametki," *Krasnaja nov'* (January 1929), pp. 234–56; N. Smirnov, "Zametki o krest'janskix pisateljax," *Novyj mir* (January 1927), pp. 223–25; P. Neznamov, "Derevnja krasivogo operenija," in *Literatura fakta,* ed. N. F. Čužak (Moskva, 1929), pp. 105–13.
2 V. I. Lenin, "Reč' na Vserossijskom s'ezde rabotnic, 19 nojabrja 1918 g.," *Sočinenija,* 30 vols. (Moskva, 1930–35), XXIII, 285–86.
3 A. Neverov, "Andron Neputevyj," *Sobranie sočinenij* (Moskva-Leningrad, 1928–30), VI, 167.
4 E.g., A. Karavaeva, *Medvežatnoe* (1925); M. Karpov, *Pjataja ljubov'* (1927); N. Bogdanov, *Pervaja devuška* (1928); Ja. Korobov, *Katja Dolga* (1925); S. Kanatčikov, *Roždenie kolxoza* (1930).
5 A. Zavališin, "Semejnaja radost'," *Pepel i drugie rasskazy* (Moskva, 1928), p. 143.
6 Ja. Švedov, *Obidy,* 2nd ed. (Moskva-Leningrad, 1931), p. 110.
7 Karpov, *Pjataja ljubov',* 5th ed. (Moskva, 1931), p. 263.
8 A. N. Tolstoj, *Xoždenie po mukam,* in *Polnoe sobranie sočinenij,* 15 vols. (Moskva, 1946–53), VIII, 99.
9 I. Šuxov, *Nenavist'* (Moskva, 1933), p. 179.
10 I. Brykin, "Sobač'ja svad'ba," *Zvezda,* No. 5 (1925), p. 182.
11 Karpov, *Pjataja ljubov'.*
12 I. Vol'nov, "Derevenskaja pestrjad'," *Krasnaja nov',* No. 2 (1923), p. 310.
13 P. Akul'šin, "Kartinki s natury," *Krasnaja nov'* (December 1926), pp. 221–29, and "O čem šepčet derevnja?" *Krasnaja nov',* No. 2 (1925), pp.

238–48; N. Kočin, "Zapiski sel'kora," *Oktjabr'* (April–June 1929); V. Polonskij, "Listki iz bloknota," *Novyj mir* (February 1929), pp. 225–36; B. Levin, "Derevenskie očerki," *Novyj mir* (March 1929), pp. 253–58; L. Rejsner, "Meščanstvo," *Krasnaja nov'* (January 1927), pp. 149–63.

14 On the scarcity of Party members and on their misuse of authority, see P. Vinogradskaja, "Sovremennaja derevnja," *Pečat' i revoljucija*, No. 6 (1924), pp. 73–98; Ja. Burov, *Derevnja na perelome* (Moskva, 1926), pp. 39–40, 228–29, 261–63; A. Zorič, "Vo t'me," *Krasnaja nov'*, No. 3 (1925), pp. 240–47.

15 *The Marriage Laws of Soviet Russia* (Russian Soviet Government Bureau, New York, 1921).

16 To mention only a few examples, A. Stel'maxovič, *Dela ob alimentax* (Moskva, 1926); P. Vinogradskaja, "Voprosy morali, pola, byta i tovarišč Kollontaj," *Krasnaja nov'*, No. 6 (1923), pp. 179–214; A. Zalkind, *Polovoj vopros v uslovijax sovetskoj obščestvennosti* (Leningrad, 1926); I. Il'inskij, "Bytovye perežitki pered licom sovetskogo suda," *Krasnaja nov'* (January 1926), pp. 189–203; A. Divil'kovskij, "Bolezni byta molodeži," *Novyj mir* (November 1926), pp. 160–75.

17 A. Jakovlev, "Bab'ja dola," *Novyj mir* (July 1926), p. 167.

CHAPTER 2

1 Akulina in D. Grigorovič's *Derevnja* (1846), Nastja in N. Leskov's *Žytie odnoj baby* (1863), and Lizaveta in A. Pisemskij's *Gor'kaja sud'bina* (1859), respectively.

2 The lascivious father-in-law (*snoxač*) is the favorite villain of Russian fiction writers, both before and after the Revolution, as, for example, in N. Leskov's "Kotin Doilec i Platonida" (1867) and F. Panferov's *Bruski* (1928–37).

3 L. N. Tolstoj, *Vlast' t'my*, in *Sobranie sočinenij* (Moskva, 1960–65), XI, 101.

4 Cf. D. Furmanov's *klassovoe čut'e* in "Lidija Sejfullina—*Virineja*," *Sočinenija* (Moskva, 1952), III, 266; P. Mireckij's *zdorovoe social'noe čuvstvo* in "Martem'janixa," *Krasnaja nov'* (May 1929), p. 66; N. Janovskij's *protest . . . stixijnyj, instinktivnyj, podsoznatel'nyj* in *Lidija Sejfullina* (Moskva, 1959), p. 92; and A. Iezuitov's *social'nyj instinkt, kotoryj javljalsja smutnoj pervonačal'noj formoj revoljucionnoj podsoznatel'nosti* in "Xarakter sovremennika v literature," *Russkaja literatura* (January 1962), p. 158.

5 As reported in A. Karavaeva's introduction to A. Neverov's *Izbrannye proizvedenija* (Moskva, 1958), p. 4.

6 E. Starikova, "*Virineja* Lidii Sejfullinoj," *Novyj mir* (August 1957), p. 213.

7 A contemporary reviewer admits that Korobov "knows his material too well, and so cannot quite manage the living reality demanding to be portrayed" (M. Luzgin, "Jakov Korobov, *Katja Dolga*, xronika sovremennoj derevni [1926]," *Oktjabr'*, No. 10 [1926], p. 131).

8 Ja. Korobov, *Katja Dolga* (Leningrad, 1926), p. 92.

9 A. Ležnev, "Literaturnoe obozrenie," *Pečat' i revoljucija*, No. 1 (1925), p. 133.

10 *Cf.* P. Mireckij, "Sejfullina i ee tipy," *Oktjabr'*, No. 6 (1926), pp. 89–93; Ju. Puxov, "M. Gor'kij i F. Gladkov," *Voprosy sovetskoj literatury* (Moskva-Leningrad, 1956), III, 410–11; Janovskij, *Lidija Sejfullina*, p. 101; Furmanov, "Lidija Sejfullina—*Virineja*," p. 266.

11 L. Sejfullina, *Virineja*, in *Sobranie sočinenij* (Moskva-Leningrad, 1926–31), III, 47.

12 L. Jakimenko, "*Tixij Don*" *M. Šoloxova* (Moskva, 1954), p. 308; I. Ležnev, *Mixail Šoloxov* (Leningrad, 1948), p. 234; V. Goffenšeffer, *Mixail Šoloxov* (Moskva, 1940), p. 124.

13 A. Neverov, "Andron Neputevyj," *Sobranie sočinenij* (Moskva-Leningrad, 1928–30), VI, 166.

14 A. Neverov, *Baby*, in *Sobranie sočinenij* (Moskva-Leningrad, 1928–30), III, 99.

15 *Ibid.*, p. 59.

16 Sejfullina, *Virineja*, p. 44.

17 Neverov, "Andron Neputevyj," p. 154.

18 For example, the "grannies" in Gorbunov's *Ledolom*, Panferov's *Bruski*, Neverov's *Povest' o babax*, Karavaeva's *Dvor*, Kočin's *Devki*. They also serve as midwives and give sensible, if seldom followed, advice to lovelorn girls, as in Karpov's *Pjataja ljubov'*.

19 Between 1928 and 1937 involved with or married to Zinka, Ula, Maša, Ela, Steška, and Fenja. He is reproved by Stalin himself for taking marriage so lightly (in F. Panferov, *Bruski* [Moskva, 1937], IV, 18). He repents and returns to Steška, who has meanwhile graduated to the status of a New Soviet Woman.

20 S. Ždanov, "Martem'janixa," *Oktjabr'* (November 1927), p. 147.

21 F. Panferov, *Bruski* (Moskva-Leningrad, 1931), I, 29.

22 P. Romanov, "Černye lepeški," *Ljubov'* (Paris, 1926), pp. 43–47.

23 M. Šoloxov, *Podnjataja celina*. Part I was published in 1932. Part II, in which the murder takes place, appeared over twenty years later (1955–60), but the mores of the earlier period have been carefully preserved.

24 A. Èrlix, "Prazdnik," *Krasnaja nov'* (January 1938), pp. 128–29; A. Korevanova, *Moja žizn'* (Leningrad, 1938), p. 8; V. Oxremenko, "Devuška iz Červonogo bora," *Novyj mir* (April 1938), p. 18, respectively. Some mothers, however, rejoice in and envy their daughters' happier lot as early as the 1920's; Tanja's mother in L. Gumilevskij's "Vragi čeloveka" (1925) is an example.

CHAPTER 3

1 A. Čistjakov, "Zadvorki," *Zvezda* (April–October 1931) and G. Alekseev, "Vozvraščenie," *Oktjabr'* (February 1934), respectively.

2 N. Kočin, "Zapiski sel'kora," *Oktjabr'* (April–June 1929), June, p. 154;

S. Babaevskij, *Svet nad zemlej* (Moskva, 1950), p. 71; S. Antonov, "Delo bylo v Pen'kove," *Povesti i rasskazy* (Moskva, 1961), p. 256.

3 F. Panferov, *Bruski* (Moskva, 1937), IV, 132.

4 *Kodeks zakonov o brake, sem'e i opeke RSFSR* (Moskva, 1950), pp. 51–55, 68–73.

5 E.g., M. Panič, "Stranicy iz raznyx tetradej," *Zvezda* (May 1961); V. Tendrjakov, "Čudotvornaja," *Znamja* (May 1958); A. Tkačenko, "Na otšibe," *Oktjabr'* (January 1962).

6 V. Panov, "Krasnyj bor," *Oktjabr'* (April–July 1940), May, p. 135.

7 B. Guber, *Bab'e leto* (Moskva, 1934), p. 47.

8 N. Kalitin, "K jasnomu beregu," *Znamja* (December 1949), p. 185.

9 K. Bukovskij, "Jasnye xaraktery," *Novyj mir* (May 1950), p. 235.

10 G. Medynskij, *Mar'ja* (Moskva, 1950), p. 521.

11 F. Gladkov, *Novaja zemlja* (Moskva-Leningrad, 1931), p. 95.

12 Panferov, *Bruski*, III, 362.

13 Ju. Konstantinov, "Sila sovetskoj sem'i," *Zvezda* (November 1950), pp. 183–85; and N. Kalitin, "Trud preobražajuščij žizn'," *Zvezda* (December 1950), pp. 165–71, respectively.

14 N. Toščakov, *Čaroma* (Leningrad, 1947), p. 84.

15 In a comic opera by V. Majkov, *Derevenskij prazdnik ili uvenčannaja dobrodetel'* (1777); and in S. Krutilin, "Rodniki," *Oktjabr'* (August–September 1953), August, p. 112, respectively.

16 G. Nikolaeva, *Žatva* (Moskva, 1951), p. 235.

17 Guber, *Bab'e leto*, p. 33.

18 Žudov, in E. Mal'cev's *Ot vsego serdca* (1948), and Proxarčev, in Medynskij's *Mar'ja*.

19 A. Ležnev, *Voprosy literatury i kritiki* (Moskva, n.d.), pp. 191–92.

20 B. Platonov, "Zametki o russkoj sovetskoj proze 1950 goda," *Zvezda* (February 1951), p. 155.

21 V. Ovečkin, "Praskov'ja Maksimovna," *Povesti i rasskazy* (Moskva, 1947), p. 276. The attitude expressed in this quotation is not new. "A woman's youth ends at forty" (*babij vek—sorok let*), says a proverb, and one peasant writer says hard work makes it true even today (E. Doroš, *Derevenskij dnevnik* [Moskva, 1958], p. 12).

22 Medynskij, *Mar'ja*, p. 182.

23 V. Fomenko, "Pamjat' zemli," *Novyj mir* (June–August 1961), July, p. 111.

24 Nikolaeva, *Žatva*, pp. 517–19.

25 E. Mal'cev, *Ot vsego serdca* (Moskva, 1949), pp. 464–71.

26 V. Čalmaev, "Oživajuščie rodniki," *Moskva* (August 1965), p. 193.

27 Doroš, *Derevenskij dnevnik*, p. 12.

28 S. Antonov, "Alenka," *Povesti i rasskazy* (Moskva, 1961), p. 402.

29 Doroš, *Derevenskij dnevnik*, p. 120; M. Žestev, "Zolotoe kol'co," *Zvezda* (July–August 1958), July, p. 13.

30 Fomenko, *Novyj mir* (June 1961), p. 17.

31 In E. Mal'cev, "Gorjačie ključi," *Oktjabr'* (August–December 1945), August, pp. 81–82; Nikolaeva, *Žatva*, p. 300.

32 A. Lavrent'eva-Krivošeeva, "Russkie ženščiny velikoj stalinskoj èpoxi," *Zvezda* (January 1950), p. 182.
33 A. Jašin, "Vologodskaja svad'ba," *Novyj mir* (December 1962), p. 6.
34 In, for example, Antonov, "Delo bylo v Pen'kove," *Povesti i rasskazy,* pp. 284–91; Jašin, *Novyj mir,* pp. 7–14; Fomenko, *Novyj mir* (June 1961), pp. 10–15.

CHAPTER 4

1 In, for example, Kočin, *Devki;* Karpov, *Pjataja ljubov';* Zamojskij, *Lapti;* Karavaeva, *Medvežatnoe.*
2 For descriptions of the life of the postrevolutionary peasant girl, see P. Akul'šin, "Zarisovki," *Krasnaja nov'* (March 1929), pp. 190–97; A. Divil'kovskij, "Naša derevnja v zerkale romana," *Krasnaja nov'* (July 1929), pp. 213–27; F. Panferov, "Svatovstvo," *Krasnaja nov'* (January 1927), pp. 219–25; P. Malov, "Derevenskoe," *Krasnaja nov'* (March 1927), pp. 164–77; T. Il'ina, "Solomennyj raj," *Krasnaja nov'* (October 1927), pp. 207–19.
3 K. Gorbunov, *Ledolom* (Moskva, 1931), p. 6.
4 *Oktjabr'* (December 1928), p. 45.
5 In a reviewer's succinct phrasing, "Kočin's books disappeared from library shelves for thirteen years while he, on false charges, was unlawfully subjected to a penalty" (V. Krasil'nikov, "Korotko o knigax," *Novyj mir* [November 1962], p. 284).
6 N. Kočin, *Devki* (Moskva, 1929), p. 186.
7 Ksjuša in G. Nikolaeva, *Žatva* (Moskva, 1951), p. 233; and Njuša in V. Panova, *Jasnyj bereg,* in *Sputniki, Kružilixa, Jasnyj bereg* (Moskva, 1951), p. 582.
8 Panova, *Jasnyj bereg,* p. 586.
9 V. Tendrjakov, *Padenie Ivana Čuprova,* in *Izbrannye proizvedenija v dvux tomax* (Moskva, 1963), I, 54.
10 Panova, *Jasnyj bereg,* p. 548.
11 S. Antonov, "Lena," *Zvezda* (July 1948), p. 28.
12 F. Panferov, *Bruski* (Moskva, 1937), IV, 290.
13 S. Krutilin, "Rodniki," *Oktjabr'* (August–September 1953), September, p. 110.
14 V. Panov, "Krasnyj bor," *Oktjabr'* (April–July 1940), June, p. 126.
15 A. Kuznecov, "U sebja doma," *Novyj mir* (January 1964), p. 47.
16 Nikolaeva, *Žatva,* p. 468.
17 A. Jašin, "Vologodskaja svad'ba," *Novyj mir* (December 1962), p. 11.
18 E. Doroš, *Derevenskij dnevnik* (Moskva, 1958), p. 247.

CHAPTER 5

1 A. Kollontaj, *Novaja moral' i rabočij klass* (Moskva, 1919), p. 7.
2 A. Kollontaj, *Sem'ja i kommunističeskoe gosudarstvo* (Moskva, 1918), pp. 13–19.
3 *The Communist Manifesto* (London, 1948), p. 147; F. Engels, *Der*

Ursprung der Familie, des Privateigentums und des Staats (Stuttgart, 1920), p. 72; and V. I. Lenin, "Velikij počin . . . ," *Sočinenija,* 30 vols. (Moskva, 1930–35), XXIV, 343.

4 M. Majzel', "F. Gladkov," *Zvezda* (April 1926), p. 230; A. Gorbov, "Itogi literaturnogo goda," *Novyj mir,* No. 12 (1925), p. 132.

5 F. Gladkov, "Cement," *Krasnaja nov'* (January–August 1925), January, p. 86.

6 *Ibid.,* pp. 92–93.

7 O. M. Brik, "Počemu ponravilsja *Cement,*" in *Literatura fakta,* ed. N. F. Čužak (Moskva, 1929), p. 86.

CHAPTER 6

1 V. Ermilov, "Bednaja Ljubaša," in *O sovetskoj literature,* ed. M. Rosental' (Moskva, 1936), p. 217.

2 I. Zverev, "Ona i on," *Znamja* (July 1964), p. 82.

3 V. Kočetov, "Brat'ja Eršovy," *Neva* (June–July 1958), June, p. 13.

4 B. Beljaev, "Pročnyj fundament," *Novyj mir* (August 1951), p. 255.

5 V. Kočetov, *Žurbiny* (Moskva, 1952), p. 7.

6 P. Nilin, "Ljubimaja devuška," *Novyj mir* (December 1936), p. 47. The use of a matronymic, facetious in 1936, did not seem so to unwed mothers after it had been in actual use for years in the Soviet Union. Nadezhda, in Vasil'ev's "Voprosov bol'še net" (published in *Moskva* [June 1964]), hopes that by the time she needs her boy's birth certificate for school registration, "the disgraceful dash in the place of the father's name will be a thing of the past" (p. 26), and that he will no longer be branded by the matronymic "son of Nadezhda" (*Nadeždovič*).

7 B. Bednyj, "Devčata," *Znamja* (July–August 1961), August, pp. 48, 50.

8 Ja. Il'ičev, "Gordaja ljubov'," *Zvezda* (June 1957), p. 78.

9 E.g., A. Musatov, "Krutye tropy," *Oktjabr'* (March 1955); E. Gerasimov, "V Stalingrade," *Novyj mir* (December 1953); I. Irošnikova, "Nadja Egorova i ee druz' ja," *Oktjabr'* (April 1948); P. Vinogradskaja, "Udarniki," *Oktjabr'* (January 1930); Ja. Il'in, *Bol'šoj konvojer* (Moskva, 1932).

10 Bednyj, *Devčata* (1961); I. Èrenburg, *Ne perevodja dyxanija* (1935); L. Kabo, "Zoloto," *Junost'* (January 1958).

11 Ja. Kamočkin, "Ščepotka soli," *Moskva* (April 1964), p. 47.

12 V. Nemcev, "Slovo o našix ženščinax," *Literaturnaja gazeta,* No. 82 (1958), pp. 1–2.

13 A. Bažanov, "Ty stanoviš'sja rabočim," *Junost'* (February 1958), p. 93.

14 A. Rybakov, *Voditeli* (Moskva, 1950), p. 158.

15 B. Reznikov, "V kavyčkax i bez kavyček," *Literaturnyj kritik* (May 1936), p. 127; A. Andreev, "Širokoe tečenie," *Oktjabr'* (January–February 1953), January, p. 22.

16 S. Beljaev and B. Pil'njak, "Mjaso," *Novyj mir* (April 1936), p. 113.

17 S. Krutilin, "Rodniki," *Oktjabr'* (August–September 1953), August, p. 121.

18 A. Vološin, *Zemlja Kuzneckaja* (Moskva, 1950), p. 34.
19 B. Gorbatov, *Donbass* (Moskva, 1951), p. 245.
20 A. Voloženin, "Dva romana," *Novyj mir* (December 1939), pp. 239–40.
21 Rybakov, *Voditeli*, p. 159.

CHAPTER 7

1 V. I. Lenin, "Zadači sojuzov molodeži . . . ," *Sočinenija*, 30 vols. (Moskva, 1930–35), XXX, 408.
2 A. Blatin, *Komsomol, pomoščnik boľševickoj partii v stroiteľstve socializma* (Moskva, 1949); *Komsomol: Sbornik statej* (München, 1960).
3 Ju. Oleša, "Strogij junoša," *Izbrannoe* (Moskva, 1936), p. 242.
4 See, for example, N. Azvolinskaja, "Zapiski vuzovki," *Oktjabr'* (January 1929), pp. 128–38; V. Zajcev, *Trud i byt rabočix podrostkov* (Moskva, 1926); I. Il'inskij, "Zametki o vysšej škole," *Novyj mir*, No. 23 (1928), pp. 225–32; A. Najštat, I. Ryvkin, N. Sosnovin, *Kommuny molodeži* (Moskva, 1931).
5 See A. Stratonickij, *Voprosy byta v Komsomole* (Moskva, 1926); M. Moskvin, *Xoždenie po vuzam* (Paris, 1933); *Komsomol: Sbornik statej;* E. Troščenko, "Vuzovskaja molodež'," *Molodaja gvardija* (April 1927), pp. 129–43.
6 A. Zalkind, *Polovoj vopros v uslovijax sovetskoj obščestvennosti* (Leningrad, 1926), p. 13; A. Kollontaj, *Novaja moraľ i rabočij klass* (Moskva, 1919), p. 47.
7 P. Vinogradskaja, "Voprosy morali, pola, byta i tovarišč Kollontaj," *Krasnaja nov'*, No. 6 (1923), pp. 179–214.
8 A. Zalkind, *Revoljucija i molodež'* (Moskva, 1925); S. Škotov, *Byt molodeži* (Ivanovo-Voznesensk, 1925); A. Divil'kovskij, "Bolezni byta molodeži," *Novyj mir* (November 1926), pp. 160–75; *Pravda*, No. 156 (1926).
9 E.g., G. Jakubovskij, "Psixologičeskij neorealizm Sergeja Malaškina," *Zvezda* (January 1927), pp. 147–61; R. Messer, "O molodoj proletarskoj proze," *Zvezda* (September 1929), pp. 176–84; V. Polonskij, *Očerki sovremennoj literatury* (Moskva, 1930), pp. 225, 285, 290; A. Ležnev, "Molodež' o molodeži," *Novyj mir* (June 1929), pp. 191–200; A. Tarasenkov, "Novye kadry," *Na literaturnom postu*, No. 8 (1929), pp. 37–41.
10 S. Malaškin, Preface, *Luna s pravoj storony*, 5th ed. (Moskva, 1928), pp. 13–15.
11 B. Gorbatov, *Moe pokolenie*, 4th ed. (Moskva, 1936), p. 297.
12 K. Zetkin, *Lenin on the Woman Question* (New York, n.d.), pp. 11–12.
13 N. Bogdanov, *Pervaja devuška* (Moskva, 1928), p. 124.
14 M. Kolosov and V. Gerasimova, *Proba* (Moskva, 1930), p. 19.
15 Troščenko, *Molodaja gvardija* (April 1927), p. 141; S. Škotov, *Perspektivy junošeskogo truda*, 2nd ed. (Ivanovo-Voznesensk, 1925), p. 32.
16 M. Kolosov, "Individual'noe vospitanie," *Oktjabr'* (March 1929), pp. 10–11.

17 A term employed by B. Gorbatov in *Jačejka* (Moskva-Leningrad, 1928), p. 144.
18 G. Nikiforov, *Ženščina* (Moskva, 1929), pp. 29, 31.
19 I. Bražnin, *Pryžok*, 4th ed. (Leningrad, 1929), pp. 98–99.
20 V. Ketlinskaja, *Natka Mičurina* (Leningrad, 1929), p. 176.
21 Zetkin, *Lenin on the Woman Question*, p. 6; M. Platoškin, *V doroge* (Moskva-Leningrad, 1929), p. 326.
22 Ketlinskaja, *Natka Mičurina*, p. 25.
23 Gorbatov, *Moe pokolenie*, p. 293.
24 AN SSSR, *Istorija russkoj sovetskoj literatury*, 3 vols. (Moskva, 1958–61), I, 517.
25 Polonskij, *Očerki sovremennoj literatury*, p. 249.
26 Platoškin, *V doroge*, p. 176; Bražnin, *Pryžok*, p. 22.
27 Gorbatov, *Jačejka*, p. 51.
28 Bogdanov, *Pervaja devuška*, pp. 169, 189.
29 E.g., Ležnev, *Novyj mir* (June 1929), p. 200; D. Tal'nikov, "Literaturnye zametki," *Krasnaja nov'* (January 1929), pp. 207–9.
30 V. Veresaev, *Sestry* (Moskva, 1933), p. 10.
31 Gorbatov, *Jačejka*, p. 50.

CHAPTER 8

1 M. Šoloxov, "Tixij Don," *Sobranie sočinenij v vos'mi tomax*, III (Moskva, 1956), 318.

CHAPTER 9

1 A. Jakovlev, *Povol'niki* (Moskva-Petrograd, 1923), p. 37; F. Gladkov, *Ognennyj kon'* (Moskva, 1926), p. 133.
2 Tain'ka in N. Nikitin, *Rvotnyj Fort;* Ninočka in A. Jakovlev, *Povol'niki;* Elena in A. Tarasov-Rodionov, *Šokolad.*
3 Nikitin, *Rvotnyj Fort* (Moskva-Leningrad, 1926), p. 29.
4 A. Jakovlev, "Bez beregov," *Nedra*, No. 5 (1924), p. 234.
5 *Ibid.*, p. 228.
6 Gladkov, *Ognennyj kon'*, p. 90; L. Lavrenev, "Veter," *Izbrannoe* (Moskva, 1948), pp. 31–32.
7 G. Gorbačev, "Boris Lavrenev," *Zvezda*, No. 5 (1925), p. 246. Thirty years later in his posthumously published autobiography, Lavrenev notes that he "wore the label until RAPP's peaceful demise in 1932 when, having escorted the corpse to the cemetery of history, I remained just a Soviet writer. This suited me fine" ("Avtobiografija," *Novyj mir* [April 1959], p. 66).
8 D. Romanenko, *Aleksandr Fadeev* (Moskva, 1956), p. 51.
9 In *Malen'kie rasskazy o bol'šoj žizni* (Moskva, 1924).
10 D. Furmanov, *Čapaev*, in *Sočinenija* (Moskva, 1952), I, 40.
11 A. Čarnyj, "Aleksej Nikolaevič Tolstoj," *Oktjabr'* (January–February 1940), February, p. 203.

12 Furmanov, *Čapaev*, p. 36; D. Furmanov, "Marusja Rjabinina," *Sočinenija* (Moskva, 1952), III, 126–27.
13 Furmanov, "Marusja Rjabinina," p. 128.

CHAPTER 10

1 For example, the heroine of P. Romanov's "Na Volge," *Krasnaja nov'* (June 1932).
2 A. Starčakov, "Zametki o istoričeskom romane," *Novyj mir* (May 1935), p. 269.
3 V. Goffenšeffer, "Parxomenko Vsevoloda Ivanova," *Literaturnyj kritik* (August/September 1939), p. 143.
4 A. Karavaeva, *Lena iz žuravlinoj rošči* (Moskva, 1938), p. 153.
5 E. Usievič, "Novaja povest' Alekseja Tolstogo," *Literaturnyj kritik* (March 1938), p. 112.
6 A. N. Tolstoj, *Xoždenie po mukam*, in *Polnoe sobranie sočinenij*, 15 vols. (Moskva, 1946–53), VIII, 397.
7 A. Pervencev, *Kočubej* (Moskva, 1948), p. 211.
8 V. Grossman, "V gorode Berdičeve," *Žizn'* (Moskva, 1947), p. 40.
9 E.g., L. Toom, "Anna Karavaeva, *Lena iz žuravlinoj rošči*," *Krasnaja nov'* (July/August 1940), pp. 303–5.

CHAPTER 11

1 A. Lejtes, "S pomoščju ženščiny," *Znamja* (November 1933), p. 170.
2 K. Simonov, *Dni i noči* (Praga, 1945), p. 99.
3 Compare this scene in F. Panferov's *Bor'ba za mir* in the 1945 edition (Moskva, p. 121) with that in the 1952 edition (Moskva, p. 154).
4 For example, Galina Petrova, prototype of the heroine in A. Pervencev's *Ognennaja zemlja*.
5 V. Ketlinskaja, *V osade* (Leningrad, 1960), p. 147. This was first serialized in *Zvezda* (June–October 1947).
6 L. Solov'ev, "Ivan Nikulin, russkij matros," *Novyj mir* (May/June 1943), p. 34.
7 V. Grossman, *Za pravoe delo* (Moskva, 1956), p. 670.
8 In B. Polevoj, *Povest' o nastojaščem čeloveke* (Moskva, 1947), pp. 20–21; and A. Kalinin, "Tovarišči," *Novyj mir* (October–November/December 1945), October, p. 16.
9 Grossman, *Za pravoe delo*, p. 666.
10 E. Kazakevič, *Vesna na Odere* (Moskva, 1950), p. 124.
11 B. Lavrenev, "Neukrotimoe serdce," *Stalinskoe plemja* (Moskva, 1943). The woman's name was Ljudmila Pavličenko.
12 A. Mackin, "Ob ukrašatel'stve i ukrašateljax," *Znamja* (November/December 1943), p. 278.
13 A. Makarov, "Roman o Stalingrade," *Novyj mir* (October 1944), p. 144.

14 V. Kataev, *Za vlast' sovetov,* in *Sobranie sočinenij,* III (Moskva, 1956), 600.

15 A. Fadeev, *Molodaja gvardija* (Moskva, 1946), p. 61.

16 Compare F. Panferov, "V strane poveržennyx," *Oktjabr'* (November–December 1948), December, pp. 28–31, with the book edition (Moskva, 1950), pp. 256–57.

17 M. Škerin, "Romany Feodora Panferova," *Zvezda* (March 1951), p. 176; L. Vol'pe, "F. I. Panferov," in AN SSSR, *Istorija russkoj sovetskoj literatury* (Moskva, 1958–61), II, 262.

18 V. Pankov, "Vysšij dolg," *Znamja* (February 1965), p. 201.

CHAPTER 12

1 L. N. Tolstoj, *Anna Karenina,* in *Sobranie sočinenij* (Moskva, 1960–65), IX, 64.

2 L. N. Tolstoj, *Vojna i mir,* in *Sobranie sočinenij* (Moskva, 1960–65), V, 344.

CHAPTER 13

1 For example, Ljudmila in Sologub's *Melkij bes,* Anfisa in L. Andreev's *Anfisa,* and Lidija in Arcybašev's *Sanin.*

2 P. Romanov, "Voprosy pola," *Krasnaja nov'* (April 1926), p. 65.

3 G. Jakubovskij, "Psixologičeskij neorealizm Sergeja Malaškina," *Zvezda* (January 1927), p. 153; V. Polonskij, *Očerki sovremennoj literatury* (Moskva, 1930), p. 256.

4 A. Kollontaj, *Sem'ja i kommunističeskoe gosudarstvo* (Moskva, 1918), p. 23.

5 G. Nikiforov, *Ženščina* (Moskva, 1929), p. 229.

6 P. Stepnoj, *Sem'ja* (Samara, 1922), p. 47.

7 V. Grossman, "Povest' o ljubvi," *Povesti i rasskazy* (Moskva, 1950), p. 201.

8 V. Grossman, "Koordinaty," *Krasnaja nov'* (January 1941), p. 146.

9 O. Ziv, *Gorjačij čas* (Moskva, 1954), p. 330.

10 E. Dobin, "Roždenie geroja," *Zvezda* (May 1930), p. 130.

11 I. Grinberg, "Antonina i drugie," *Zvezda* (September 1936), p. 221; M. Levidov, "Roman i ego podrobnosti," *Literaturnyj kritik* (October 1936), p. 120; A. Margolina, "Jurij German," *Literaturnyj sovremennik* (March 1935), p. 171.

CHAPTER 14

1 G. Nikolaeva, "Povest' o direktore MTS i glavnom agronome," *Znamja* (September 1954), p. 61.

2 V. Dobrovol'skij, *Ženja Maslova* (Moskva, 1953), p. 227.

3 *Sonet Petrarki* (1956), a much-discussed play by N. Pogodin, is perhaps the best example. "Nelegkij razgovor," a poem by P. Sevak, translated from the Armenian by E. Evtušenko (*Novyj mir* [June 1956]), is another.

4 V. Ketlinskaja, *Inače žit' ne stoit* (Leningrad, 1961), p. 141; and M. Kolosov and A. Gerasimov, *Proba* (Moskva, 1930), p. 36.

5 In K. Kloss, *Signaly bedstvij*; A. Storoženko, "Kambuznica Katja"; V. Oxremenko, "Devuška iz Červonogo bora"; E. Sobolevskij, "Tovarišči"; B. Gorbatov, *My i radist Vovnič*, respectively.

6 I. Nusinov, "B. Gorbatov: *Obyknovennaja Arktika*," *Krasnaja nov'* (July/August 1940), p. 302.

7 Ju. Berezin, "Èliksir molodosti," *Zvezda* (April 1935), p. 28.

8 A. Koptjaeva's *Ivan Ivanovič* (1949), *Družba* (1954), and *Derzanie* (1958).

9 In V. Igišev, *Šaxtery*; V. Kočetov, *Pod nebom rodiny*; V. Zakrutkin, *Plovučaja stanica*; L. Voronkova, *Bespokojnyj čelovek*, respectively.

10 I. Èrenburg, *Den' vtoroj* (Paris, 1933), p. 11.

11 G. Konovalov and B. Losin, "Dvorec brakosočetanij" (*fotoreportaž*), *Neva* (February 1960), photo 8.

12 N. Strokovskij, "Istorija odnoj noči," *Oktjabr'* (September 1963), p. 40.

13 I. Bražnin, *Pryžok*, 4th ed. (Leningrad, 1929), pp. 77–78; V. Grossman "Povest' o ljubvi," *Povesti i rasskazy* (Moskva, 1950), p. 220.

14 E. Uspenskaja, "Žena šagajuščego," *Novyj mir* (January 1958), p. 45.

15 B. Polevoj, *Na dikom berege* (Moskva, 1963), p. 30.

16 N. Evdokimov, "Vysokaja dolžnost'," *Oktjabr'* (September 1950), p. 164.

17 Ju. Kapusto, "Xleboroby," *Novyj mir* (April 1950), p. 179.

18 Nikolaeva, "Povest' o direktore MTS i glavnom agronome," p. 32.

19 V. Kočetov, "Brat'ja Eršovy," *Neva* (June–July 1958), June, p. 14.

20 E. Katerli, "Dal'njaja doroga, " *Oktjabr'* (November 1954), p. 75; G. Nikolaeva, "Bitva v puti," *Oktjabr'* (March–July 1957), July, p. 82.

21 B. Isaev, "Tvorčestvo Very Panovoj," *Zvezda* (August 1950), p. 171.

22 V. Panova, *Kružilixa* (Moskva-Leningrad, 1959), p. 451.

23 D. Granin, *Iskateli* (Moskva, 1959), p. 429.

24 D. Pavlova, "Sovest'," *Moskva* (January–February 1962), January, p. 17.

25 L. Zajcev and G. Skul'skij, "V dalekoj gavani," *Oktjabr'* (July–August 1951). The play is K. Simonov's *Russkij vopros* (1946).

26 L. Žak, "Poprygun'i, ix druz'ja i vragi," *Oktjabr'* (September 1961), p. 210.

27 V. Kaverin, *Doktor Vlasenkova* (Moskva, 1953), p. 384.

28 A. Šiškina, "Moral' i moralisty," *Neva* (January 1963), p. 166.

29 A. Kirnosov, "Zolotaja ryba," *Zvezda* (May 1964), p. 92. This sentiment is also expressed by a speaker at a fictional "readers' conference," in E. Levakovskaja, "Sentjabr'—lučšij mesjac," *Moskva* (September–October 1964), September, pp. 55–56.

30 I. Irošnikova, *Načalo puti* (Moskva, 1951), p. 31.

31 V. Ketlinskaja, *Dni našej žizni*, 2 vols. (Leningrad, 1953), II, 218–19.
32 G. Konovalov, "Stepnoj majak," *Oktjabr'* (October–November 1949), October, p. 125; Dobrovol'skij, *Ženja Maslova*, p. 30.
33 M. Škerin, "O bogatstve," *Oktjabr'* (February 1948), p. 145.
34 O. Kolesnikova, "Molodost' social'na," *Oktjabr'* (June 1934), p. 189; and B. Platonov, "Zametki o russkoj proze 1949 goda," *Zvezda* (January 1950), p. 170, respectively.
35 E. Flejšic, "Sem'ja i zakon," *Oktjabr'* (June/July 1940), p. 239.
36 Z. Guseva, "Dve formy sem'i, dva ponimanija nravstvennosti," *Oktjabr'* (July 1949), p. 172.
37 Ju. Trifonov, "Studenty," *Novyj mir* (October–November 1950), October, p. 157.

CHAPTER 15

1 Editorial, "God 1959–yj," *Voprosy literatury* (January 1960), commenting on N. Xruščev's pronouncements on current Soviet literature.
2 Ju. Žukov, "Pesok i samorodki," *Neva* (October 1964), p. 4; A. Mixajlov, "Velikomu vremeni, velikuju literaturu," *Moskva* (January 1965), p. 193.
3 V. Dudincev, "Ne xlebom edinym," *Novyj mir* (August–October 1956), October, p. 98.
4 For example, T. Trifonova, "Kniga o kotoroj sporjat," *Novyj mir* (March 1958), pp. 211–13; K. Muridzi, "O sovremennosti i glubine konflikta," *Literaturnaja gazeta*, No. 116 (1957). Most of the offending details were deleted when the novel appeared in book form.
5 L. Popova, review in *Zvezda* (August 1960), p. 208; I. Vinogradov, "Po povodu odnoj večnoj temy," *Novyj mir* (June 1962), p. 240.
6 A. Èl'jaševič, "Budni ili prazdniki?" *Zvezda* (October 1954), p. 175; V. Pankov, "Ja umru ot Vas," *Zvezda* (August 1955), p. 174.
7 For example, A. Šiškina, "Moral' i moralisty," *Neva* (January 1963), pp. 164–67; K. Pozdnjaev, "Zvezdnyj bilet, kuda?" *Oktjabr'* (October 1961), p. 213; V. Rebrin, "Dva pis'ma," *Novyj mir* (October 1956), p. 182; V. Baskakov, "O smelosti podlinnoj i mnimoj," *Oktjabr'* (December 1956), pp. 69–72.
8 St. Zlobin, "Bitva v puti," *Znamja* (June 1958), p. 208.
9 G. Nikolaeva, "Bitva v puti," *Oktjabr'* (March–July 1957), July, p. 93.
10 Vinogradov, *Novyj mir* (June 1962), p. 251.
11 I. Leščevskij, "Ljubov' po špargalke," *Znamja* (August 1960), p. 218.
12 V. Bavina, "Optimističeskij konflikt," *Oktjabr'* (January 1962), p. 202; and a letter from A. Dmitrieva in "Tribuna čitatelja" [readers' tribune], *Neva* (November 1958), p. 216.
13 I. Gončarov, *Obryv* (1869), in *Sobranie sočinenij*, 6 vols. (Moskva, 1959–60), VI, 137.
14 A. Volodin, "Fabričnaja devčonka," *Teatr* (September 1956), p. 58.
15 G. Lenobl', "Na novom ètape," *Voprosy literatury* (July 1959), p. 39; also compare Zlobin, *Znamja* (June 1958), p. 211.

Glossary

Note: Terms appearing only once in the text and followed by an explanation are not included in this glossary.

BABA—A married peasant woman in prerevolutionary Russia; a foolish, ignorant woman.

BESPRIZORNYE (masc. *besprizornik*, fem. *besprizornitsa*)—Homeless children orphaned in the Civil War, who throughout the 1920's roamed the country begging and stealing in order to survive, often forming large criminal bands.

BYT—The complex of customs, beliefs, and manners which determine the way of life of a nation or social group: mores.

CHEKA—Abbreviation for Extraordinary Commission (1918-22), the police organization famed for its ruthless struggle against counter-revolutionaries.

DEKULAKIZATION—A purge of the Soviet village of kulaks (*q.v.*) through the requisition of their property and through deportation, as part of the agricultural reform (collectivization) during the years 1928-33; also known as "liquidation of the kulaks as a class."

"DIZZY WITH SUCCESS"—The title of the famous article by Stalin (*Pravda*, 2 March 1930) in which he called for a softening of the drastic methods used in the enforcement of the collectivization.

FELLOW TRAVELER—The term, coined by Trotsky, applied to writers who, while politically loyal to the Soviet regime, were not members of the Communist Party and did not adjust their artistic work to its aims.

KOLKHOZ—Collective farm.

KOMSOMOL (members: masc. *Komsomolets*, fem. *Komsomolka*)—Communist Youth League, organized in 1917, with members aged 14-26.

KULAK—A prosperous peasant, ruthless exploiter of hired labor.

MTS—Machine and Tractor Station. These technical and political district centers, each serving several collective farms, were established in 1929, abolished in 1958.

NEP—New Economic Policy (1921–28): a period of relaxation of government controls in Soviet national economy and of numerous divergent trends in literature.

OCTOBERING—A short-lived effort in the 1920's at replacing baptism with a ceremony of naming the baby, so-called in honor of the October Revolution.

PARTORG—A local Party member who serves as adviser and watchdog and is responsible for the working performance and ideological soundness of his unit (kolkhoz, factory, etc.).

PIONEERS—The Children's Corps of the Pioneers of Communism, established in 1922, with members aged 9–14.

POLITRUK—A Party member assigned to a military unit and in charge of its political morale.

PRIVILIGENTSIA—A term coined in the West in analogy to *intelligentsia*, of which this new social stratum is a part. It denotes the Soviet elite who enjoy the privileges of better living conditions and wield considerable power as bureaucrats, professionals, industrial and Party executives, high-ranking military, and successful writers and artists.

RABFAK—A school to prepare peasants and workers for college studies. Such schools were introduced in 1919 and lasted through the 1930's.

RAPP—The Russian Association of Proletarian Writers, which led a vituperative crusade against bourgeois influences in Soviet literature from 1925 to 1932, when it was supplanted, along with other literary organizations, by the Professional Union of Soviet Writers. The latter body has had the avowed duty to adhere to and promote the principles of Socialist Realism (*q.v.*) as the only correct literary method.

SOCIALIST REALISM—The exclusive Soviet literary method, whose guidelines for writers have been endorsed by the Communist Party since 1934. Its officially stated aims are "a genuine, historically concrete portrayal of reality in its revolutionary development" and "the education of the toiling masses in the spirit of Communism."

SOVIET PATRIOTISM—A nationalist trend prominent in the Soviet Union after World War II, evinced both in exaggerated appreciation of everything Russian and in repudiation of all things Western. In literature the trend was launched by the Communist Party spokesman, Andrey Zhdanov, in 1946 in his address to the Leningrad branch of the Soviet Writers' Union.

STAKHANOVITE—An honored worker who consistently overfulfills production norms. The name was derived from that of Aleksey Stakhanov, a miner who initiated the efficiency movement in 1935.

THAW—The term, derived from I. Erenburg's novel *The Thaw* (1954), popularly applied to the relaxation of Party controls in Soviet literature during the post-Stalinist period, especially 1954–57.

TRUDODEN—A workday pay unit on a collective farm.

ZHENOTDEL—A women's section of the Communist Party established in 1919 and discontinued in 1929.

Bibliography

This bibliography is a list of English translations of Russian literature mentioned or discussed in the text, both prerevolutionary and postrevolutionary. Of course, the ever-increasing number of translations of Soviet literary works may soon date this list, but it should be of assistance to those interested in reading the literary works mentioned.

Abramov, F. [*Vokrug da okolo*, 1963.] *The Dodgers.* Tr. David Floyd. London: Flegon, with assoc. of A. Blond, 1963. Also as: *The New Life: A Day on a Collective Farm.* Tr., with Introd., George Reavey. New York: Grove, 1963. Also as: *One Day in the New Life.* Tr. David Floyd. New York: Praeger, 1963.

Aksyonov, V. [*Kollegi*, 1960.] *Colleagues.* Tr. Alec Brown. London: Putnam, 1962.

———. [*Zvezdnyj bilet*, 1961.] *A Starry Ticket.* Tr. Alec Brown. London: Putnam, 1962. Also as: *A Ticket to the Stars.* Tr. Andrew R. MacAndrew. New York: Signet, 1963.

Alyoshin, S. [*Odna*, 1956.] "Alone," in *The Year of Protest, 1956.* Tr. and ed. Hugh McLean and Walter Vickery. New York: Vintage, 1961.

Antonov, S. [*Alenka*, 1956.] *Alyona.* Tr. Helen Altschuler. Moscow: Foreign Languages, n.d.

———. [*Delo bylo v Pen'kove*, 1956]. *It Happened at Penkovo.* Tr. Olga Shartse. Moscow: Foreign Languages, 1959.

———. [*Lena*, 1948.] *Lena*, in *Spring: Short Stories.* Tr. Margaret Wettlin. Moscow: Foreign Languages, 1954.

———. ["Poddubenskie častuški," 1950.] *Poddubki Songs.* Moscow: Foreign Languages, 1953.

Artsybashev, M. [*Sanin,* 1909.] *Sanine.* Tr. P. Pinkerton, with Preface by Gilbert Cannon. New York: Huebsch, 1915.

Azhaev, V. [*Daleko ot Moskvy,* 1948.] *Far from Moscow.* Moscow: Foreign Languages, 1950.

Babel, I. [*Konarmija,* 1926.] *The Red Cavalry.* Tr. Nadia Helstein. New York: Knopf, 1929.

Baklanov, G. [*Pjad' zemli,* 1959.] *The Foothold.* Tr. R. Ainsztein. London: Chapman and Hall, 1962.

———. [*Južnee glavnogo udara,* 1958.] *South of the Main Offensive.* Philadelphia: Dufour, 1963.

Bely, A. [*Peterburg,* 1913.] *St. Petersburg.* Tr., with Introd., John Cournos, with Foreword by George Reavey. New York: Grove, 1959.

Blok, A. [*Dvenadcat',* 1918.] "The Twelve," in *An Anthology of Russian Verse, 1812–1960.* Ed. Avrahm Yarmolinsky. New York: Doubleday-Anchor, 1962.

Chekhov, A. ["Dušečka," 1898.] "The Darling," in *The Darling and Other Stories.* Tr. Constance Garnett, with Introd. Edward Garnett. New York: Macmillan, 1916.

———. ["Poprygun'ja," 1893.] "The Grasshopper," in *The Grasshopper and Other Stories.* Tr., with Introd., A. E. Chamot. Philadelphia: McKay, 1926.

———. [*Dom s mezaninom,* 1895.] "House with the Mezzanine," in *House with the Mezzanine and Other Stories.* Tr. S. S. Koteliansky and Gilbert Cannon. New York: Scribner, 1917.

———. [*V ovrage,* 1900.] *In the Ravine,* in *The Grasshopper and Other Stories.* Tr., with Introd., A. E. Chamot. Philadelphia: McKay, 1926.

———. [*Tri sestry,* 1901.] *Three Sisters,* in *Plays.* Tr. Constance Garnett. New York: Modern Library, 1930.

Chernyshevsky, N. [*Čto delat'?* 1863.] *What's to Be Done?* Tr. B. R. Tucker. Boston: Tucker, 1886.

Dostoevsky, F. [*Prestuplenie i nakazanie,* 1866.] *Crime and Punishment.* Tr. Constance Garnett. New York: Macmillan, 1928.

Dudintsev, V. [*Ne xlebom edinym,* 1956.] *Not By Bread Alone.* Tr. Edith Bone. New York: Dutton, 1957.

Erenburg, I. [*Den' vtoroj,* 1933.] *Out of Chaos.* Tr. Alexander Bakshy. New York: Holt, 1934.

———. [*Ottepel',* 1954; *Vesna,* 1956.] Part I as: *The Thaw.* Tr. Manya Harari. Chicago: Regnery, 1955. Part II as: *The Spring.* Tr. Humphrey Higgins. London: Macgibbon and Kee, 1961. Both parts as: *A Change of Seasons.* Tr. Manya Harari and Humphrey Higgins. New York: Knopf, 1962.

Fadeev, A. [*Razgrom,* 1925.] *The Nineteen.* Tr. R. D. Charques. New York: International, 1929. Also as: *The Rout.* Tr. O. Gorchakov. Moscow: Foreign Languages, n.d.

———. [*Molodaja gvardija,* 1945.] *Young Guard.* Tr. Violet Dutt; ed. D. Skvirsky. London: Universal Distributors, 1959.

Fedin, K. [*Pervye radosti*, 1945.] *Early Joys*. Tr. G. Kazanina, with Introd. Ernest J. Simmons. New York: Random House, 1960.

———. [*Neobyknovennoe leto*, 1948.] *No Ordinary Summer*. Tr. Margaret Wettlin. 2 vols. Moscow: Foreign Languages, 1950.

Furmanov, D. [*Čapaev*, 1923.] *Chapaev*. Tr. George Kittel and Jeanette Kittel; ed. G. Gorchakov. Moscow: Foreign Languages, 1956.

German, Yu. [*Naši znakomye*, 1932–36.] *Antonina*. Tr. Stephen Garry. London: Routledge, 1937. Also as: *Tonia*. Tr. Stephen Garry. New York: Knopf, 1937.

———. [*Delo, kotoromu ty služiš'*, 1958.] *The Cause You Serve*. Tr. Olga Shartse. Moscow: Foreign Languages, n.d.

Gladkov, F. [*Cement*, 1925.] *Cement*. Tr. A. S. Arthur and C. Ashleigh. New York: Ungar, 1960.

Goncharov, I. [*Obryv*, 1869.] *The Precipice*. Tr. M. Bryant. New York: Knopf, 1916.

Gorbatov, B. [*Donbass*, 1951.] *Donbass*. Tr. Bernard Isaacs. Moscow: Foreign Languages, 1953.

Gorky, M. [*Mat'*, 1906.] *Mother*. Tr. Margaret Wettlin. New York: Collier, 1961.

Granin, D. [*Iskateli*, 1953.] *Those Who Seek*. Tr. Robert Daglish. Moscow: Foreign Languages, 1957.

Griboedov, A. [*Gore ot uma*, 1823.] *Wit Works Woe*, in *Masterpieces of the Russian Drama*. Ed. G. R. Noyes. 2 vols. New York: Dover, 1961.

Gumilevsky, L. [*Sobačij pereulok*, 1927.] *Dog's Lane*. Tr. N. R. Wreden. New York: Vanguard, 1930.

Ilf, I. and E. Petrov. [*Dvenadcat' stul'ev*, 1927.] *Diamonds to Sit On*. Tr. Elizabeth Hill and Doris Mudie. London: Methuen, 1930. Also as: *The Twelve Chairs*. Tr. John H. C. Richardson, with Introd. Maurice Friedberg. New York: Vintage, 1961.

Karamzin, N. [*Bednaja Liza*, 1792.] *Poor Liza*, in *The Literature of Eighteenth-Century Russia: A History and Anthology*. Tr. and ed. Harold Segal. 2 vols. New York: Dutton, 1967.

Kataev, V. [*Kvadratura kruga*, 1928.] *Squaring the Circle*. Tr. N. Goold-Verschoyle. London: Wishart, 1934.

———. [*Vremja vpered!* 1932.] *Time Forward;* Tr. Charles Malamuth. New York: Farrar and Rinehart, 1933.

Kaverin, V. [*Xudožnik neizvesten*, 1931.] *The Unknown Artist*. Tr. P. Ross. London: Westhouse, 1947.

Kazakevich, E. [*Serdce druga*, 1953.] *Heart of a Friend*. Tr. R. Dixon. Moscow: Foreign Languages, 1956.

———. [*Vesna na Odere*, 1949.] *Spring on the Oder*. Tr. Robert Daglish. Moscow: Foreign Languages, 1953.

———. ["Pri svete dnja," 1961.] "By Light of Day," tr. Darya Efremova, *Soviet Literature Monthly*, No. 6 (1963).

Kazakov, Yu. ["Adam i Eva," 1962.] "Adam and Eve," in *Going to Town and Other Stories*. Tr. Gabriella Azrael. Boston: Houghton Mifflin, 1964.

———. ["Man'ka," 1956.] "Manka," in *Going to Town and Other Stories*. Tr. Gabriella Azrael. Boston: Houghton Mifflin, 1964.

———. ["Na ostrove," 1963.] "On the Island," in *Going to Town and Other Stories*. Tr. Gabriella Azrael. Boston: Houghton Mifflin, 1964.

Ketlinskaya, V. [*Dni našej žizni*, 1952.] *Days of Our Life*. Tr. A. Bostock. London: Lawrence, 1956.

Kochetov, V. [*Žurbiny*, 1952.] *The Zhurbins*. Tr. R. Daglish. Moscow: Foreign Languages, 1953.

Kollontay, A. [*Ljubov' pčel trudovyx*, 1923.] *Free Love*. Tr. J. C. Hogarth. London: Dent, 1934. Also as: *A Great Love*. Tr. Lily Lore. New York: Vanguard, 1929. Also as: *Red Love*. New York: Seven Arts, 1927.

Koptyaeva, A. [*Ivan Ivanovič*, 1949.] *Ivan Ivanovich*. Tr. Margaret Wettlin. Moscow: Foreign Languages, 1952.

Korolenko, V. ["Son Makara," 1885.] "Makar's Dream," in *Makar's Dream and Other Stories*. Tr., with Introd., Marian Fell. New York: Duffield, 1916.

Krymov, Yu. [*Tanker Derbent*, 1938.] *The Tanker Derbent*. Tr. John S. Spink. New York: Penguin, 1944.

Lavrenyov, B. [*Sorok pervyj*, 1924.] *The Forty-First*. Tr. M. Wettlin and N. Jochel. Moscow: Foreign Languages, 1958.

Leonov, L. [*Barsuki*, 1924.] *The Badgers*. Tr. Hilda Kazanina. New York: Hutchinson, 1947.

———. [*Doroga na okean*, 1935.] *Road to the Ocean*. Tr. Norbert Guterman. New York: Fischer, 1944.

———. [*Sot'*, 1930.] *The Soviet River*. Tr. Ivor Montegu and Sergei Nolbandov, with Foreword by Maxim Gorky. New York: MacVeagh-Dial, 1932.

———. [*Vor*, 1927.] *The Thief*. Tr. Hubert Butler. New York: MacVeagh-Dial, 1931. Also: with Introd. by Rufus W. Mathewson, Jr. New York: Vintage, 1960.

Leskov, N. [*Ledi Makbet Mcenskogo uezda*, 1865.] *Lady Macbeth of the Mzensk District*, in *The Sentry and Other Stories*. Tr. A. E. Chamot, with Introd. Edward Garnett. New York: Knopf, 1923.

———. ["Kotin Doilec i Platonida," 1867.] "Kotin and Platonida," in *The Musk-Ox and Other Tales*. Tr. R. Norman. London: Routledge, 1945.

Libedinsky, Yu. [*Nedelja*, 1922.] *A Week*. New York: Heubsch, 1923.

Lidin, V. [*Otstupnik*, 1927.] *The Apostate*. Tr. H. Chrouschoff Matheson. London: Cape, 1931. Also as: *The Price of Life*. New York: Harper and Brothers, 1932.

Nagibin, Yu. ["Molodožen," 1958.] "The Newlywed," in *Soviet Short Stories*. Ed. A. Yarmolinsky. New York: Doubleday-Anchor, 1960.

Nekrasov, N. [*Moroz Krasnyj nos*, 1863.] *Red Nose Frost*. Tr. W. R. S. Ralston. Boston: Ticknor, 1887.

Nekrasov, V. [*Kira Georgievna*, 1961.] *Kira Georgievna*. Tr. Walter Vickery. New York: Pantheon, 1962.

Neverov, A. [*Andron Neputevyj*, 1922.] *Andron the Good-for-Nothing*, in *Modern Russian Stories*. Tr. Elisaveta Fen. London: Methuen, 1943.

——. ["Mar'ja Bol'ševička," 1921.] "Marya the Bolshevik," in *Russian Literature Since the Revolution*. Ed. Joshua Kunitz. New York: Boni and Gaer, 1948.

Nikolaeva, G. [*Žatva*, 1950.] *Harvest*. Moscow: Foreign Languages, 1952.

——. [*Povest' o direktore MTS i glavnom agronome*, 1954.] *The Newcomer*. Tr. D. Skvirsky. Moscow: Foreign Languages, 1955.

Olesha, Yu. [*Zavist'*, 1927.] *Envy*. Tr. Anthony Wolfe. London: Hogarth, 1936. Also in: *The Wayward Comrade and the Commissars*. Tr. Andrew McAndrew. New York: New American Library, 1960. Also: Tr. P. Ross, with Introd. G. Struve. London: Westhouse, 1947. Also in: *Love and Other Stories*. Introd. R. Payne. New York: Washington Square Press, 1967.

Ostrovsky, A. [*Groza*, 1860.] *The Storm*. Tr. George F. Holland and Malcolm Morley. London: Allen and Unwin, 1930. Also as: *The Thunderstorm*. Tr. Florence Whyte and George Rapall Noyes. New York: French, 1927.

Panfyorov, F. [*Bruski*, 1928–37.] *Brusski: A Story of Peasant Life in Soviet Russia*. Tr. Z. Mitrov and J. Tabrisky. London: Lawrence, 1930. Parts III and IV also as: *And Then the Harvest*. Tr. Stephen Garry. London: Putnam, 1939.

Panova, V. [*Kružilixa*, 1947.] *The Factory*. Tr. Moura Budberg. London: Putnam, 1949. Also as: *Looking Ahead*. Tr. David Skvirsky. Moscow: Foreign Languages, n.d.

——. [*Vremena goda*, 1953.] *Span of the Year*. Tr. Vera Traill. London: Harvill, 1957.

——. [*Sereža*, 1955.] *A Summer to Remember*. New York: Yoseloff, 1962. Also as: *Time Walked*. Cambridge, Mass.: Arlington, 1959.

——. [*Sputniki*, 1946.] *The Train*. Tr. Marie Budberg. New York: Knopf, 1949.

Pavlenko, P. [*Sčast'e*, 1947.] *Happiness*. Tr. J. Fineberg. Moscow: Foreign Languages, 1950.

Perventsev, A. [*Kočubej*, 1937.] *Cossack Commander*. Tr. Stephen Garry. London: Routledge, 1939.

Pilnyak, B. [*Golyj god*, 1922.] *The Naked Year*. Tr. Alec Brown. New York: Payson and Clark, 1928.

Pisemsky, A. [*Gor'kaja sud'bina*, 1859.] *A Bitter Fate*, in *Masterpieces of the Russian Drama*. Tr. and ed. G. B. Noyes. 2 vols. New York: Dover, 1961.

Polevoy, B. [*Povest' o nastojaščem čeloveke*, 1946.] *Story About a Real Man*. Moscow: Foreign Languages, 1949.

Pushkin, A. ["Metel'," 1830.] "The Snowstorm," in *Tales of Bielkin*. London: Drummond, 1947. Also as: "The Blizzard," in *The Tales of Ivan Belkin*. Tr. Ivy and Tatiana Litvinov. Moscow: Foreign Languages, 1954.

Romanov, P. ["Černye lepeški," 1925.] "Black Fritters," in *Russian Literature Since the Revolution*. Ed. Joshua Kunitz. New York: Boni and Gaer, 1948.

————. ["Na Volge," 1932.] "On the Volga," in *On the Volga and Other Stories*. Tr. Ann Gretton. New York: Scribners, 1934.

————. ["Voprosy pola," 1926.] "Sex Problems," in *Modern Russian Stories*. Tr. Elisaveta Fen. London: Methuen, 1943.

————. [*Tovarišč Kisljakov*, 1930.] *Three Pairs of Silk Stockings*. Tr. L. Zarine; ed. Stephen Graham. New York: Scribner, 1931.

————. ["Bez čeremuxi," 1926.] *Without Cherry Blossom*. Tr. L. Zarine; ed. Stephen Graham. New York: Scribner, 1932.

Sholokhov, M. [*Tixij Don*, 1927/28–1940.] Part I as: *And Quiet Flows the Don*. Tr. Stephen Garry. New York: Knopf, 1934. Part II as: *The Don Flows Home to the Sea*. Tr. Stephen Garry. London: Putnam, 1940. Both parts as: *The Silent Don*. Tr. Stephen Garry. New York: Knopf, 1942.

————. [*Podnjataja celina*, 1932, 1960.] Part I as: *Virgin Soil Upturned*. Tr. Stephen Garry. London: Putnam, 1935. (American edition: *Seeds of Tomorrow*. New York: Knopf, 1935.) Part II as: *Harvest on the Don*. Tr. H. C. Stevens. New York: Knopf, 1960; Signet, 1962; London: Putnam, 1960. Part II also as: *Virgin Soil Upturned, Book II*, tr. Robert Daglish, *Soviet Literature Monthly*, Nos. 1–3, 7 (1960).

Simonov, K. [*Dni i noči*, 1943–44.] *Days and Nights*. Tr. Joseph Barnes. New York: Simon and Schuster, 1945; Ballantine, 1962.

————. [*Živye i mertvye*, 1959.] *The Living and the Dead*. Tr. R. Ainsztein. New York: Doubleday, 1962.

————. [*Russkij vopros*, 1946.] *The Russian Question*. Sydney: Current Book Distributors, 1947.

Smirnov, V. [*Synov'ja*, 1928–37.] *Sons*. Tr. Naomi Y. Yohel, with Introd. Paul Hollister, Jr. Garden City: Doubleday, 1947.

Sologub, F. [*Melkij bes*, 1907.] *The Little Demon*. Tr. Ronald Wilks. London: New English Library, 1962. Also as: *The Petty Demon*. Tr., with Preface and Notes, Andrew Field; Introd. Ernest J. Simmons. New York: Random House, 1962.

Solzhenitsyn, A. ["Matrenin dvor," 1963.] "Matryona's Home," in *Halfway to the Moon: New Writings from Russia*. Ed. Patricia Blake and Max Hayward. London: Weidenfield and Nicolson, 1964.

————. [*Odin den' Ivana Denisoviča*, 1962.] *One Day in the Life of Ivan Denisovich*. Tr. Max Hayward and Ronald Hingley. New York: Praeger, 1963. Also: Tr. Thomas P. Whitney. New York: Crest Books, 1963.

Tarasov-Rodionov, A. [*Šokolad*, 1922.] *Chocolate*. Tr. Charles Malamuth. New York: Doubleday, 1932.

Tendryakov, V. [*Ne ko dvoru*, 1954.] *Son-in-Law*. Tr. Y. Rebrov. Moscow: Foreign Languages, 1956.

Tolstoy, A. N. [*Xleb*, 1937.] *Bread*. Tr. Stephen Garry. New York: Ryerson, 1938.

————. [*Xoždenie po mukam*, 1920/21–1940/41.] *Ordeal*. Tr. Ivy and Tatiana Litvinova. 3 vols. Moscow: Foreign Languages, 1953. Also as: *The Road to Calvary*. Tr. Edith Bone. 2 vols. New York: Knopf, 1946.

————. [*Gadjuka*, 1928.] *The Viper*, in *Modern Russian Stories*. Tr. Elisaveta Fen. London: Methuen, 1943.

Tolstoy, L. N. [*Anna Karenina*, 1875–77.] *Anna Karenina*. Tr. C. Garnett. 2 vols. New York: McClure and Phillips, 1901.

————. [*D'javol*, 1889.] *The Devil*. (*The Works of Leo Tolstoy*, Vol. XVI.) Oxford: Oxford University Press, 1934.

————. [*Xozjain i rabotnik*, 1895.] *Master and Man*. Tr. S. Rapport and John C. Kenworthy. New York: Crowell, 1895.

————. [*Vlast' t'my*, 1887.] *The Power of Darkness*, in *Plays*. Tr. Louise and Aylmer Maude. London: Oxford University Press, 1923.

————. [*Vojna i mir*, 1865–69.] *War and Peace*. Tr. C. Garnett. 3 vols. London: Heinemann, 1904.

Trifonov, Yu. [*Studenty*, 1950.] *Students*. Tr. Ivy Litvinova and Margaret Wettlin. Moscow: Foreign Languages, 1953.

Turgenev, I. [*Mumu*, 1854.] *Mumu*. Tr. Jessie Domb and Zlata Shoenberg. London: Harrup, 1945.

————. [*Dvorjanskoe gnezdo*, 1859.] *A Nest of Gentry*. Moscow: Foreign Languages, 1947, 1951. Also as: *A Nobleman's Nest*. Tr. Isabel F. Hapgood. New York: Scribner, 1924.

————. [*Nakanune*, 1860.] *On the Eve*. Tr. Gilbert Gardiner. Harmondsworth, Eng.: Penguin, 1951.

————. [*Dym*, 1867.] *Smoke*. Tr. I. F. Hapgood. New York: Scribner, 1907.

————. [*Nov'*, 1877.] *Virgin Soil*. Tr. T. S. Perry. New York: Holt, 1877.

Veresaev, V. [*Sestry*, 1933.] *The Sisters*. Tr. Juliet Soskice. London: Hutchinson, 1936.

————. [*V tupike*, 1922.] *The Deadlock*. Tr. Nina Wissotzky and C. Coventry. London: Faber and Gwyer, 1927.

Voloshin, A. [*Zemlja Kuznetskaja*, 1950.] *Kuznetsk Land*. Tr. Rose Prokofieva. Moscow: Foreign Languages, 1953.

Yashin, A. ["Ryčagi," 1956.] "Levers," in *Bitter Harvest*. Tr. Miriam B. London; ed. Edmund Stillman. New York. Praeger, 1959. Also in: *The Year of Protest, 1956*. Tr. and ed. Hugh McLean and Walter Vickery. New York: Vintage, 1961.

Zakrutkin, V. [*Plovučaja stanica*, 1950.] *Floating Stanitsa*. Tr. Bernard Isaacs. Moscow: Foreign Languages, 1954.

Zhdanov, N. ["Poezdka na rodinu," 1956.] "A Trip Home," in *The Year of Protest, 1956*. Tr. and ed. Hugh McLean and Walter Vickery. New York: Vintage, 1961. Also as: "Journey Home," in *Bitter Harvest*. Tr. Miriam B. London; ed. Edmund Stillman. New York: Praeger, 1959. Also as: "The Trip Home," in *Great Soviet Short Stories*. Ed. F. D. Reeve. New York: Dell, 1962.

Zoshchenko, M. ["Aristokratka," 1923.] "The Aristocrat," in *Scenes from the Bathhouse, and Other Stories from Communist Russia*. Tr. Sidney Monas. Ann Arbor: University of Michigan Press, 1961.

Index

DATE DUE